BIRDS OF MADAGASCAR

A PHOTOGRAPHIC GUIDE

Birds of Madagascar

A Photographic Guide

Pete Morris and Frank Hawkins

Yale University Press
New haven and London

Published 1998 in the United Kingdom by Pica Press (an imprint of Helm Information Ltd) and in the United States by Yale University Press.

ISBN 0-300-07755-6

Library of Congress Cataloging in Publication Number 98-86266.

Printed in Hong Kong

A catalogue record for this book is available from the British Library.

The paper in this book meets the guidelines for permanence and durability of the Committee on Production Guidelines for Book Longevity of the Council on Library Resources.

10 9 8 7 6 5 4 3 2 1

CONTENTS

INTRODUCTION

Two factors inspired the production of this book. First, on visiting Madagascar one is instantly struck by how confiding and beautiful many of the birds are. Many species show remarkable plumage coloration and this, together with their often confiding nature, makes them perfect photographic subjects. Second, many advances have been made in the last decade of Malagasy ornithology and in particular since the publication of Olivier Langrand's *Guide to the Birds of Madagascar* in 1990. New species have been discovered and described, many species have been rediscovered, the vocalisations of many species have been recorded for the first time and our knowledge of many of the more difficult species has grown considerably.

The aim of this book is to update and expand our knowledge of the Malagasy avifauna. With this book, the user should be able to identify all species occurring in Madagascar. Many groups which have caused identification problems in the past, such as the jeries and newtonias, are now clearly described with the best means of separating them from one another summarised in the identification sections. Through the use of colour photographs, the true, often vivid, colours of the Malagasy birds will have been brought to life for the first time. We have also spent much time researching, recording and describing the calls of Malagasy birds and hope that this will prove useful to fieldworkers and visiting birders alike.

More than anything else, however, we hope that the publication of this book will be the catalyst that will inspire people to visit Madagascar and take an interest in the Malagasy avifauna and its plight. We also hope that it will help to promote greater interest in wildlife and conservation among the Malagasy people. Visiting birdwatchers and other naturalists bring much-needed revenue to Madagascar and thereby help to promote the preservation of natural areas and the conservation of wildlife. Increased interest in, and study of, Madagascar's birds, many of which are threatened with extinction, will contribute to their conservation and long-term survival. If this book is able to generate greater levels of interest in the Malagasy avifauna it will, as far as we are concerned, have achieved its aim.

ACKNOWLEDGEMENTS

While preparing this book, we have drawn upon the knowledge and work of many ornithologists, birdwatchers and collectors. We are indebted to all these people for devoting their time to furthering our knowledge of these fascinating birds and for putting their findings in a format accessible to us. Perhaps our biggest debt of gratitude should go to Olivier Langrand and Vincent Bretagnolle who in 1990 published their groundbreaking *Guide to the Birds of Madagascar*. That book has inspired countless ornithologists and birdwatchers to visit Madagascar and it was an invaluable source of reference during the preparation of this book. During that preparation a great number of people have kindly offered their help and support. We would like to thank everyone who assisted us and apologise to anyone who has been erroneously omitted from the list below.

This book could never have worked without the submission of thousands of excellent photographs. We would like to thank all the photographers who have submitted their work and offered helpful advice. In particular we would like to thank Simon Harrap and Alan Lewis who kindly loaned their entire slide collections and Alan Greensmith and Ray Tipper who repeatedly supplied transparencies to plug gaps. Of no less importance are the other photographers who have all made an invaluable contribution: Björn Anderson, Magnus Aurivillius, Jem Babbington, Jeff Blincow, Marc de Bont, Robin Chittenden, David Cottridge, Charles Domergue, Joanna Durbin, Brian Field, Nick Garbutt, Kerry Harrison, Jon Hornbuckle, Olivier Langrand, E. McCabe, Robert Morris, Tony Morris, René Pop, Richard Porter, Bosse Söderström, Don Taylor, David Tipling (Windrush), Gavin and Val Thomson, Russell Thorstrom (The Peregrine Fund), Margaret Welby and Barry Wright. We are particularly grateful to Mark Andrews whose excellent artwork, complementing the photographs, has completed the illustrations for all of the species.

We would also like to thank David Dupuy at the Royal Botanic Gardens, Kew, for allowing us to reproduce the excellent habitat map; Robert Prys-Jones and the staff at the Natural History Museum, Tring, for allowing us access to their skin collection; Richard Ranft at the National Sound Archive of the British Library for supplying a number of tape recordings; and Alan Greensmith and Simon Harrap for supplying recordings. We would also like to thank the following who have commented on or helped with the text for particular species/families: Simon Harrap (chats), Claus König (owls), Simon Mustoe (Appert's Greenbul) and Glyn Young (ducks).

Pete Morris would also like to thank Nina Higgins for her patience and tremendous assistance during the preparation of this book, and Nigel Redman for his encouragement during its gestation. He would also like to thank all those who have assisted with field observations, either as travelling companions or for supplying useful birding or logistical information. These include Nina Higgins, Pete Davidson and Barry Wright, Simon Harrap, and all of the Birdquest participants who have travelled to Madagascar with him, Russell Thorstrom for his invaluable help in the Masoala Peninsula, Brian Field and Jem Babbington, Nik Borrow, Nick Gardner, Nick Garbutt, Frank Lambert, Alan Lewis, Simon Mustoe, Steve Smith, and all the excellent local guides, including Maurice and Patrice at Perinet, Fidy at Ranomafana National Park, Mosa and family at Ifaty and Tiana who has accompanied him throughout.

Frank Hawkins would also like to extend his special thanks to Joanna Durbin, the Ministère des Eaux et Forêts, the Association Nationale pour la Gestion des Aires Protégées, WWF International, BirdLife International and the ZICOMA team and the Jersey Wildlife Preservation Trust. The following have all provided valuable input to this project and he would like to thank them all: Andriamasimanana Rado, Andrianarimisa Aristide, Andrianarivo Chantal, Andriantsalama Voahirana, Andriantsilavo Fleurette, Will Duckworth, Joanna Durbin, Lee Durrell, Emahalala Rayonné Ellis, Mike Evans, Faramalala Miadana, Lincoln Fishpool, Joerg Ganzhorn, Steve Goodman, Dominique Halleux, Olivier Langrand, Richard Lewis, Raoul Mulder, Sheila O'Connor, Mark Pidgeon, Mike Putnam, Rabarisoa Rivo, Rabenandrasana Marc, Rabeony Orly, Rakotofiringa Sylvère, Rakotondravony Daniel, Rakotonomenjanahary Odon, Ramanampamonjy Julien, Ramanitra Narisoa Andriamboavonjy, Ramiarison Robert, Raminoarisoa Voninavoko, Randriamanindry Jean-Jacques, Randrianasolo Harison, Ratsirarson Joelisoa, Razafimahaimodison Jean-Claude, Don Reid, Réné de Roland Lily-Arison, Peter Robertson, Roger Safford, Tom Schulenberg, Russell Thorstrom, Patrick de Valois, Glyn Young, and Steve Zack.

The following organisations have provided support to fieldwork in Madagascar: World Wide Fund for Nature - Madagascar, the People's Trust for Endangered Species, Flora and Fauna International, Jersey Wildlife Preservation Trust, the British Ecological Society, the British Ornithologists' Union and British Airways - Assisting Nature Conservation. We are very grateful to all of them.

ILLUSTRATION CREDITS

Mark Andrews	3, 74, 81b, 85, 88, 153, 206, 218b, 241

PHOTOGRAPHIC CREDITS

Björn Anderson	80a
Magnus Aurivillius	160b, 172b, 185b, 186b, 212b, 243b
Jem Babbington	20a, 262a
Jeff Blincow	14a, 19a, 65a, 101, 148, 178a
Marc de Bont	223b
Robin Chittenden	87
Joanna Durbin	fig.6, fig.8
Brian Field	8a, 59c
Nick Garbutt	13a, 57b, 172a, 223a
Alan Greensmith	1, 4b, 20b, 86, 93b, 122,131, 139, 161b, 170b, 188a, 188b, 192a, 192b, 194b, 196, 251b, 254
Simon Harrap	9, 10a, 10b, 19b, 19c, 21a, 40a, 62a, 66b, 80b, 83, 124a, 132a, 138b, 149b, 156, 161a, 163, 179b, 185a, 191a, 191b, 195b, 197, 202a, 213a, 213b, 215a, 222c, 229b, 230b, 233, 235a, 235c, 236, 243a, 244, 245a, 246, 257c, 262b
Frank Hawkins	figs.1–5, fig.7, fig.9, fig.10, 40b, 55b, 56, 69, 79b, 144a, 169a, 200a, 203b, 205
Jon Hornbuckle	15a, 15b, 18, 41b, 62b, 71, 136b
Olivier Langrand (BIOS)	53, 81a, 247
Alan Lewis	24b, 33a, 33b, 38b, 50a, 59b, 67a, 72a, 72b, 72c, 91b, 99a, 100, 144b,158b, 162b, 173, 184b, 186a, 200b, 202b, 209b, 220a, 220b, 224c, 225b, 245b, 251a
E. McCabe	180a, 181a, 252

HOW TO USE THIS BOOK

TAXONOMY AND NOMENCLATURE

There is no recent authority for the taxonomy of Madagascar's birds. The most recent complete treatment of the birds of Africa is Dowsett and Forbes-Watson (1993); however, this does not take into consideration some of the less well-known Malagasy taxonomic issues which have been raised as a result of recent fieldwork and have been discussed in recent ornithological literature. Our general approach has been to use the most widely accepted taxonomic treatment, thus minimising unnecessary or as yet unjustified departures from convention. In this book, the family order follows the sequence of Morony, Bock and Farrand (1975) as adopted by del Hoyo *et al.* (1992–1996). The order within families and nomenclature largely follows that in Dowsett and Forbes-Watson (1993), though some changes have been made.

We have not included Malagasy names in this book as there are few species that have the same name throughout Madagascar. It would be potentially confusing to publish a name used only in one area, as in other places that name might be used for another species or conversely that species might be known under another name. A comprehensive, geographically referenced glossary of Malagasy names is a worthwhile exercise but it is beyond the scope of this book.

A few taxa which have previously not generally been considered full species have been treated as such by us if they are biogeographically, morphologically or ecologically separate, pending more detailed taxonomic reviews. For some which are not generally recognised in the literature, we present evidence for our treatment. We would like to underline our belief that even this is a conservative approach, and that further fieldwork and genetic analysis will doubtless produce further distinct species, and even some surprises at the generic and family levels.

Some of the more contentious and difficult species groups are discussed below:

Dimorphic Egret *Egretta dimorpha*

It seems possible that the medium-sized egrets inland and on the coast of Madagascar may not be the same taxon, given that the coastal population is composed of roughly equal proportions of dark and white morphs while the inland populations are almost exclusively white morphs. Dowsett and Forbes-Watson consider that the Malagasy birds are a subspecies of Little Egret *Egretta garzetta*, but this seems a minority view and is not discussed fully by them. The situation warrants further investigation.

Madagascar White Ibis *Threskiornis bernieri*

This species is distinct from Sacred Ibis in that it is smaller overall, has pale blue eyes, a shorter and finer bill, white wing-tips and appears to occur almost exclusively on estuaries and the muddy borders of lakes, in contrast to the Sacred Ibis *Threskiornis aethiopica* of mainland Africa which is largely a bird of grasslands. Recent reviews of the status of *Threskiornis* ibises lacked the ecological information supporting the treatment of the Madagascar form as a separate species.

Madagascar Hoopoe *Upupa marginata*

This species has different calls, in particular territorial calls, compared to other hoopoes (see species text). In line with Dowsett and Forbes-Watson, we thus treat the Madagascar Hoopoe as a separate species.

Rock Thrushes

We agree with Dowsett & Dowsett-Lemaire (1993) and earlier authors that the Malagasy rock thrushes show more variation between them than there is between the genus *Pseudocossyphus* and *Monticola*, and thus do not warrant their own genus (*Pseudocossyphus*). In addition, we consider that the **Amber Mountain Rock Thrush** is a good species (*Monticola erythronotus*) on the basis of its strikingly different structure and plumage (in both the male and female) and its isolated distribution. We are confident that ongoing field and genetic studies will reveal other differences to support this treatment.

Madagascar Yellowbrow *Crossleyia xanthophrys*

Some recent literature has treated this species in the same genus (*Oxylabes*) as the White-throated Oxylabes. We would like to emphasise that apart from their terrestrial habits, these two species are extremely different both in their morphological and their vocal characteristics. Thus we retain the monotypic genus *Crossleyia* as well as the distinct common name.

Subdesert Brush Warbler *Nesillas lantzii*

This species has already been treated as separate from Madagascar Brush Warbler (Schulenberg *et al.* 1993) and we support this view, as the calls of the two species are quite distinct and the distributions overlap in the region of Fort Dauphin.

Wedge-tailed Jery *Hartertula flavoviridis*

This species is very distinct from the other jeries and should not be treated as a *Neomixis*. It also does not bear the slightest resemblance, as has been suggested, to *Thamnornis*. We thus retain the monotypic genus *Hartertula*.

There are a few other forms which further study may prove to be good species. These include the endemic form of **African Black Swift** *Apus barbatus balstoni* which is considered to merit specific status by some authors. A recent monograph on swifts (Chantler and Driessens 1995) considered it to be a subspecies of African Black Swift. In addition, further studies of the **Madagascar Scops Owl** *Otus rutilus* may result in the recognition of more than one species based largely on vocal differences.

SPECIES INCLUDED IN THE BOOK

All naturally occurring resident species, breeding and non-breeding visitors and vagrants are included in the main body of the book. Also included are introduced species which have established, or show signs of establishing, a feral population. Those seabirds which have not been recorded from land and are only on the Madagascar list on the basis of observations made from boats in Malagasy waters are included in Appendix A. Species which have definitely become extinct have generally been excluded from the book. These include, among others, the amazing elephant birds, but the beautiful Snail-eating Coua *Coua delalandei* which was last recorded from Ile Sainte-Marie off the east coast in 1834 is treated briefly in Appendix B. Other species on the verge of extinction, such as Alaotra Little Grebe *Tachybaptus rufolavatus* and Madagascar Pochard *Aythya innotata*, are included, though the future does not look good for either. There are also two historically recorded species, Long-crested Eagle *Lophaetus occipitalis* and Lesser Striped Swallow *Hirundo abyssinica* which have been omitted as it seems possible that the records are erroneous and it is unlikely that these species will occur again. These species are also included in Appendix B.

SPECIES ACCOUNTS

These are treated under a number of headings:

DESCRIPTION

The text begins with an introductory sentence indicating the general size and type of bird. This is followed by a detailed description of all plumages likely to be encountered in Madagascar. Where there are distinct differences in plumage between adult male and adult female, between breeding and non-breeding plumages, distinctive immature plumages or more than one colour morph, these are described. For the definition of technical terms the reader is referred to the Glossary.

VOICE

Many of the bird calls have been described using written descriptions which attempt to mimic the sound and form of the call. The voice descriptions are largely based on the field experience and tape recordings of the authors.

HABITAT/BEHAVIOUR

The habitat types in which the species is most likely to be seen are listed. Characteristics of the species' behaviour are briefly described, including whether it is generally of a solitary or gregarious nature, what it feeds on and how it finds its prey. For species breeding in Madagascar, a brief description of the structure and location of the nest is given except in cases where no data are available.

RANGE/STATUS

The following information is given:

1. The species' world range. This indicates briefly where else the species is known to occur, or if the species is endemic to Madagascar or the Malagasy region.

2. The global conservation status of the species as given in Collar *et al.* (1994). The categories used are as defined in this book and are outlined in the table below.

Criteria	Main numerical thresholds		
	Critical	**Endangered**	**Vulnerable**
Rapid Decline	>80% over 10 years or 3 generations	>50% over 10 years or 3 generations	>50% over 20 years or 5 generations
Small Range	Extent of occurrence <100km^2 or area of occupancy <10km^2	Extent of occurrence <5,000km^2 or area of occupancy <500km^2	Extent of occurrence <20,000km^2 or area of occupancy <2,000km^2
Small Population (declining)	<250 mature individuals	<2,500 mature individuals	<10,000 mature individuals
Very Small Population	<50 mature individuals	<250 mature individuals	<1,000 mature individuals
Very Small Range	–	–	<100km^2 or <5 locations
Unfavourable PVA*	Probability of extinction >50% within 5 years	Probability of extinction >20% within 20 years	Probability of extinction >10% within 100 years

* PVA = Population Viability Analysis

In addition, some species are considered to be Near Threatened. This is a subjective category based on reduced levels of research. The species deemed near threatened are those which did not meet the criteria of the above three categories but are nevertheless a cause for concern or further study. By listing these species as Near Threatened it emphasises the need to continue to gather data and monitor populations of these species.

3. The subspecies occurring in Madagascar is/are given along with a brief summary of the world range(s) of the subspecies. Where a species is monotypic this is stated. If the subspecies is endemic to the Malagasy region the distinctions between it and the subspecies found in mainland Africa are described.

4. The range of the species within Madagascar is described.

5. The known altitudinal range of the species is given.

6. Any taxonomic notes are placed at the end of this section. This includes reasons for taxonomic decisions employed in this book and also highlights other taxa which may merit full specific status or subspecies which are treated by other authors as full species.

WHERE TO SEE
This part gives an indication of the abundance of the species, and the sites at which a visiting birdwatcher is most likely to encounter them. The sites mentioned in this section are largely selected from those detailed below under Birdwatching Sites in Madagascar.

SIMILAR SPECIES
This section aims to provide the user with a concise summary of identification pitfalls within Madagascar. Similar species known to occur are brought to the reader's attention and the main identification criteria summarised. In a few cases, potential vagrants which have not yet been recorded in Madagascar but which may cause identification pitfalls should they do so, are also mentioned.

THE PHOTOGRAPHS
The photographs selected have been chosen to show, wherever possible, the salient identification features of the species. In species which show distinct sexual dimorphism or age related plumage differences, a number of photographs have been used where they were available. In addition, where species are represented by more than one distinct subspecies or morph, these have been illustrated whenever possible. Most of the photographs were taken in the wild in Madagascar but inevitably some were not, and in these cases we have attempted to use photographs of the form occurring in Madagascar. In a few cases where these were not available photographs of a similar form have been selected.

or Balsaminaceae, which may grow to a couple of metres in height in damp valleys, making observation of terrestrial birds difficult. Often *Pandanus* trees and tree-ferns are abundant, the former particularly on ridges. There are large numbers of epiphytes, particularly orchids and ferns. This forest type may be found to about 1,600m or even higher in sheltered dells, although the transition to montane forest occurs at around 1,200m on exposed ridges. Many species of bird find their upper limit with the limit of mid-altitude forest. They include many terrestrial and understorey species such as Short-legged Ground-roller, Long-billed and Spectacled Greenbuls, Crossley's Babbler and Madagascar Magpie-Robin. Equally, there is a wide range of canopy species that drop out at this level, including Rand's Warbler, Stripe-throated and Common Jeries, and Blue, Red-tailed, Hook-billed and White-headed Vangas. At least Common Sunbird-Asity is restricted to mid-altitude forest, being rare in lowland forest and replaced at higher altitudes by Yellow-bellied Sunbird-Asity.

Several species of bird only appear in mid-altitude forest, being largely absent from lowland forest. They include Rufous-headed Ground-roller, Grey-crowned Greenbul, Madagascar Yellowbrow, Brown Emutail, and Cryptic Warbler. They are all also common in montane forest.

Montane forest is characterized by a low canopy, rarely more than 5-8m, with very heavy moss growth, carpeting the forest floor and most tree limbs and trunks. Many of the canopy species are of the family Ericaceae. Other epiphytes are also abundant, and the herb-layer, understorey and canopy merge in many places to form an almost solid wall of tangled vegetation. There may be very dense growths of parasites such as *Bakerella* and members of the Mistletoe family. Bamboo is also common in such habitats, being frequently of a species with unpleasant irritating hairs on the leaf-sheaths. Tree-ferns, palms and *Pandanus* trees may be locally common, and in such places as Andringitra, almost monotypic stands of *Podocarpus* trees may occur. Yellow-bellied Sunbird-Asity is commonest in this habitat.

Above the montane forest (mostly above 1,600-2,000m) may occur sclerophyllous or ericoid scrub, which is essentially a dwarfed form of the montane forest, up to a couple of metres in height. It may be interspersed with areas of grass, bamboo, or bare rock, depending on exposure. In areas where the scrub is high, dense mats of moss may form on the ground. There are no species limited to this habitat, but some (for instance Stonechat) may appear in this habitat when they are absent from true forest.

Figure 3: Western deciduous forest on Tsingy, Ankarana.

Forest (Western deciduous, seasonally dry forest)

Western Malagasy deciduous forest (figures 3 and 4) occurs on sandy, calcareous, lateritic or more rarely ferralitic or basaltic soils over the entire west of Madagascar, from Cap d'Ambre in the north, to south of Ihosy and Isalo, where it grades into southern spiny forest. It probably originally covered an area of 13 million hectares, but now it occurs in a large number of small fragments, the sum of which only covers about 1.5 million hectares. Only about 55 of these blocks are larger than 3,500 hectares and only five are larger than 50,000 hectares.

Western Malagasy deciduous forest structure and species composition varies somewhat with a humidity and rainfall gradient that declines to the south. It varies additionally (often more substantially) with substrate, with forest on the calcareous 'tsingy' pinnacle karst being extremely stunted. The usual structure is that of a canopy at between 8 and 20 metres, usually closed and formed of between 10% and 80% deciduous trees. Especially in the south, there are many bottle-trunked trees, the best known being the baobabs (figure 10). There are many epiphytes, in particular lianas and orchids, although not as wide a selection as are found in the east. The understorey is often fairly dense, sometimes spiny, and often difficult to penetrate, especially in areas near rivers. There is often very little herb layer, although in some areas carpets of *Lissochilus* orchids cover the ground.

There are four species of bird largely or wholly restricted to western forest; White-breasted Mesite, Coquerel's Coua, Appert's Greenbul, and Van Dam's Vanga. There are additionally some species that occur only in either western or southern forest. This is perhaps not surprising given the similarity in structure and climate between the two forest types. These species include Red-capped and Giant Couas, Sickle-billed Vanga and Sakalava Weaver.

Figure 4: Western deciduous forest, Ampijoroa.

Forest (Southern deciduous dry forest)

Southern Malagasy spiny forest is a very particular forest formation, characterised in many places by the cactus-like trees of the endemic Didiereaceae family. The forest occurs on mostly sandy and calcareous substrates not far from the coast between just north of the Mangoky river in the west to just west of Fort Dauphin in the east. It currently covers an area of about 1.4 million hectares.

There are several different forms of this forest type that hold rather different bird communities. The north-western sector of spiny forest, between Toliara and the Mangoky (figure 5), is fairly tall forest, 5-15m high and with many species in common with western Malagasy deciduous forest. The presence of abundant *Didierea* trees is characteristic. The Subdesert Mesite and Long-tailed Ground-roller are found only in this habitat. South of Toliara and near the coast, especially on calcareous soils, euphorbia forest (figure 6) is more common. This is lower (2-3m), and denser, being almost impenetrable. Verreaux's Coua, Littoral Rock Thrush and Red-shouldered Vanga are largely limited to this forest type. Towards the east and somewhat inland, the spiny forest resembles that to the north of Toliara but is dominated by *Alluaudia* species, which resemble *Didierea*. Again many species of more conventional tree are shared between this forest type and western Malagasy deciduous forest. The Thamnornis Warbler occurs in this forest and in that to the north of Toliara, but not in coastal euphorbia scrub. Running Coua, Archbold's Newtonia, Subdesert Brush-Warbler and Lafresnaye's Vanga are found all over the southern Malagasy spiny forest domain, but nowhere else.

Figure 5: Spiny forest, Andohahela.

Figure 6: Euphorbia scrub.

Savanna

Malagasy savannas (figure 7), which cover the greater proportion of the high plateau, the west and the south, are dominated by alien grass and tree species. In the high plateau, there are only three or four species of grass over vast areas of sterile landscape. In the west and south, the savanna may be colonised by a few species of fire-resistant native tree, and there are often huge and spectacular populations of the endemic palm *Bismarckia nobilis*. In some areas of the plateau, notably near Isalo and Fianarantsoa, tree-savanna with the endemic, fire-resistant Tapia Tree *Uapaca bojeri* occurs. Very few species of bird occur in this habitat and few of them are endemic to Madagascar. The most frequent is the Madagascar Bush Lark, which with the Madagascar Cisticola is found all over the island in savanna habitats. The Réunion Harrier is found rarely in savanna grasslands, mostly on the plateau. The Madagascar Partridge, Buttonquail, Sandgrouse and Hoopoe can be found in tree-savanna, particularly in the west, where other non-endemic species such as the Namaqua Dove and Helmeted Guineafowl are also common. Benson's Rock Thrush is found in areas of Tapia forest and rocks near Isalo, and in low-altitude tree-savanna in the south-west the local race of the Stripe-throated Jery is very common. In areas of scrubby savanna not far from primary forest the Red-capped Coua may be found.

Figure 7: Savanna near Ankaramem.

Wetlands (East)

Eastern Malagasy wetlands occur in the form of lakes (figure 8), rivers and marshes (figure 9). There are few large lakes in the region; however there is the largest in the country, Alaotra, plus the system of sterile acid coastal lagoons called the Pangalanes. Alaotra is nowadays heavily polluted with fertilisers and insecticides, clogged with sediments and what vegetation occurs on the lake is mostly introduced *Salvinia* and Water-hyacinth. In the past, the lake was home to huge populations of waterbirds, including the Alaotra Grebe and Madagascar Pochard, as well as colonies of African Spoonbills, Yellow-billed Storks, and many species of Heron. Nowadays the grebe and the pochard are on the verge of extinction, if not already extinct, while the colonies of large waterbirds are just a memory. There are still fairly good numbers of Meller's Ducks around the lake, and Humblot's Herons can still be seen, but it is not clear if these species really breed at the lake. There are few species of waterbird recorded from the Pangalanes, but more extensive searches might reveal a significant population of Meller's Ducks.

The rivers of the east are mostly fairly short, descending rapidly to the Indian Ocean down the scarp. Some among them, in particular those of the centre-east, provide shelter for pairs of Meller's Ducks where the rivers flow through rainforest.

The most important eastern wetlands are the marshes. These are usually small areas of swampy vegetation, usually at moderate or high altitude and often in narrow valleys or on the fringes of lakes. They are dominated by *Cyperus* sedges, *Phragmites* reeds, rushes, grasses and often contain

Figure 8: Lake near Alaotra.

Figure 9: Torotorofotsy Marsh.

large numbers of orchids. The marshes of Vohiparara, in Ranomafana National Park, are one such example. In inhabited areas, these valley-bottom marshes are much in demand for rice cultivation. Some such marshes, Torotorofotsy and Didy being good examples, are very large. The vegetation is often up to 3m tall, especially on the fringes of larger lakes such as Alaotra. In marshes with no or little free-standing water, such as Torotorofotsy, the vegetation is about a metre high and there may be 15-20cm of water underneath. There are several species of bird limited to these habitats. The Slender-billed Flufftail is an extremely secretive bird, currently known from only two eastern marshland sites, both in or near abandoned rice-fields. However it is probably much more widespread. The Madagascar Snipe, Madagascar Rail and Grey Emutail are widespread and are much easier to see. Other species, not limited to the habitat but common within it, are Madagascar Little Grebe, Madagascar Swamp Warbler and Common Stonechat.

Figure 10: Baobab relicts, western deciduous forest, Morondava.

Wetlands (West)

As in the east, western wetlands occur as rivers, lakes and marshes. However, their character is rather different from those of the east. The typical western wetland is a shallow, perhaps seasonal, lake, with patches of *Phragmites* along certain of the banks, others that were open and muddy, and much native *Nymphea* lily-pad growth over the surface. Western lakes are often slightly alkaline and thus richer in vegetation and more productive than their eastern counterparts. Unfortunately these lakes are becoming increasingly rare, as they are much in demand by local people for the growing of rice. Other wetland types present in western Madagascar include the banks and waters of the larger rivers, such as the Betsiboka, Tsiribihina and Mahavavy, the soda lake of Tsimanampetsotsa in the far south-west and the salt lake of Ihotry, north of Toliara. These two waterbodies appear to be the relicts of a much more extensive system of freshwater wetlands that extended from Morondava to Fort Dauphin around four thousand years ago. The disappearance of these wetlands had a major effect on the biodiversity of the area, with at least three species of hippopotamus, a *Vanellus* lapwing, a large goose, a shelduck, and at least two rails now extinct.

Several species of waterbird are found nowhere else but in these wetlands. The Sakalava Rail is a close relative of the African Black Crake *Amaurornis flavirostris*, but seems strangely rare or is extremely secretive. It has only been recorded once recently, from Bemamba Lake near Antsalova. The Madagascar Teal is less secretive than the Sakalava Rail but is probably much more threatened. It seems unlikely that there are more than 500 of this attractive small duck left. They are restricted to an area between Morondava and the Sambirano where they breed in large mangrove tree-holes and feed on mudflat edges and muddy lake fringes. Humblot's Heron is a large species related to the rare White-bellied and Great-billed Herons of South and South-east Asia. It is also rather rare, usually found singly on lake shores or estuaries.

Table 1. Threatened bird species of Madagascar (contd.)

English Name	Scientific Name	Status
Scaly Ground-roller	*Brachypteracias squamigera*	Vulnerable
Rufous-headed Ground-roller	*Atelornis crossleyi*	Vulnerable
Long-tailed Ground-roller	*Uratelornis chimaera*	Vulnerable
Yellow-bellied Sunbird-Asity	*Neodrepanis hypoxantha*	Endangered
Appert's Greenbul	*Phyllastrephus apperti*	Vulnerable
Grey-crowned Greenbul	*Phyllastrephus cinereiceps*	Vulnerable
Dusky Greenbul	*Phyllastrephus tenebrosus*	Endangered
Pollen's Vanga	*Xenopirostris polleni*	Vulnerable
Van Dam's Vanga	*Xenopirostris damii*	Vulnerable
Bernier's Vanga	*Oriolia bernieri*	Vulnerable
Benson's Rock Thrush	*Monticola bensoni*	Vulnerable
Madagascar Yellowbrow	*Crossleyia xanthophrys*	Vulnerable
Red-tailed Newtonia	*Newtonia fanovanae*	Vulnerable

Table 2. Near threatened bird species of Madagascar

Madagascar Pond Heron	*Ardeola idae*
Madagascar Crested Ibis	*Lophotibis cristata*
Lesser Flamingo	*Phoeniconaias minor*
Meller's Duck	*Anas melleri*
Réunion Harrier	*Circus maillardi*
Henst's Goshawk	*Accipiter henstii*
Madagascar Sparrowhawk	*Accipiter madagascariensis*
Verreaux's Coua	*Coua verreauxi*
Pitta-like Ground-roller	*Atelornis pittoides*
Schlegel's Asity	*Philepitta schlegeli*
Helmet Vanga	*Euryceros prevostii*
Forest Rock Thrush	*Monticola sharpei*
Brown Emutail	*Dromaeocercus brunneus*
Rand's Warbler	*Randia pseudozosterops*
Wedge-tailed Jery	*Hartertula flavoviridis*
Ward's Flycatcher	*Pseudobias wardi*

DISTRIBUTION OF BIRDS WITHIN PROTECTED AREAS

Malagasy wetlands are very poorly protected. Of the wetland birds in the threatened bird list above, only Slender-billed Flufftail and Madagascar Plover have significant populations in protected areas. Even such critically threatened species such as Madagascar Fish Eagle and Sakalava Rail have no (or in the case of Madagascar Fish Eagle probably three) pairs in protected areas. The Alaotra Grebe and the Madagascar Pochard are probably on the edge of extinction, although stalwart efforts to conserve the last vestiges of useful habitat at Lake Alaotra are underway. The Madagascar Teal is probably the most threatened of the remaining species, as it nests in tree holes in mangroves, which are under considerable pressure for prawn-pond construction and timber extraction. The recent increase in prawn-pond development in Madagascar threatens almost the entire breeding range of this species, both by destruction of breeding trees and the massive increase in hunting pressure that results from the prawn-pond workers.

Almost all the threatened forest bird species of Madagascar are found within protected areas. Only Subdesert Mesite and Long-tailed Ground-roller have no formal protection; the Red-shouldered Vanga, also not yet known from any protected area, has not been treated under any Red-Data Book as it was only described in 1997, but will probably come under the Vulnerable category if no further populations are found. Zombitse and Vohibasia forests, long exploited for charcoal and cleared for maize planting, and the home to the entire world population of Appert's Greenbul, will shortly become a national park. The Subdesert Mesite and Long-tailed Ground-roller share an almost identical range between Toliara and the Mangoky river. The southern part of this habitat is very degraded through canopy tree extraction for charcoal, but there are fairly large intact forest blocks to the west of the main road between Toliara and Morombe, where presumably fairly large populations of these two species still exist. The Red-shouldered Vanga is only known from a very limited area of forest between the Onilahy river and Toliara, a distance of perhaps 20km, in coastal euphorbia scrub, so its population may be very small. However the habitat extends for long distances north and south and the species may well be found more widely.

PRIORITIES FOR CONSERVATION ACTION

The recent upsurge in interest in Malagasy birds has lead to the description of two new species (one in a new genus) since 1996. There are probably more to be discovered, and investigation of the status of forms currently treated as subspecies will probably reveal previously unrecognised distinct species. Thus a first priority for conservation action is more data on the distribution and status of as many species as possible. This need is being addressed by the BirdLife International Important Bird Area programme (ZICOMA - Zones d'Importance pour la Conservation des Oiseaux à Madagascar), which aims to visit and inventory as many hitherto unsurveyed sites as possible. In addition, studies on the taxonomic status of these indeterminate forms will permit the recognition of sites where they are found as important centres of endemicity. However there are clearly many places that current research programmes (including ZICOMA) will not be able to visit, so information on any site outside the major tourist centres is invaluable.

Population estimates of some of the rarer species are also vital. For only a handful of Malagasy bird species has there even been an order of magnitude estimate made. For species such as Benson's Rock Thrush and Madagascar Plover, even an approximate estimate might reveal that they are not really threatened. For others, such as Humblot's Heron or Madagascar Pond Heron, a population estimate might reveal that the chances of random events or the elimination of a single particularly favoured piece of habitat having a profound effect on their population might be very high, so that their level of menace is currently underestimated.

Clearly, as regards habitat conservation, wetlands are effectively unprotected at present, so effort to manage wetlands to maintain their biodiversity interest as well as their essential human support functions is primordial. The Malagasy government are currently addressing the possibilities of signing the Ramsar Convention, which should help in introducing a legal and conceptual framework for the conservation of wetlands.

WHAT BIRDWATCHERS CAN DO

A major contribution to the conservation of the biodiversity of a country can be made simply by letting the government of the country know that you are coming to the country to observe the wildlife. Making it clear that Madagascar's bird life is fascinating and of great value to you, the evidence being the money you paid to come to and stay in Madagascar, will help to convince decision-makers that it is worth investing money in biodiversity conservation for purely financial reasons.

As far as the priorities for conservation action are concerned, there are many places that have never been fully explored for birds. Even those that have are still turning up some major surprises. Of the last two species discovered in Madagascar, the Cryptic Warbler and the Red-shouldered Vanga, the former is one of the commoner (and certainly most easily detectable) birds of montane forest, first collected at Maromizaha, a mere 8km from Perinet, the most studied site on the island. The Red-shouldered Vanga was found within 10km of the centre of Toliara, a major provincial capital. There are undoubtedly more such discoveries to be made. The ranges of many species are poorly known and a casual visit to a roadside forest away from the major centres could easily turn up something very interesting. Aside from the usual description (and photographs if possible), there are two pieces of information that will prove invaluable in such circumstances and that might not be collected by every birdwatcher; the first is a tape-recording of any calls made, and the second is an exact geographical locality. The latter is most easily gathered using a hand-held Geographical Positioning System receiver, (a GPS), a remarkable and affordable instrument costing nowadays less then 200 US dollars. Having obtained such data, the essential thing is to make sure that they are deposited where they will be best exploited. The BirdLife Madagascar office (see below for address) will ensure that all such data reaches the people who will make best use of them.

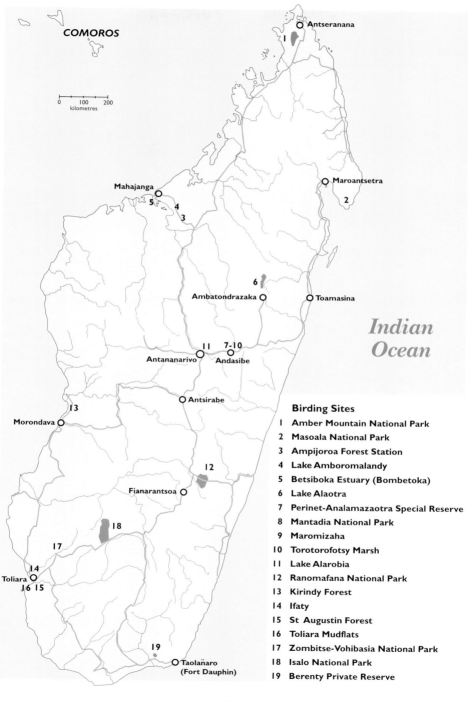

COMOROS

0   100   200
kilometres

Antseranana
1

Maroantsetra
2

Mahajanga
5
4
3

6

Ambatondrazaka
Toamasina

Indian Ocean

11   7-10
Antananarivo   Andasibe

Antsirabe

13
Morondava

12

Fianarantsoa

18

17

14
Toliara
16 15

19

Taolañaro
(Fort Dauphin)

Birding Sites

1   Amber Mountain National Park
2   Masoala National Park
3   Ampijoroa Forest Station
4   Lake Amboromalandy
5   Betsiboka Estuary (Bombetoka)
6   Lake Alaotra
7   Perinet-Analamazaotra Special Reserve
8   Mantadia National Park
9   Maromizaha
10   Torotorofotsy Marsh
11   Lake Alarobia
12   Ranomafana National Park
13   Kirindy Forest
14   Ifaty
15   St Augustin Forest
16   Toliara Mudflats
17   Zombitse-Vohibasia National Park
18   Isalo National Park
19   Berenty Private Reserve

BIRDWATCHING SITES IN MADAGASCAR

1. Amber Mountain National Park

Habitat: Submontane rainforest.

Access: About 30km south of Antseranana (Diégo-Suarez) in northern Madagascar. A taxi from Antseranana will take you to the park along a road that runs through Joffreville.

Accommodation: Take tents and all food with you, and camp near the tree nursery.

Permits: Available from the ANGAP office in Antseranana.

Best time of the year: October-November.

Key species: The Amber Mountain subspecies of the Forest Rock Thrush is probably a good species. The local subspecies of the Spectacled Greenbul is also very distinctive. Otherwise Pitta-like Ground-rollers are fairly common.

2. Masoala National Park

Habitat: Lowland and submontane rainforest.

Access: From Maroantsetra, which is most easily reached by scheduled flights from Antananarivo, the park is most easily accessible by boat. It is a three-hour trip each way and the charter may be arranged through hotels in Maroantsetra.

Accommodation: Very basic facilities (camping and a shelter) are available at Ambanizana. Best to take tents and all provisions with you, though some basics may be available at Ambanizana.

Permits: Available from the ANGAP office in Antananarivo or in the National Park office in Maroantsetra.

Best time of the year: September-November.

Key species: Helmet Vanga and Bernier's Vanga are both present around Ambanizana as are Scaly and Short-legged Ground-rollers and Brown Mesite. Red-breasted Coua is common. Madagascar Red Owl and Madagascar Serpent Eagle are both present though difficult to see. The Peregrine Fund are sometimes able to assist visitors in finding these species and should be contacted in advance by prospective visitors wishing to find them. Pools, beaches and estuarine habitats around the town of Maroantsetra are worth exploring for wetland species including herons, cormorants, ducks, waders and terns.

3. Ampijoroa Forest Station

Habitat: deciduous western forest, freshwater lake.

Access: Ampijoroa Forest Station is on the main N4 Antananarivo-Mahajanga road, 130km south of Mahajanga (Majunga). Trails lead all over the forest.

Accommodation: It is possible to camp at the Forest Station. The nearest hotels are in Mahajanga.

Permits: Obtainable on site.

Best time of the year: September-December.

Key species: White-breasted Mesite, Madagascar Fish Eagle, Coquerel's Coua, Schlegel's Asity, Van Dam's Vanga.

4. Lake Amboromalandy

Habitat: large freshwater reservoir, flooded rice fields in season.

Access: Amboromalandy lake is between Ampijoroa and Mahajanga on the main N4 route, about 95km south of Mahajanga. The far north-eastern portion of the lake, where there are marshes, is the most interesting. This is most easily accessed by walking the length of the southern shore. If the rice paddies on the western side of the road are flooded, there may be interesting species on them.

Accommodation: There are many hotels in Mahajanga, about 1.5h drive away.

Permits: Not necessary.

Best time of the year: November-January.

Key species: Madagascar Teal, Humblot's Heron, Madagascar Jacana, Madagascar Pond Heron, Madagascar Little Grebe.

❏	Rock Dove/Feral Pigeon	*Columba livia*	180
❏	Madagascar Turtle Dove	*Streptopelia picturata*	180
❏	Namaqua Dove	*Oena capensis*	182
❏	Madagascar Green Pigeon	*Treron australis*	182
❏	Madagascar Blue Pigeon	*Alectroenas madagascariensis*	184
❏	Greater Vasa Parrot	*Coracopsis vasa*	184
❏	Lesser Vasa Parrot	*Coracopsis nigra*	186
❏	Grey-headed Lovebird	*Agapornis canus*	186
❏	Thick-billed Cuckoo	*Cuculus audeberti*	188
❏	Madagascar Lesser Cuckoo	*Cuculus rochii*	188
❏	Giant Coua	*Coua gigas*	190
❏	Coquerel's Coua	*Coua coquereli*	190
❏	Running Coua	*Coua cursor*	192
❏	Red-breasted Coua	*Coua serriana*	192
❏	Red-fronted Coua	*Coua reynaudii*	194
❏	Red-capped Coua	*Coua ruficeps*	194
❏	Crested Coua	*Coua cristata*	196
❏	Verreaux's Coua	*Coua verreauxi*	196
❏	Blue Coua	*Coua caerulea*	198
❏	Madagascar Coucal	*Centropus toulou*	198
❏	Madagascar Red Owl	*Tyto soumagnei*	200
❏	Barn Owl	*Tyto alba*	200
❏	Madagascar Scops Owl	*Otus rutilus*	202
❏	White-browed Owl	*Ninox superciliaris*	202
❏	Madagascar Long-eared Owl	*Asio madagascariensis*	204
❏	Marsh Owl	*Asio capensis*	204
❏	Collared Nightjar	*Caprimulgus enarratus*	206
❏	Madagascar Nightjar	*Caprimulgus madagascariensis*	206
❏	Madagascar Spinetail	*Zoonavena grandidieri*	208
❏	African Palm Swift	*Cypsiurus parvus*	208
❏	Alpine Swift	*Apus melba*	210
❏	African Black Swift	*Apus barbatus*	210
❏	Little Swift	*Apus affinis*	212
❏	Madagascar Malachite Kingfisher	*Alcedo vintsioides*	212
❏	Madagascar Pygmy Kingfisher	*Ceyx madagascariensis*	214
❏	Madagascar Bee-eater	*Merops superciliosus*	214
❏	European Bee-eater	*Merops apiaster*	216
❏	Broad-billed Roller	*Eurystomus glaucurus*	216
❏	Short-legged Ground-roller	*Brachypteracias leptosomus*	218
❏	Scaly Ground-roller	*Brachypteracias squamigera*	218
❏	Pitta-like Ground-roller	*Atelornis pittoides*	220

SPECIES ACCOUNTS

1   Rockhopper Penguin *Eudyptes chrysocome*

DESCRIPTION Size: 55-62cm. Sexes similar, though male averages larger. Plumage varies slightly with age. The only penguin to have been recorded in Madagascar. **Adult:** Head and upperparts dark blue-black, black occipital crest with a narrow golden-yellow plumes on the sides of the head. Underparts white. Iris red, bill thick and dull red, legs and feet pink with black soles. Immature: as adult, though crest shorter, and may show some pale on the chin and throat. **Juvenile:** Smaller than adult, bill duller and only a faint crest. Some white on the chin and throat.
VOICE Raucous braying calls.
HABITAT/BEHAVIOUR Marine and pelagic.
RANGE/STATUS Circumpolar in the subantarctic zone with the nearest breeding sites to Madagascar being on Saint Paul and Amsterdam Islands. Not globally threatened. Monotypic. Recorded once in Madagascar, an individual taken at the south tip of Betanty in January 1956. It may have been released by sailors.
WHERE TO SEE A very rare vagrant and therefore no regular sites. Most likely to turn up on south-coast beaches.

2   Little Grebe *Tachybaptus ruficollis*

DESCRIPTION Size: 25-29cm. A small grebe. Sexes alike, though marked seasonal variation. **Adult breeding:** Distinctive rufous patch extending over the ear-coverts, throat, foreneck and sides of neck, merging into the dark brown breast and lower foreneck. Crown, hindneck and upperparts blackish-brown, paler and browner on the flanks. Underparts dark brown, mottled paler, especially on the belly. In flight, upperwing dark brown with variable white inner webs of secondaries showing as an indistinct white bar. **Adult non-breeding:** Much drabber. Upperparts including crown and hindneck dark brown, underparts, cheeks and rest of neck paler buff-brown. Iris dull red, bill black with white tip and in breeding plumage a prominent yellow spot at the base which is usually visible in non-breeding plumage. Legs and feet greyish-green. **Immature:** Similar to adult non-breeding.
VOICE A loud and distinctive whinnying trill and a short, clipped whit in alarm.
HABITAT/BEHAVIOUR Freshwater or brackish pools and rivers usually with marginal and/or floating vegetation. Found in pairs in the breeding season, small groups at other times. Dives for food and often dives to escape predators.
RANGE/STATUS Found throughout much of Europe and Asia east to New Guinea and the Solomons, northern and sub-Saharan Africa. Not globally threatened. Subspecies *T. r. capensis*, common in Africa and is probably recently established in Madagascar where the first reference dates from around 1930. Now a common resident throughout in suitable habitats from sea level to 1,500m, though less common in the east. Studies indicate that the introduction of Tilapia fish have aided its establishment and the species may be out-competing the two endemic grebe species.
WHERE TO SEE Common in many deeper lakes in the highlands in the east and west, sometimes in large numbers. Also occurs in wetlands in the west such as Lake Amboromalandy, north-west of Ampijoroa Forest Station.
SIMILAR SPECIES In breeding plumage distinguished from Madagascar and Alaotra Little Grebes by the extensive rufous neck patch and yellow spot at the base of the bill. In non-breeding plumage more difficult to identify. Madagascar Little Grebe tends to show a trace of the breeding plumage with a pale line between the dark cap and the greyish cheeks, absent in Little Grebe. Compared to Alaotra Little Grebe, Little Grebe shows less mottling on the breast and flanks and typically lacks the white iris shown by Alaotra.

Rockhopper Penguin, adult.

a. Little Grebe, adult breeding.

2b. *Little Grebe, adult non-breeding.*

3 Alaotra Little Grebe *Tachybaptus rufolavatus*

DESCRIPTION Size: 25cm. A small, short-winged grebe. Sexes alike, though marked seasonal variation. **Adult breeding:** Glossy black cap to the nape and continuing as a narrow line down the hindneck. The black cap extends as a line below the eye and meets the chin, isolating the pale eye. Rest of head and neck pale cinnamon, paler, whitish on the throat. Upperparts dark brown, underparts dusky buff, mottled with white and dark grey, palest on the centre of the belly. Wings show a distinct white wing-bar on the secondaries and inner primaries. **Adult non-breeding:** Drabber than adult breeding. Cap brown not black, and cinnamon on the face much less distinct. Breast and flanks mottled. Iris pale, whitish, bill long and thick, dark with a pale tip, legs and feet olive-grey. **Immature:** Similar to adult non-breeding. Note, this species is known to hybridise with Little Grebe and hybrids may show mixed characters of the two species.
VOICE Unknown, though probably similar to previous species.
HABITAT/BEHAVIOUR Previously inhabited the densely vegetated shallows of Lake Alaotra and adjacent swamps. Thought to be strongly sedentary as indicated by its short wings. Behaviour assumed to be similar to other two species.
RANGE/STATUS Endemic to Madagascar. Globally threatened and currently classified as **Critically Endangered.** Monotypic. On the verge of extinction probably due to habitat destruction, pollution, introduction of exotic fish and competition and hybridisation with Little Grebe. Only definitely recorded from the Lake Alaotra region in north central Madagascar where it was apparently last recorded in 1985 despite many searches since then. Records from other parts of Madagascar may relate to hybrids.
Where to see: Although possibly extinct it may be worth searching any wetland habitats around Lake Alaotra.
SIMILAR SPECIES In all plumages the exceptionally long bill (much longer than the other two small grebes occurring in Madagascar) should be apparent. In breeding plumage identified by the combination of the black cap contrasting with pale cinnamon cheeks. In non-breeding plumage Madagascar Little Grebe usually shows a trace of a pale line between the dark cap and the greyish cheeks which is absent in Alaotra Little Grebe. In addition Alaotra Little Grebe shows far more dark mottling on the breast and flanks than the other two species, though this may be difficult to see in the field. The pale iris should be diagnostic in all plumages.

4 Madagascar Little Grebe *Tachybaptus pelzelnii*

DESCRIPTION Size: 25cm. A small grebe. Sexes alike, though marked seasonal variation. **Adult breeding:** Black cap extending to the nape and as a narrow line down the hindneck, restricted rufous patch on the rear cheeks and sides of neck. Chin, throat and rest of the neck fawn-grey. Rufous cheeks partly separated from the dark crown by a whitish line which is broadest below the eye. Upperparts dark blackish-brown, underparts whitish with grey-brown breast and flanks. In flight the upperwing shows a distinctive narrow wing-bar which extends on to the primaries. **Adult non-breeding:** Drabber than breeding plumage. Upperparts, including the cap and hindneck, dark brown, cheeks and rest of neck grey-brown, with an indistinct paler line on the face. Rest of underparts whitish. Iris red, bill dark with a pale tip, legs and feet greyish-green. **Immature:** Similar to adult non-breeding.
VOICE A loud whinnying, similar to Little Grebe, though sounding less hysterical, being slightly lower-pitched and harsher.
HABITAT/BEHAVIOUR Prefers temporary or permanent, usually shallow, bodies of fresh water with abundant aquatic vegetation, especially lilypads. Behaviour similar to Little Grebe.
RANGE/STATUS Endemic to Madagascar. Globally Threatened and currently classified as **Vulnerable.** Threats include habitat loss, introduction of exotic fish and competition and hybridisation with Little Grebe. Monotypic. Previously common and widespread, now declining, Most common in suitable habitat in the north, west and the high plateau. Found from sea level to 2,000m.
WHERE TO SEE Can be seen in Antananarivo at Tsimbazaza Park, on small lakes (e.g. Lake Rouge) at Perinet-Analamazaotra, on the river near Vohiparara and at Lake Amboromalandy, north-west of Ampijoroa Forest Station.
SIMILAR SPECIES Breeding plumage distinctive and best recognised by the extent of rufous on the cheeks, lack of rufous on the neck and the white line on the face. Lacks the yellow patch at the base of the bill of Little Grebe. In non-breeding and immature plumage, very difficult to separate from the two other small grebe species.

Alaotra Little Grebe, adults.

Madagascar Little Grebe, adult breeding.

4b.   Madagascar Little Grebe, adult non-breeding.

5   Black-browed Albatross *Diomedea melanophris*

DESCRIPTION Size: 83-93cm . Wingspan: 240cm.Huge, heavy, long-winged seabird. Sexes alike, plumage varies with age. **Adult:** Head and neck white with a black mark around the eye. Upperparts and upperwing dark greyish-black except for white rump and uppertail-coverts and grey tail. Underparts largely white with a thick blackish border to the underwing, broadest on the leading edge. Iris brown, bill bright yellow-orange becoming redder at the tip. Legs and feet fleshy-grey. **Juvenile/Immature:** Upperparts similar to adult. Bill dull horn becoming yellower with a dark tip with age. A grey wash extends from the nape across the breast forming a collar. Underwings darker than the adult, though gradually take on the adult's pattern with age.
VOICE Usually silent away from breeding areas.
HABITAT/BEHAVIOUR Feeds and winters at sea. Covers vast areas of ocean, sometimes close inshore, flying effortlessly, gliding with just the occasional flap of the wings. Habitually follows ships.
RANGE/STATUS Circumpolar in the southern oceans, as far north as the Tropic of Capricorn. Not globally threatened. Previously reported as frequent at sea off Madagascar, though few recent records. Nearest breeding islands are Crozet and Kerguelen.
Where to see: Unlikely to be seen from land. Presumably most likely to be seen at sea in the austral winter.
SIMILAR SPECIES Underwing pattern, head pattern and bill colour of the adult easily separate it from Shy and Yellow-nosed Albatrosses and other potential confusion species such as Grey-headed and Wandering Albatrosses. Immature very similar to immature Grey-headed Albatross (which has not yet been recorded from Malagasy waters). Juvenile Grey-headed shows an all-dark bill and darker head and breast-band and the bill becomes yellow on the tip with age, as opposed to Black-browed which shows a yellow bill with a dark tip. Wing patterns of immatures of the two species are very similar. For a full discussion of potential seabirds in Malagasy waters see Langrand (1990), and for photographs of the species see Harrison (1987) and Enticott and Tipling (1997).

6   Shy Albatross *Diomedea cauta*

DESCRIPTION Size: 90-99cm. Wingspan: 220-256cm. Huge, heavy, long-winged seabird. Sexes alike, plum-age varies with age. **Adult:** Head and neck mostly white with a darker eyebrow and greyish cheeks. Upperparts grey-brown with darker greyish-black upperwing. Outer primary shafts whitish, rump and uppertail-coverts white and tail grey. Underparts largely white, with a uniformly narrow blackish border to the underwing and a diagnostic dark notch at the base of the leading edge. Iris brown, bill bright yellowish-grey becoming yellower at the tip. Legs and feet fleshy, though blue at the joints. **Juvenile/Immature:** Similar to adult, though bill dull grey with a black tip and more extensive grey on the head. Wing pattern same as adult. Bare parts and head gradually become the same as the adult with age.
VOICE Usually silent away from breeding areas.
HABITAT/BEHAVIOUR Marine, occurring in both pelagic and inshore waters. Feeds and winters at sea. Covers vast areas of ocean, sometimes close inshore, flying effortlessly, gliding with just the occasional flap of the wings. Habitually follows ships.
RANGE/STATUS Circumpolar in the southern oceans, north to about 25°S. Not globally threatened. The nominate subspecies is rare in Malagasy waters.
WHERE TO SEE Rare visitor, most likely to be encountered from southern headlands in the austral winter.
SIMILAR SPECIES Best distinguished from Black-browed and Yellow-nosed, and other possible vagrants such as Grey-headed and Wandering Albatrosses, by the diagnostic underwing pattern and the bill colour of the adult.

. *Black-browed Albatross, adult. 5b (inset) immature in flight.*

6a. *Shy Albatross, adult. 6b (inset) Shy Albatross, adult.*

7   Yellow-nosed Albatross *Diomedea chlororhynchos*

DESCRIPTION Size: 71-81cm. Wingspan: 180-220cm. Large, heavy, long-winged seabird. Sexes alike, plumage varies with age. **Adult:** Head and neck mostly white with darker eyebrow and greyish cheeks. Upperparts dark grey with dark greyish-black upperwing slightly darker than saddle, though outer primary shafts whitish, rump and uppertail-coverts white and tail grey. Underparts largely white, with a narrow blackish border to the underwing, which is slightly broader on the leading edge, and black tips to the outer primaries. Iris brown, bill black with a conspicuous yellow line along the culmen and a pinkish red tip. Legs and feet fleshy grey. **Juvenile/Immature:** Similar to adult, though head entirely white and bill all-dark. Wing pattern same as adult, though may show slightly more black on the underwing. Bare parts and head gradually become the same as the adult with age.
VOICE Usually silent away from breeding areas.
HABITAT/BEHAVIOUR Marine, occurring in both pelagic and inshore waters. Feeds and winters at sea. Covers vast areas of ocean, sometimes close inshore, flying effortlessly, gliding with just the occasional flap of the wings. Habitually follows ships.
RANGE/STATUS Occurs in the southern Atlantic and Indian Oceans as far north as the Tropic of Capricorn. Not globally threatened. Recent records refer to the nominate subspecies. A rare visitor to southern Malagasy waters, especially between May and August.
WHERE TO SEE Rare visitor which may be encountered by seawatching off the south coast.
SIMILAR SPECIES The smallest and most slender albatross. Best distinguished from Black-browed and the possible vagrant Grey-headed Albatross by the bill pattern and the restricted black on the underwing. Separated from Shy Albatross by the dark bill and the lack of that species' diagnostic dark notch at the base of the leading edge.

8   Southern Giant Petrel *Macronectes giganteus*

DESCRIPTION Size: 86-89cm. Wingspan: 185-205cm. A huge, heavy seabird. Sexes alike, though male averages larger than female. Occurs in two colour morphs. **Adult (white morph):** The rarer colour morph, all-white with irregular dark feathers scattered through the plumage. **Adult (dark morph):** Head off-white mottled brown on the nape. Upperparts and underparts greyish-brown, slightly paler on the underparts, especially on the breast. Iris pale grey or brown, bill pale yellow-horn with a greenish tip, legs and feet flesh or grey. **Juvenile/Immature:** White morph similar to adult white morph, though iris darker. Dark morph begins sooty-black all over, gradually lightening to warmer brown. Progresses to paler adult plumage gradually over approximately seven years. Iris begins dark brown, gradually becoming paler. Bill as adult.
VOICE Usually silent away from breeding areas.
HABITAT/BEHAVIOUR Marine, feeding on carrion in coastal and pelagic waters. Habitually follows ships. Breeds colonially on coastal plateaux and headlands on grassy or bare ground.
RANGE/STATUS Circumpolar in southern hemisphere, as far north as the Tropic of Capricorn, occasionally further north. Not globally threatened. Monotypic. Frequently sighted at sea off Madagascar, and several have been taken on the coast, including individuals ringed on the South Shetlands and the South Orkneys. Nearest breeding islands are Crozet and Kerguelen.
WHERE TO SEE Unlikely to be seen from land, though may be seen following stormy conditions. Presumably most likely to be seen at sea in the austral winter.
SIMILAR SPECIES Distinguished from albatrosses by heavier, plump 'hunchbacked' body with comparatively shorter wings, giving a distinctive jizz. Dark morph very similar to Northern Giant Petrel (*M. hallii*) which could theoretically occur, and only safely identified by bill pattern. Northern Giant Petrel shows a horn-coloured bill with a darker, reddish tip.

1. *Wilson's Petrel, adults.*

12a. *Red-tailed Tropicbird, adult in flight.*

12b. *Red-tailed Tropicbird, adult. 12c (inset) juvenile.*

13 White-tailed Tropicbird *Phaethon lepturus*

DESCRIPTION Size: 37-40cm (+ 33-45cm tail-streamers). Wingspan: 90-95cm. An elegant white seabird. Sexes alike, though tail-streamers of males average longer. Plumage varies with age. **Adult:** Head white with a conspicuous black mask. Rest of upperparts white with black-tipped scapulars. Tail white, with elongated, white central streamers. Upperwing white with a black wedge in the outer primaries and a black diagonal wing-bar formed by black median coverts, inner secondaries and their coverts. Underparts and underwing white, though longest flank feathers tipped black. Iris brown, bill yellow, legs and feet yellowish. **Juvenile:** Differs from adult in having a dull yellow, black-tipped bill, blackish barring on the crown, nape and upperparts and the black-tipped tail lacks streamers. The upperwing lacks the black diagonal bar of the adult, the upperwing-coverts being barred with black.
VOICE Usually silent away from breeding areas. In breeding colonies, gives a variety of loud, raucous calls, similar to, though shriller than, Red-tailed.
HABITAT/BEHAVIOUR Tropical and subtropical seas. The least pelagic tropicbird, and will fish inshore. Flight pigeon-like, though more graceful than the other tropicbirds, usually high above the surface of the water. Feeds mainly by plunge-diving. Usually solitary at sea where it is attracted to ships. Breeds in loose colonies on remote oceanic islands, where it nests on cliffs, in rock crevices and under dense cover of bushes.
RANGE/STATUS Found in tropical and subtropical zones of the Indian, Pacific and Atlantic Oceans. Not globally threatened. Most numerous of the tropicbirds. In Madagascar, represented by the nominate subspecies which breeds on rocky northern and north-western coasts including near Antsiranana, Nosy Bé, Nosy Tanikely and Nosy Mitsio. Breeding has been observed between March and September. Unlike previous species, this species suffers human predation where colonies are accessible.
WHERE TO SEE Most easily seen on the north coast near to Antsiranana and at Nosy Bé.
SIMILAR SPECIES Large, stocky white seabird. Smallest of the tropicbirds. Adult easily separated from the two other tropicbirds by a combination of yellow bill, upperwing pattern and long white tail-streamers. For discussion on the identification of juveniles, see comments under Red-tailed Tropicbird.

14 Pink-backed Pelican *Pelecanus rufescens*

DESCRIPTION Size: 125-132cm. Wingspan: 250-290cm. A massive grey and white waterbird with a long broad bill with a large distensible pouch characteristic of all pelicans. Sexes alike, though female slightly smaller. Plumage varies slightly with age and season. **Adult breeding:** Head mostly white with some black around the eye and a short grey crest on the nape. Rest of upperparts off-white tinged pink. Underparts greyish tinged pink with some paler streaking. Iris dark, orbital-ring pink, bill dull yellow, tinged pink, legs dull orange. In flight, there is contrast between the pale upperwing- and underwing-coverts and the darker grey flight feathers. **Adult non-breeding:** As adult breeding but upperparts sullied with brown and orbital-ring grey. **Immature:** As adult, though bare parts generally greyer and the plumage appears dirtier, tinged grey-brown.
VOICE Silent away from the breeding colonies where guttural calls are given.
HABITAT/BEHAVIOUR Coastal estuaries and freshwater wetlands where they forage, usually solitarily. Typically breeds in colonies in trees by water and occasionally on the ground on islets.
RANGE/STATUS Found in much of sub-Saharan Africa. Not globally threatened and is generally tolerant of humans. Monotypic. In Madagascar a very rare visitor, though a colony existed for several years in the late 1950s and early 1960s in the west in the Antsalova Lake region. This colony was almost certainly exterminated by local villagers, and probably made vulnerable by the species general lack of fear of humans. The species has not been recorded in Madagascar since.
WHERE TO SEE A very rare visitor, most likely to be encountered at lakes or estuaries in the west.
SIMILAR SPECIES Unlikely to be confused with any other species in Madagascar. Great White Pelican (*Pelecanus onocrotalus*) which occurs in southern Africa is larger and generally whiter with darker, blackish, flight feathers.

13a. White-tailed Tropicbird, adult. 13b (inset) White-tailed Tropicbird, adult in flight.

14a. Pink-backed Pelican, adult.

14b. Pink-backed Pelican, adult.

15 Red-footed Booby *Sula sula*

DESCRIPTION Size: 66-77cm. Wingspan: 91-101cm. A large seabird. Sexes alike, though female averages larger. A polymorphic species, with four morphs occurring in Malagasy waters. All adults show diagnostic pink facial skin and bright red feet and legs. **Adult light morph:** All-white but for black primaries and secondaries, black mark on the carpal on the underwing and variable yellow wash, particularly around the head. Iris brown, orbital-ring blue, bill pale blue with pink base, legs and feet red. Adult white-headed intermediate morph: head, underparts and tail white, wings and back brown. Bare parts as light morph. **Adult white-tailed intermediate morph:** Wholly brown but for white uppertail-coverts, tail and vent. May show a yellowish wash on the head. Bare parts as light morph. **Adult dark morph:** Wholly brownish with a variable yellowish wash on the head and neck. Bare parts as light morph. **Immature:** As dark morph, though at close range plumage appears streaked. Also show duller bare parts: bill blackish-brown; facial skin dull purple; legs dull yellow. Birds in transitional plumage may resemble intermediate morph adults, though the bare parts are duller.
VOICE Usually silent at sea.
HABITAT/BEHAVIOUR Strictly marine and largely pelagic. Gregarious, feeds on fish by plunge-diving, often from a considerable height. The smallest booby.
RANGE/STATUS A pantropical species. Not globally threatened, one of the commonest sulids. However tree destruction has resulted in the loss of some colonies. Represented in Madagascar by the subspecies *S. s. rubripes* which is seen occasionally from the north and west coasts of Madagascar. The nearest breeding colonies to Madagascar are on Europa, Aldabra, Cosmoledo, Farquhar and Tromelin.
WHERE TO SEE An uncommon visitor, most likely to be seen from the north or west coast.
SIMILAR SPECIES A large pelagic species with long wings, a stout bill and a wedge-shaped tail. The only similar species regularly occurring in Malagasy waters is Brown Booby which is larger, always shows a dark head and pale underparts and has a yellow bill and legs. Pale morph easily separated from the rare Masked Booby (see Appendix) by the diagnostic dark carpal patches on the underwing, the wholly white tail and the lack of that species' blackish mask.

16 Brown Booby *Sula leucogaster*

DESCRIPTION Size: 64-74cm. Wingspan: 132-150cm. A large seabird. Sexes alike, though female averages larger. Plumage varies with age. **Adult:** Head, neck and upperparts dark chocolate-brown, underparts (excluding neck) white, underwing-coverts white, rest of underwings dark brown. Iris yellow, bill yellow with blue or green (male) or pale green (female) facial skin. Legs and feet yellowish-green. **Immature:** Similar to adult, though bill and facial skin grey and white areas of plumage sullied brown.
VOICE Usually silent at sea, though vocal at colonies.
HABITAT/BEHAVIOUR Strictly marine, feeding mostly in inshore waters. Feeds either solitarily or in small groups on fish by plunge-diving, often at a shallow angle from a low elevation. Breeds colonially on bare rocky islands and coral atolls often on cliffs or slopes but sometimes on flat ground.
RANGE/STATUS A pantropical species. Not globally threatened, possibly the commonest booby. Represented in Madagascar by the subspecies *S. l. plotus* which is common to the Indian and West Pacific Oceans. It occurs on the north-west coast of Madagascar where it has been found breeding on small rocky islets near Nosy Mitsio off Nosy Bé.
WHERE TO SEE Best looked for from the north-west coast of Madagascar around Nosy Bé and in particular at Nosy Mitsio.
SIMILAR SPECIES A large pelagic species with long wings, a stout bill and a wedge-shaped tail. The only similar species regularly occurring in Malagasy waters is Red-footed Booby (see above). Immature similar to immature Masked Booby (see Appendix) which differs in showing paler, more mottled upperparts, a white collar and a white, as opposed to brown, upper breast.

a. Red-footed Booby, adult light morph.

b. Red-footed Booby, white-tailed intermediate morph in flight.   16.   Brown Booby, adult.

17 Long-tailed Cormorant *Phalacrocorax africanus*

DESCRIPTION Size: 50-60cm. Wingspan: 80-90cm. A small cormorant. Sexes alike, plumage varies with season and age. **Adult breeding:** Entire plumage blackish with a silver gloss to the upperparts, especially on the coverts and scapulars. Small, erect crest on the forehead and some white flecking above and behind the eye. Iris red, bill pinkish with darker culmen, facial skin yellowish, legs and feet blackish. **Adult non-breeding:** Similar to adult breeding, though overall much browner. Lacks the crest and has a white throat, pale brown breast and whitish belly. Upperparts brown, fringed with buff. Iris duller red and bill yellowish. **Immature:** Similar to adult winter but upperparts browner and more uniform. Underparts paler.
VOICE Usually silent but utters a variety of cackling and hissing calls at breeding colonies.
HABITAT/BEHAVIOUR Freshwater lakes, slow-moving rivers, coastal lagoons, mangroves and estuaries. Feeds mostly on small fish which it catches by pursuit diving. Usually fishes alone. Usually nests in small numbers in heronries.
RANGE/STATUS Common and widespread in suitable habitat throughout much of sub-Saharan Africa. Not globally threatened. Resident in Madagascar where it is represented by the endemic subspecies *P. a. pictilis* which is larger than the nominate, with bigger, less rounded spots on the upperparts. Found throughout the island from sea level to 1,500m, though most common in suitable habitat in the north, west and east.
WHERE TO SEE Can be found in small numbers at suitable wetland sites such as around Maroantsetra, wetlands around Ampijoroa and lakes at Perinet-Analamazaotra.
SIMILAR SPECIES The only cormorant occurring on Madagascar. Far smaller and darker than African Darter with a much shorter bill.

18 African Darter *Anhinga rufa*

DESCRIPTION Size: 80-90cm. Wingspan: 120cm. A large, slender, cormorant-like species. Sexes differ. **Male breeding:** Dark-brown crown and nape, buff chin and throat becoming dull-rufous on the sides of the neck and upper breast. A narrow lateral white line separates the darker crown from the paler neck. Rest of the plumage glossy-black with fine white speckling on the wing-coverts and elongated scapulars. Iris yellow, bill fleshy, legs and feet blackish. **Male non-breeding:** Similar to male breeding, though overall duller, plumage less black and the neck stripe is less prominent. **Female:** Similar to non-breeding male.
VOICE Usually silent, though may give croaking calls on breeding grounds.
HABITAT/BEHAVIOUR Inland lakes and swamps and slow-flowing rivers with wooded or vegetated surrounds. Occasionally found in brackish waters and mangroves. Feeds on fish which are speared underwater. Often swims with body submerged, and flies with neck extended producing a distinctive silhouette. Habitually soars. Usually nests in small numbers in trees among heron colonies.
RANGE/STATUS Common to locally abundant in much of sub-Saharan Africa. Not globally threatened. Resident in Madagascar where it is represented by the endemic subspecies *A. r. vulsini* which differs from the nominate in being duller and browner, slightly larger, and having a tendency to wider streaks on the lower scapulars and tertials. It is commonest in suitable habitat in the west, north-west and north. Rather rare elsewhere. Found from sea level to 1,500m. (The taxonomy of the darter complex is unclear, with some authors recognising two species and others recognising four allopatric species. *A. rufa* is often lumped in the *melanogaster* complex using the name Darter for the enlarged species.)
WHERE TO SEE Most easily seen on the lakes around Ampijoroa Forest Station.
SIMILAR SPECIES A large, long-necked, cormorant-like waterbird with a small head and long slender bill which is unlikely to be confused with any other species.

Reed Cormorant, adult non-breeding.

African Darter, male breeding.

19　Greater Frigatebird　*Fregata minor*

DESCRIPTION Size: 85-105cm. Wingspan: 205-230cm. A huge piratical seabird. Sexes and immature plumages differ. Female averages slightly larger than male. **Adult male:** Plumage all-black with a green gloss to the head and upperparts. In flight usually shows a brownish bar across the upperwing-coverts. Has a bright red throat pouch which is inflated on the breeding grounds. Iris brown, orbital-ring black, bill usually blue-grey, long and hook-tipped, legs and feet reddish. **Adult female:** Similar to adult male, though browner on the upperparts, greyish-white chin and throat, white upper breast not extending on to the axillaries. Orbital-ring pinkish, legs fleshy-red. **Immature:** Immature plumages are extremely complex. Juveniles show extensive yellowish-white on the head and white on the belly, often with a darker breast-band. Plumage gradually darkens to match that of the adults. Note that the axillaries are always dark and the throat always pale. Bill may be pinkish in youngest birds.
VOICE Usually silent at sea.
HABITAT/BEHAVIOUR A highly aerial oceanic species usually seen in groups high over the sea. Sociable, often gathering on thermals and sometimes flying over land near the coast. Feeds mainly on fish, especially flying fish which it takes from the surface. Occasionally pursues other seabirds in skua-like fashion and will take eggs and nestlings at seabird colonies. Does not settle on the surface of the sea due to the incomplete waterproofing of the plumage.
RANGE/STATUS A tropical species with a mainly Indo-Pacific distribution, though also occurs in two outposts in the intertropical zone of the Atlantic. Not globally threatened. Represented in Madagascar by the subspecies *F. m. aldabrensis*. The nearest breeding sites to Madagascar are Aldabra, Europa and Tromelin. A casual visitor to Madagascar where it is most likely to be encountered on the north, west and south-west coasts, especially in stormy conditions.
WHERE TO SEE Best looked for anywhere on the north, west or south-west coasts such as around Toliara or Mahajanga.
SIMILAR SPECIES A huge, long-winged dark seabird with a long, deeply forked tail. Similar to Lesser Frigatebird. Male distinguished by the lack of white in the plumage. Females and immatures best identified by their black axillaries (there is a white axillary spur in all plumages of Lesser Frigatebird). In addition, Lesser tends not to show white on the belly and females show complete black heads (including the throat).

20　Lesser Frigatebird　*Fregata ariel*

DESCRIPTION Size: 71-81cm. Wingspan: 175-195cm. A large piratical seabird. Sexes and immature plumages differ. Female averages slightly larger than male. **Adult male:** Plumage entirely glossy-black with white flank patches which extend on to the axillaries and a paler bar across the coverts on the upperwing. Has a bright red throat pouch which is inflated on the breeding grounds. Iris brown, orbital-ring black, bill greyish or black, long and hook-tipped, legs and feet reddish or black. **Adult female:** Browner upperparts than the male with white edging to the hindneck which forms a narrow collar. There is a prominent pale bar across the coverts on the upperwing. Blackish chin and throat, white of upper breast extending down the flanks and joining the white axillary spurs. Rest of underparts blackish. Orbital-ring pinkish-blue, legs fleshy-red. **Immature:** Immature plumages complex. Similar to female, though juveniles show a russet head, more white on the upper belly, and browner upperparts. Plumage gradually darkens to match that of the adults. Note that there is always a white axillary spur and the throat is not usually pale. Bill and legs may be paler than adults.
VOICE Usually silent at sea.
HABITAT/BEHAVIOUR Similar to Greater Frigatebird.
RANGE/STATUS A tropical species with a mainly Indo-Pacific distribution, though also occurs at two outposts in the intertropical zone of the Atlantic. Not globally threatened. Represented in Madagascar by the subspecies *F. a. iredalei*. Nearest breeding sites to Madagascar are Aldabra, Chagos and Tromelin. A casual visitor to Madagascar where it is most likely to be encountered anywhere on the west coast. Often forced inshore by stormy conditions.
WHERE TO SEE Best looked for anywhere on the west coast. Regularly seen around Nosy Bé. May also be encountered in the Toliara area.
SIMILAR SPECIES A huge, long-winged dark seabird with a long, deeply forked tail. Similar to Greater Frigatebird. For differences, see that species. When seen together, the considerably smaller size and lighter build of Lesser should be apparent.

19. Greater Frigatebird. 19a (top) adult female. 19b (above) adult males. 19c (left) immature.

20a. Lesser Frigatebird, adult male in flight.

20b. Lesser Frigatebird, adult female in flight.

21 Little Bittern *Ixobrychus minutus*

DESCRIPTION Size: 27-36cm. Wingspan: 40-58cm. A tiny heron. Sexes and immature plumages differ. **Adult male breeding:** Black (with a slight green gloss) crown, mantle, back, tail and flight feathers contrasting with buffy face, neck, wing-coverts and underparts. The greater coverts are paler than rest of the secondary wing-coverts. Iris yellow, lores yellow or green, bill yellowish with a dark brown culmen, legs and feet vary from greyish-green to yellow. **Adult male non-breeding:** Plumage duller with drabber, less glossy plumage and duller bare parts. **Adult female:** Similar to male but duller, upperparts browner and streaked. Underparts with broad longitudinal brown streaks. **Immature:** Generally similar to the female but duller with an overall mottled appearance formed by dark feather centres and extensive pale fringes. In all plumages the pale secondary coverts contrast strongly with the dark flight feathers, particularly when seen in flight.
VOICE Short and quiet *kuk* or *kek*. In flight or when excited has a louder *keck eck eck eck* or *kreh-eh*. Courtship call at night, *kock*, repeated at 2-second intervals.
HABITAT/BEHAVIOUR Freshwater marshes, lakes and pools with reedbeds. Also in wooded swamps, wet grassland and mangroves. Generally solitary but sometimes in pairs or small groups. Very secretive, active around dawn and dusk when most often seen in flight. Mainly insectivorous, feeding on aquatic insects and their larvae captured when standing motionless or when walking slowly through vegetation. Nests in dense aquatic vegetation or low bushes, usually solitarily, though occasionally in loose colonies.
RANGE/STATUS Widely distributed in Europe, Asia, Africa and Australasia. Not globally threatened. Represented in Madagascar by the endemic subspecies *I.m. podiceps* which is brighter rufous on the neck, wing-coverts and underparts than the nominate race. It is an uncommon breeder in Madagascar that may migrate to East Africa in the dry season. It is known from scattered locations from sea level up to 1,500m throughout north, central and west Madagascar but appears to be absent in the south and south-east. The subspecies *I.m. minutus*, which breeds in Eurasia and winters in sub-Saharan Africa, may also winter in Madagascar.
WHERE TO SEE Scarce and difficult to see. Can be found in small numbers at suitable wetland sites such as wetlands around Ampijoroa (including Lake Amboromalandy), at Lake Ranobe (north of Toliara/Ifaty), Lake Alaotra and in marshes around Maroantsetra.
SIMILAR SPECIES The smallest heron in Madagascar. Unlikely to be confused with any other species.

22 Black-crowned Night Heron *Nycticorax nycticorax*

DESCRIPTION Size: 56-65cm. Wingspan: 95-112cm. A medium-sized heron. Sexes alike. Plumage varies seasonally and with age. **Adult breeding:** Glossy-black crown, nape and back with a dark grey tail and paler grey wings with darker grey remiges. Forehead, supercilium, face, neck and underparts greyish-white, greyer on the flanks. Two or three long, thin white plumes extend from the back of the head. Iris red, lores greenish-yellow, bill black, legs and feet yellow. **Adult non-breeding:** Similar to adult breeding, though the black crown and back is duller, the plumes are absent, the bill and lores are greenish and the legs are paler yellow. **Immature:** Juvenile is dark brown on the upperparts streaked and spotted with buff and white. Underparts whitish, heavily streaked with brown. Undertail-coverts white. Iris yellowish-orange, becoming brown, bill greyish-pink, lores greenish, legs and feet yellowish-green. Attains adult plumage gradually over two years. At one year, resembles adult non-breeding but much duller and browner with some paler spotting in the coverts and streaked underparts.
VOICE A harsh *kwark*, often heard when flying to and from roosts.
HABITAT/BEHAVIOUR Margins of shallow fresh, brackish or salt water including streams, lakes, rice paddies and mangroves. Roosts in trees with thick cover sometimes in large groups. Mainly crepuscular and nocturnal although may feed in the daytime during the breeding season. Often seen flying at dusk when its characteristic silhouette, formed by a combination of the short neck and broad, rounded wings, is apparent. Feeds on a variety of prey including invertebrates, amphibians and fish, which are usually captured in shallow water when standing still or walking slowly. Nests colonially, usually in trees or bushes in mixed heronries.
RANGE/STATUS Very widely distributed, occurring in Europe, Africa, Asia and the Americas. Not globally threatened.
WHERE TO SEE Most easily found in wetlands around Antananarivo (such as Lake Alarobia) and in wetlands around Ampijoroa.
SIMILAR SPECIES Unlikely to be confused with any other species in Madagascar.

21a. Little Bittern, male.

21b. Little Bittern, female.

22a. Black-crowned Night Heron, adult.

22b. Black-crowned Night Heron, immature.

23   Squacco Heron *Ardeola ralloides*

DESCRIPTION Size: 42-48cm. Wingspan: 80-92cm. A small heron. Sexes similar, though plumage varies seasonally and with age. **Adult breeding:** Crown and nape bright buff with long, black-edged white plumes. Mantle and scapulars tawny buff and long, almost entirely concealing the white wings, rump and tail when on ground. Underparts white with face and breast bright buff. Iris bright yellow, lores green or blue, bill blue tipped with black, legs and feet yellowish, becoming red during courtship. **Adult non-breeding:** Similar to adult breeding; but duller buff-brown upperparts with brown streaking on the head and hindneck, plumes reduced or lacking and duller bare parts. Underparts buff, streaked with dark brown. **Immature:** Similar to non-breeding adult but drabber with more heavily streaked neck and chest. Belly greyish and wings tinged brown. In all plumages, the predominantly white wings are a conspicuous feature in flight.
VOICE Generally quiet but may utter a *kaw* at dusk. Makes a duck-like *kek-kek-kek* if disturbed.
HABITAT/BEHAVIOUR Shallow, preferably fresh-water habitats with abundant marginal vegetation. May occur in coastal areas on migration. Stands and waits for prey to approach. Feeds on fish, insects and small invertebrates. Secretive. Becomes gregarious at roosts. Nests colonially, usually in trees or bushes in mixed heronries.
RANGE/STATUS Occurs in south-west and central Europe, south-west Asia and Africa where it is a widespread winter visitor and breeds in a number of scattered areas. Not globally threatened. Monotypic. In Madagascar it is a common resident except in the south.
WHERE TO SEE Common in many wetland areas including Lake Alarobia and Tsimbazaza Park (both in Antananarivo) and wetlands around Ampijoroa.
SIMILAR SPECIES A small to medium-sized heron with a short-necked and hunched appearance. In all plumages, separated from all egrets in flight by smaller size and contrast between white wings and buff-brown upperparts and breast. In breeding plumage, distinguished from breeding-plumage Cattle Egret by shorter neck, more extensively buff plumage (often with little or no white visible when perched) and blue bill (yellow in Cattle Egret). Distinguished from Madagascar Pond Heron in non-breeding plumage by paler upperparts (darker brown in Madagascar Pond Heron), paler crown (often appearing very dark due to heavy blackish streaking in Madagascar Pond Heron) and lighter streaking on the head, neck and underparts. Madagascar Pond Heron also appears bigger headed, thicker necked and heavier billed.

24   Madagascar Pond Heron *Ardeola idae*

DESCRIPTION Size: 45-48cm. A small heron. Sexes alike, though plumage varies seasonally and with age. **Adult breeding:** Whole plumage white with fluffy appearance due to long nuptial plumes on crown, upperparts and breast. May show a faint buff wash to the plumage. Iris yellow, lores greenish, bill bright blue with a black tip, legs pink and feet duller, greenish. **Adult non-breeding:** Similar to non-breeding Squacco Heron, though darker and more heavily marked. Crown and nape brown, heavily streaked with black, sides of head and throat buff with dark brown streaking. Mantle, scapulars and inner secondaries dark brown with buff shaft-streaks broadening at feather tips. White flight feathers, rump and tail. Underparts buff, streaked with dark brown. Iris yellow, lores greenish, bill greenish-grey with a black tip, legs and feet yellowish or greenish-grey. **Immature:** As non-breeding adult but with dark brown on outer flight feathers and tail. Iris pale green, bill orange with sooty tip.
VOICE A low, deep guttural croak given from dense vegetation.
HABITAT/BEHAVIOUR Habitat as for Squacco Heron. A secretive and solitary feeder. Rarely forms groups. Feeds on fish, insects and small invertebrates by walking stealthily or by standing motionless at waters edge or on floating vegetation. Nests colonially, usually in trees or bushes in mixed heronries.
RANGE/STATUS **Regional Endemic Breeder**. Breeds only in Madagascar and Aldabra, where it is present from approximately October to May, and winters in central and eastern Africa. Currently considered **Near Threatened** globally. Monotypic. Formally bred throughout Madagascar but has declined dramatically in the last 50 years, possibly due to competition with Squacco Heron which appears to be spreading and appears to be more adaptable to man-made habitats. Occurs throughout Madagascar, though is rare in the south. Recorded from sea level to 1,800m. Most common in suitable wetlands in the west.
WHERE TO SEE Most easily seen at Lake Alarobia and Tsimbazaza Park (both in Antananarivo), wetlands around Ampijoroa and at Berenty.
SIMILAR SPECIES For separation from Squacco Heron, see that species. Adult in breeding plumage may be identified by its small size, stocky and short-necked appearance and heavy, blue bill. In flight separated from Cattle Egret by black-tipped, blue bill and short legs not projecting beyond the tail.

. Squacco Heron, adult in transitional plumage.

23b. Squacco Heron, adult breeding.

. Madagascar Pond Heron, adult breeding.

24b. Madagascar Pond Heron, adult breeding in flight.

25　Cattle Egret　*Bubulcus ibis*

DESCRIPTION Size: 50-56cm. Wingspan: 88-96cm. A small, stocky egret. Sexes alike, though plumage varies seasonally and with age. **Adult breeding:** White except for rufous-buff plumes on crown, nape, foreneck, chest and mantle. Iris orange-yellow, lores pink or red, bill orange-red, legs and feet reddish. These colours intensify during the courtship period of 10-20 days. Not all birds acquire this plumage when breeding while some retain the buff plumes throughout the non-breeding season. **Adult non-breeding:** Entirely white, male with slightly longer creamy-white feathers on the lower throat and mantle. Iris, lores and bill yellow, legs and feet grey-green. **Juvenile:** As non-breeding adult, plumage sometimes with a grey tinge. Bill, legs and feet greyish.
VOICE A variety of harsh, throaty calls given at colonies and roosts, relatively quiet elsewhere.
HABITAT/BEHAVIOUR Least aquatic of all herons, prefers pastures, arable fields and lake shores, sometimes in suburban areas. Diurnal, usually in small flocks feeding alongside cattle or large mammals which help to disturb their prey. Prey includes insects, grasshoppers, frogs, lizards and rodents. Where food is abundant gatherings of hundreds may occur. Often seen on the backs of cattle. Roost and nest colonially often in mixed heronries.
RANGE/STATUS Found on all continents except Antarctica. Not globally threatened. Represented in Madagascar by the nominate subspecies which occurs in Africa, southern and western Europe and the Americas. A very common resident throughout Madagascar from sea level to 1,700m.
WHERE TO SEE Common and widespread, occurring in most open areas. Easily seen at the heronry at Lake Alarobia.
SIMILAR SPECIES The smallest egret in Madagascar. Much smaller and shorter necked than Great Egret. Separated from Dimorphic Egret by the stockier shape, smaller size, yellow-orange bill and yellow-green legs. Tends to prefer drier habitats than other herons. See also Squacco and Madagascar Pond Herons for separation from these species.

26　Green-backed Heron　*Butorides striatus*

DESCRIPTION Size: 35-45cm. Wingspan: 52-60cm. A small heron. Sexes alike, plumages vary seasonally and with age. **Adult breeding:** Striking head pattern with crown and nape black glossed green, forming an elongated crest. White supercilium and broad white moustachial stripe contrast with the black eye-stripe. Rest of the head, nape and upperparts grey, except for long, dark, green-glossed scapulars and upperwing-coverts which are pale fringed. Flight feathers and tail dark grey. Underparts grey mottled with rufous on the lower neck and upper breast. Iris orange, lores yellow, bill black, legs and feet yellow-orange. **Adult non-breeding:** Duller plumage and bare parts, no plumes. Iris yellow, lores greenish, bill sooty, legs and feet duller yellow. **Immature:** Upperparts brownish, crown dull green, wings spotted with white. Grey underparts heavily streaked with brown. Soft parts as non-breeding adult although bill browner.
VOICE Generally quiet but calls when alarmed with a *kyah* or *skeow*. Also various calls when breeding.
HABITAT/BEHAVIOUR Shallow fresh or salt-water habitats, common in mangroves or dense wooded vegetation fringing streams, lakes or estuaries. Also seen in reedbeds, grassy marshlands and rice paddies. Fairly secretive and sometimes crepuscular. Solitary feeder, often seen moving through waterside vegetation. Prey includes fish, mudskippers, insects and crustaceans which are stalked when perching motionless in a hunched position. Usually a solitary nester, preferring trees and bushes close to feeding areas.
RANGE/STATUS Occurs in Africa, Asia, the Americas and Australasia. Not globally threatened. Represented in Madagascar by *B. s. rutenbergi* which is found in Madagascar and Réunion. It differs from the African subspecies *B. s. atricapillus* in being slightly smaller, with a tendency to be darker on the upperparts and redder on the foreneck. The fringes of the upperwing-coverts are buffy rather than whitish. Resident, occurring throughout the island from sea level to 1,500m, least common on the high plateau and in the south. Thirty subspecies are usually recognised worldwide which in turn are sometimes split into three species: *B. striatus* (Green-backed Heron) and *B. virescens* (Green Heron), each with many subspecies, and *B. sundevalli* (Lava Heron).
WHERE TO SEE Fairly common in wetlands and coasts such as the fishponds at Perinet-Analamazaotra, around Maroantsetra, the coast at Toliara and wetlands around Ampijoroa.
SIMILAR SPECIES A small stocky heron with distinctive plumage pattern. Larger than Little Bittern and lacks that species pale wing-patch.

29a. *Great Egret, adult breeding.*

29b. *Great Egret, adult non-breeding.*

30a. *Purple Heron, adult.*

30b. *Purple Heron, immature.*

31   Grey Heron *Ardea cinerea*

DESCRIPTION Size: 90-98cm. Wingspan: 175-195cm. A large heron. Sexes alike, though female averages smaller. Plumage varies with age. **Adult breeding:** White head with a broad black line from above the eye to the nape where it joins and forms two long black plumes. Upperparts blue-grey but for elongated whitish scapulars, a white patch on the lesser coverts and blackish flight feathers. Throat white, neck grey with two rows of black streaks on the foreneck. Rest of the underparts white except for grey flanks and black sides to the belly. Elongated white plumes on the breast. There is a prominent black patch visible at the bend of the wing when perched. Iris and lores yellow, orbital skin greenish, bill yellow (orange to red during courtship) and legs and feet yellow-orange. **Adult non-breeding:** As breeding adult but lacks the plumes and bare parts duller. **Immature:** Overall greyer than adult and more uniform. Extent of black in plumage varies with age. Typically shows a dark grey crown, drab grey upperparts, and grey underparts with grey-brown streaking on the foreneck. Bill brown, legs greenish-grey. Takes around two years to attain adult plumage.
VOICE A loud harsh *krarnk* call uttered in flight. Various softer calls at the nest.
HABITAT/BEHAVIOUR Shallow fresh, brackish or salt water including rivers, lakes, marshes, rice paddies, mangroves and mudflats. Mainly a solitary feeder preying largely on fish and eels but also amphibians, crustaceans, insects, reptiles and small mammals which it captures by stalking. Breeds colonially, often in mixed colonies, usually in trees, though occasionally in bushes and even on cliffs.
RANGE/STATUS Widespread in Europe, Africa and Asia. Not globally threatened. In Madagascar represented by the subspecies *A. c. firasa* which also occurs in Aldabra and the Comoros. It averages larger in the bill and longer in the leg than the nominate race. Common throughout Madagascar except on the high plateau where it is uncommon. Found from sea level to 1,500m.
WHERE TO SEE Fairly common on the coast around Toliara and in wetlands around Ampijoroa.
SIMILAR SPECIES A large, grey, black and white heron. For separation from Purple and Black-headed Herons see the respective species accounts. The similar Humblot's differs in its larger size and much darker and more uniform plumage. In addition, Humblot's always lacks the white on the lesser coverts of Grey, shows an indistinct black face and cap and has a more powerful build with a heavier and longer bill.

32   Black-headed Heron *Ardea melanocephala*

DESCRIPTION Size: 85-90cm. Wingspan: 160-180cm. A large heron. Sexes alike, plumage varies with age. **Adult:** Head, nape and hindneck black. Chin and throat white. Upperparts dark grey with pale-tipped plumes on the scapulars. Wing-coverts grey, flight feathers dark grey. Foreneck spotted white on black. Rest of the underparts grey with paler plumes on the breast. In flight shows contrasting white underwing-coverts. Iris yellow, reddening during courtship. Lores yellow-green, bill black with yellow on the lower mandible, legs and feet black. **Immature:** Similar to adult but duller. Crown dark grey, neck brownish-grey and underparts white with buff streaking.
VOICE Away from roost or nest utters a loud raucous *kuark*.
HABITAT/BEHAVIOUR Typically found in damp, open pastures and grasslands but also in wetland habitats. A solitary, partially nocturnal feeder preying mainly on terrestrial vertebrates and invertebrates. Partial migrant, with movements related to dry seasons.
RANGE/STATUS Common in sub-Saharan Africa. Not globally threatened. Monotypic. A vagrant to Madagascar, recorded once.
WHERE TO SEE A very rare vagrant and therefore no regular sites.
SIMILAR SPECIES A large heron, separated from Grey and Humblot's Herons by the contrast between the black head and white throat and foreneck. In flight, the diagnostic white underwing-coverts are easily seen.

1a. Grey Heron, adult.

2a. Black-headed Heron, adult.

31b. Grey Heron, immature.

32b. Black-headed Heron, adult in flight.

33   Humblot's Heron   *Ardea humbloti*

DESCRIPTION Size: 100cm. A very large, stocky heron. Sexes alike, plumage varies with age. **Adult:** Front of face and crown black with two long black plumes on the nape. Rest of plumage dark grey except for blackish flight feathers and some paler elongated feathers on the scapulars and breast. Iris pale yellow, lores green, bill long, stout and greyish-green changing to greyish-pink or even orange when breeding, often darker at the base. Legs and feet stout and usually grey-brown. **Immature:** Similar to adult but the head pattern is less distinct with the black replaced by dark grey, the throat is usually white and the bill dull greyish-yellow.
VOICE Usually quiet, though a loud and harsh *kra-ark* given in flight.
HABITAT/BEHAVIOUR Prefers coastal areas but also frequents lakes, rivers, mangroves, estuaries and rice paddies. Usually solitary when feeding although may associate with other heron species. Feeds on large fish and crustaceans which it catches by stalking. Nests alone or in mixed colonies, often with Grey Heron, usually in trees or occasionally rock hollows on offshore islands.
RANGE/STATUS Endemic to Madagascar although recorded as a vagrant on Aldabra and possibly breeds on the Comoros. **Globally Threatened** and currently classified as **Vulnerable**. Monotypic. Uncommon in coastal regions in the north, west and south, rare on the high plateau and east coast. Fairly common at a few favoured localities in the west. Young birds disperse and may wander widely. Found from sea level to 1,500m.
WHERE TO SEE Uncommon but best looked for in wetlands around Ampijoroa including Lake Amboromalandy and along the coast between Toliara and the Onilahy River mouth at St. Augustin.
SIMILAR SPECIES A very large, dark heron which is only likely to be confused with Grey Heron or possibly Goliath Heron, which see for identification discussions.

34   Goliath Heron   *Ardea goliath*

DESCRIPTION Size: 135-140cm. A huge heron. Sexes alike, plumage varies with age. **Adult:** Face, crown and rear of neck chestnut with a bushy crest on the rear of the crown. Rest of the upperparts blue-grey with a chestnut patch at the bend of the wing. Scapulars and mantle plumes longer and lanceolate. Throat and foreneck white with black streaking. Rest of the underparts deep chestnut. Underwing-coverts paler chestnut. Iris yellow, lores yellow-green, bill black often with paler lower mandible, legs and feet black. **Immature:** Similar to adult, though the upperparts are drabber and browner, the chestnut coloration is less intense and the black and white streaking on the underparts more extensive.
VOICE A series of deep, loud croaks, *kwoorrk - kwoorrk - roorrk - roorrk*, which is audible at great range. Also a deep *aark* when disturbed.
HABITAT/BEHAVIOUR Near shallow fresh or salt water including lakes, rivers, marshes, estuaries, mangroves and reefs. A diurnal and solitary feeder preying mainly on large fish but also amphibians and crustaceans.
RANGE/STATUS Occurs in sub-Saharan Africa where generally frequent or locally common. Not globally threatened. Monotypic. A vagrant to Madagascar where it has been recorded twice in the west.
WHERE TO SEE A very rare vagrant and therefore no regular sites.
SIMILAR SPECIES A huge heron, the largest in the world. Easily identified by its large size and chestnut, black and white plumage. Much larger than the superficially similar Purple and Humblot's Herons and differs in having a chestnut crown and underwing-coverts and a heavy black bill.

. Humblot's Heron. 33a. (inset left) adult. 33b (centre) immature. 33c (inset right) adult in flight.

. Goliath Heron, adult.

35 Hamerkop *Scopus umbretta*

DESCRIPTION Size: 50-60cm. Wingspan: 90-94cm. A strange, small, stork-like bird. Sexes and all plumages alike. Whole bird dull brown, paler on the chin and throat and slightly darker brown on the primaries. The bushy crest on the head and the heavy bill give rise to its name. Iris dark brown. Bill black, stout and laterally compressed. Legs and feet black.
VOICE Usually silent when alone but vocal when in a group. Social call is a loud, nasal cackle, *wek - wek - wek - warrk*. This call is often given at night. Also gives a high-pitched *nyit* call in flight.
HABITAT/BEHAVIOUR Shallow fresh or salt water including lakesides, river banks, marshes, estuaries, rice paddies and other irrigated areas. Diurnal and usually found alone or in pairs. Frequently soars. Feeds mainly on amphibians and small fish. Builds a huge dome-shaped nest, usually in the fork of a tree.
RANGE/STATUS Occurs throughout sub-Saharan Africa and south-west Arabia. Not globally threatened. Represented in Madagascar by the subspecies *S. u. bannermani* which differs slightly from the nominate by having a more slender bill and being somewhat darker. This subspecies is not always recognised and is sometimes included within the nominate subspecies. Widespread in Madagascar, locally common on the high plateau and west coast. Found from sea level to 1,700m.
WHERE TO SEE Fairly widespread. Best looked for in rice paddies such as near Antananarivo and Vohiparara, and at wet areas in the south-west such as the Onilahy River mouth at St. Augustin.
SIMILAR SPECIES A medium-sized, short-legged, dark brown stork-like species. Unique and unlikely to be confused with any other species.

36 Yellow-billed Stork *Mycteria ibis*

DESCRIPTION Size: 95-105cm. Wingspan: 150-165cm. A large stork. Sexes alike but males average larger. Plumage varies seasonally and with age. **Adult breeding:** White head with bright red facial skin. Flight feathers and tail black, rest of plumage white with a pink tinge on the breast and upperparts. Iris brown, bill bright yellow and slightly decurved towards the tip, legs and feet red. **Adult non-breeding:** As adult breeding but bare parts duller, red facial skin less extensive and the pink tinge is fainter. **Immature:** Generally grey-brown with dark brown wing and tail feathers. Facial skin dull orange, bill greyish-yellow and legs and feet brown.
VOICE Generally silent. During breeding season utters loud squeaks and hisses.
HABITAT/BEHAVIOUR Large areas of marsh or shallow water including river banks, lakes, rice paddies, lagoons and mudflats. Diurnal and gregarious, often associating with African Spoonbill. Feeds on amphibians, fish, crustaceans and aquatic insects. Feeds for short periods of time and often seen resting near feeding grounds. Usually nests in trees in mixed colonies.
RANGE/STATUS Occurs widely in sub-Saharan Africa. Not globally threatened. Monotypic. Locally common in the central west area of Madagascar from sea level to 150m, occasionally to 1,500m.
WHERE TO SEE Most likely to be encountered at large wetlands in the west such as Lake Amboromalandy near Ampijoroa.
SIMILAR SPECIES A large, black and white stork which is unmistakable. In flight differs from Pink-backed Pelican in that it holds its neck outstretched and the legs project well beyond the tail.

35. Hamerkop, adult.

36a. Yellow-billed Stork, adult.

36b. Yellow-billed Stork, immature.

37 African Openbill *Anastomus lamelligerus*

DESCRIPTION Size: 80-85cm. A small dark stork. Sexes alike, males average larger. Plumage varies seasonally and with age. **Adult:** All-black plumage, feathers on breast and mantle are long, stiff and glossed purple, brown or green during the breeding season. Iris brown, facial skin black. Bill brown, paler at the base, the lower mandible is curved forming a gap in the bill. Bill thinner and has more pronounced longitudinal ridges than in the African race. Legs and feet black. **Immature:** Dull brown, hindneck flecked with white, bill shorter and straighter.
VOICE Generally quiet, may utter a deep croak or cackle when disturbed or at colonies.
HABITAT/BEHAVIOUR Mainly large freshwater habitats including lakes, marshes, rice paddies and floodplains. Occasionally at river mouths and estuaries. Diurnal and gregarious. Feeds mainly on aquatic snails and freshwater mussels using its specialised bill. Nests colonially in trees near water or in dense aquatic vegetation.
RANGE/STATUS Occurs widely in sub-Saharan Africa. Not globally threatened. In Madagascar, represented by the endemic subspecies *A. l. madagascariensis* which has more strongly marked longitudinal ridges on the bill than the nominate, and more white spots on the neck of juveniles. Formally locally common in the central west area but range and numbers are declining due in part to habitat loss and destruction of colonies by villagers. Found from sea level to 150m and occasionally to 1,500m.
WHERE TO SEE Most likely in wetlands on the west coast in areas not often visited by birdwatchers. Occasionally seen at the Onilahy River mouth at St. Augustin, south of Toliara and recently a single bird has been present on a number of occasions in the roost at Lake Alarobia in Antananarivo.
SIMILAR SPECIES An all-dark-brown stork. In flight differs from Hamerkop by its larger size, outstretched neck and legs projecting well beyond the tail.

38 Madagascar White Ibis *Threskiornis bernieri*

DESCRIPTION Size: 70-85cm. Wingspan: 112-124cm. A large predominantly white ibis. Sexes alike plumage varies with age. **Adult:** Bare, wrinkled black skin covers the head and neck. Rest of the plumage white, often stained brownish-yellow with black lower scapulars and tertials. These form ornamental plumes that may show a blue or green gloss and are most prominent in the breeding season. The wings, including the tips of the flight feathers, are usually entirely white, though there may be small dark tips to some primaries. Iris pale grey, bill thick, decurved and black, legs and feet black. **Immature:** As adult except head and neck feathered black with white streaks, lacks the ornamental plumes on the back and may show some black on the wing-tips.
VOICE Generally silent, may utter a harsh croak in flight.
HABITAT/BEHAVIOUR Appears to be largely restricted to coastal mudflats estuaries and mangrove swamps. More rarely found on freshwater and coastal wetlands. Diurnal, feeds alone or in small groups. Feeds mainly on crustaceans and vegetable refuse. Nests colonially in trees, bushes or on the ground on islands.
RANGE/STATUS **Regional Endemic** occurring in Madagascar and Aldabra. Conservation status unknown, though may well be **Globally Threatened**. Represented in Madagascar by the endemic nominate subspecies which is now a rare bird confined to the west of Madagascar from sea level to 150m. The population is believed to suffer from human exploitation of nests. Madagascar White Ibis (here including *T. b. abbotti* from Aldabra) is often considered to be a subspecies of the widespread African species Sacred Ibis *T. aethiopica,* but is morphologically distinct, being smaller with a proportionally much shorter, slimmer bill and white (or with restricted black tips) as opposed to black wing-tips. In addition, Sacred Ibis is found in a much greater variety of habitats including dry areas, whereas Madagascar White Ibis is largely restricted to estuaries and coastal areas. Although Sacred Ibis is not globally threatened, giving Madagascar White Ibis specific status means that it is likely to be considered globally threatened, being uncommon and declining in Madagascar and with only a small population of 150-200 existing on Aldabra. It is possible that Sacred Ibis may occur as a vagrant, though there are no confirmed records.
WHERE TO SEE A rare bird only likely to be encountered on the west coast. Best looked for in the Bombetoka Estuary south of Mahajanga which is accessible by boat from Boanamary.
SIMILAR SPECIES A large, heavily built ibis, unlikely to be confused with any other species. However the similar Sacred Ibis is a possible vagrant. For differences see Range/Status above.

a. African Openbill, adult.

a. Madagascar White Ibis, adult.

37b. African Openbill, adult in flight.

38b. Madagascar White Ibis, adult in flight.

39 Glossy Ibis *Plegadis falcinellus*

DESCRIPTION Size: 50-65cm. Wingspan: 80-95cm. A small, dark, wetland ibis. Sexes alike, plumage varies slightly with season and age. **Adult breeding:** Head, neck, mantle, scapulars and underparts chestnut. Wings and back dark metallic green, glossed purple. Iris dark brown, lores bluish edged with white, olive-brown bill is long and decurved and often paler towards the tip. Legs and feet olive-brown. **Adult non-breeding:** Duller than adult breeding, head and neck dark brown, streaked with white. **Immature:** As adult non-breeding but darker overall.
VOICE Generally silent, may utter soft croaks and grunts in flight or at the nest.
HABITAT/BEHAVIOUR Shallow fresh or brackish water including lakes, rivers, swamps, flooded cultivated areas and estuaries. Diurnal and gregarious. Feeds mainly on insects, worms, leeches, crustaceans and small vertebrates. Nests colonially often with herons in trees near water or in dense aquatic vegetation.
RANGE/STATUS Occurs in Europe, Africa, Asia, the Americas and Australasia. Not globally threatened. Represented in Madagascar by the nominate subspecies which occurs throughout most of the world range. Widespread except in the south, fairly common in the west, though numbers are declining, probably as a result of human exploitation of nests. Found from sea level to 1500m.
WHERE TO SEE Most likely to be seen in wetlands around Ampijoroa including those around Lake Amboromalandy and other western wetlands.
SIMILAR SPECIES Easily identified by a combination of its long decurved bill and all-dark plumage. Flies with the neck and legs extended.

40 Madagascar Crested Ibis *Lophotibis cristata*

DESCRIPTION Size: 50cm. A small forest ibis. Sexes alike, though plumage varies with age. Two subspecies. **Adult nominate:** Bright red, bare facial skin, green crown and elongated metallic green and white or yellowish nape feathers which form a bushy crest. Upperparts rufous with white wings. Throat and foreneck dark brown, rest of underparts rufous. Iris chestnut, bill olive-brown, legs and feet reddish. **Adult *L. c. urschi*:** Similar to the nominate subspecies, though the crest tends to show a darker greenish-blue hue with little or no white. **Immature:** As adult but bare parts duller, head browner and crest shorter.
VOICE Fairly vocal, utters a flat, monotonous, grating *onk - onk - onk - onk - onk - onk* during the day from the ground or more frequently at dusk, from a perch or in flight. This is similar to the call of Madagascar Scops Owl, though is more grating.
HABITAT/BEHAVIOUR Found in all native forest types and seems to be able to adapt to secondary forest and dense plantations adjacent to primary forest. Shy, usually feeds in pairs on the forest floor. Feeds on invertebrates including insects, worms, spiders and snails and small vertebrates including frogs and reptiles. When disturbed usually flies up into a tree. Nests in a large tree within the forest.
RANGE/STATUS Endemic to Madagascar and found throughout except in the south-west and is rare or absent from much of the south. Currently considered **Near Threatened** globally. Subspecies *L. c. urschi* is locally common in the west, while the nominate subspecies is found in eastern forests and seems to be declining. Found from sea level to 2,000m.
WHERE TO SEE May be seen in most areas of forest, though often difficult to find. Good sites include Perinet-Analamazaotra, Ampijoroa, Ranomafana and the Masoala Peninsula.
SIMILAR SPECIES The combination of white wings, rufous plumage, red face with green crest and decurved bill render this species unmistakable.

43a. Lesser Flamingo, adult.

43b. Lesser Flamingo, adults in flight.

44a. Fulvous Whistling Duck, adult.

44b. Fulvous Whistling Duck, adult.

45 White-faced Whistling Duck *Dendrocygna viduata*

DESCRIPTION Size: 43-50cm. A medium-sized duck. Sexes alike, plumage varies slightly with age. **Adult:** Front half of head, chin and foreneck white. Back of head, nape and hindneck black. Variable black stripe across the throat. Upperparts olive-brown, scapulars fringed with tawny-buff. Rump, uppertail-coverts and tail black. Upper breast chestnut, lower breast, belly and undertail-coverts black. Sides of breast and flanks finely barred black and buff. Wings blackish, lesser wing-coverts chestnut. Iris brown, bill black with blue-grey subterminal band, legs and feet blue-grey. **Immature:** As adult but duller, face and throat grey.

VOICE Vocal. Usual call is a distinctive three note whistle, *swee-swee-sweeoo* or *swee swee-oo*, used when feeding and in flight.

HABITAT/BEHAVIOUR Open waterbodies with some emergent vegetation. Gregarious and often associates with Fulvous Whistling Duck and other duck species. Mainly feeds at night on grass, seeds, rice and aquatic invertebrates. Nests in long grass or reedbeds in single pairs or small groups.

RANGE/STATUS Occurs in sub-Saharan Africa and Central and South America. Not globally threatened. Monotypic. In Madagascar, common in suitable habitat throughout, particularly in the west and around Antananarivo.

WHERE TO SEE Fairly common in most wetlands. Easily seen at Lake Alarobia and in wetlands around Ampijoroa and Maroantsetra.

SIMILAR SPECIES Often first noticed by its distinctive and frequent calls. If seen well, the white face and dark uppertail-coverts render the species unmistakable.

46 White-backed Duck *Thalassornis leuconotus*

DESCRIPTION Size: 35-44cm. A small diving duck which tends to sit low in the water. Sexes alike, plumage varies slightly with age. Females average smaller. **Adult:** Head and hindneck buff, heavily speckled with black, densest on the forecrown and hindneck. Prominent white oval patch on the lores. Chin and throat blackish, front and sides of the neck buff. Upperparts tawny-buff, broadly barred black except for the white back which is usually concealed. Flight feathers brown. Underparts tawny barred blackish, belly and undertail-coverts dusky. Iris dark brown, bill large, blackish with green and yellow mottling, legs and feet grey. **Immature:** As adult but duller and less clearly marked, neck more freckled and the white loral spot is smaller.

VOICE Described as a clear whistled *tit-weet*, similar to a whistling duck.

HABITAT/BEHAVIOUR Quiet, shallow freshwater lakes, pools and marshes with much emergent and floating vegetation. Secretive, usually seen in pairs or small groups. Feeds on seeds and leaves of aquatic plants. Nests among dense aquatic vegetation.

RANGE/STATUS Occurs in sub-Saharan Africa and Madagascar. Represented in Madagascar by the endemic subspecies *T. l. insularis* which is slightly smaller and more strongly marked than the nominate race, with blacker barring and a lighter ground colour, a paler belly and a darker crown. It is widespread except on the high plateau where there are few records. Numbers have declined due to hunting and it is now rare throughout. Found from sea level to 1,300m.

WHERE TO SEE Rare and difficult to find in Madagascar. Most accessible sites where there have been recent sightings are the wetlands around Ampijoroa, especially Lake Amboromalandy and small lakes around Morondava.

SIMILAR SPECIES The large-headed appearance, overall tawny-buff coloration with black barring and prominent white loral spot is unlike any other species of duck in Madagascar.

*. White-faced Whistling Duck, adult. 45b (inset) White-faced Whistling Duck, adults.

White-backed Duck, adult.

47 Comb Duck *Sarkidiornis melanotos*

DESCRIPTION Size: 50-75cm. A very large duck. Sexes differ slightly, plumage varies with age and season. Female considerably smaller than male. **Adult male breeding:** Head and neck white, speckled with black, more densely on the crown and hindneck forming a dark cap. Variable yellow wash on the neck. Upperparts black, glossed green and blue except for the grey rump. Flanks grey, rest of underparts white with a variable orange wash on the undertail-coverts. Iris dark brown. Bill black with a large, fleshy, dark grey 'knob' or 'comb' on the upper mandible. Legs and feet dark grey. **Adult male non-breeding:** Comb much smaller and no yellow wash on the neck. **Adult female:** As male non-breeding but bill grey with no comb, upperparts duller, rump white and some brown mottling on the flanks. **Immature:** As adult female but the head and neck are more densely speckled with black and the underparts are washed with buff.

VOICE Generally silent, though may give short grunts and wheezy whistles, especially when disturbed.

HABITAT/BEHAVIOUR Freshwater wetlands including marshes, lakes, rivers, rice paddies and flooded grasslands. Feeds on aquatic plants, seeds, terrestrial and aquatic insects. Forms small flocks during the non-breeding season. Often perches in trees. Nests in tree cavities in single pairs or small, loose groups.

RANGE/STATUS Occurs in sub-Saharan Africa, Asia and South America, though the South American population is sometimes recognised as a distinct species. Not globally threatened. Represented in Madagascar by the nominate subspecies which is locally frequent in suitable habitats throughout Madagascar, particularly in the north and west. Numbers are declining due to hunting. Found from sea level to 1,500m.

WHERE TO SEE Often common in the wetlands near Ampijoroa. May be seen at other wetlands such as Lake Alarobia and the Onilahy River mouth at St. Augustin.

SIMILAR SPECIES This large black and white duck is unlike any other duck in Madagascar. In flight its large size and black upperparts which contrast with the white underparts render it unmistakable.

48 African Pygmy Goose *Nettapus auritus*

DESCRIPTION Size: 30-33cm. A tiny duck. Sexes differ. **Adult male:** Forehead, face, throat and foreneck white. Crown and hindneck metallic greenish-black. A large, pale green, oval patch on the side of the neck is bordered by black. Upperparts dark metallic green, tail black. In flight, a white wing-bar is visible, formed by white upperwing-coverts and secondaries. Breast and flanks chestnut, belly white, undertail-coverts black. Iris brown, bill small, bright yellow with a black nail. Legs and feet dark grey. **Adult female:** Generally duller than the male, lacks the pale green patch on the neck. Instead the face and neck are white with grey-brown mottling and a dark eye-stripe. Bill greyish-yellow lacking the black nail. **Immature:** As adult female but less distinctly marked.

VOICE Generally silent, though male utters soft whistles and the female a soft quack.

HABITAT/BEHAVIOUR Freshwater with floating vegetation, in particular, waterlilies. Habitats include lakes, marshes and slow-flowing rivers. Occasionally on brackish lakes. Feeds on seeds, aquatic plants (especially lilies), insects and small fish. Usually in small groups, hides unobtrusively in emergent vegetation and often perches on partially-submerged branches. Usually nests in tree cavities.

RANGE/STATUS Occurs in sub-Saharan Africa. Not globally threatened. Monotypic. Widespread in Madagascar except on the high plateau, most common in the west and north. Numbers are declining due to hunting.

WHERE TO SEE Best seen at wetlands near to Ampijoroa (including Lake Amboromalandy when the water levels are low).

SIMILAR SPECIES The combination of small size and generally green and chestnut plumage render this species unmistakable.

a. Comb Duck, adult male.

b. Comb Duck, adult female.

48. *African Pygmy Goose, adults: male left, female right.*

49 Meller's Duck *Anas melleri*

DESCRIPTION Size: 55-68cm. A large dabbling duck. Sexes alike. Males slightly larger than females. **Adult:** Head and neck brown with fine, darker grey streaks. Rest of plumage dark brown with paler, buff fringes and central streaks to each feather. Speculum iridescent green with a black border and a thin white trailing edge. Underwing-coverts whitish. Iris dark reddish-brown, bill long and heavy, greyish with variable black at the base and a black nail, legs and feet dull orange. **Immature:** As adult but more reddish-brown.
VOICE Male utters a soft *kreep-kreep-kreep* and the female a harsh *quack*, similar to, though shriller than Mallard.
HABITAT/BEHAVIOUR Freshwater marshes, lakes, streams and rivers, particularly in wooded areas. Usually in pairs or small loose groups. Feeds on aquatic invertebrates, seeds and plants. Occasionally seen in rice paddies. Constructs a nest of dry vegetation on the ground.
RANGE/STATUS Endemic to Madagascar, introduced to Mauritius where it is almost extinct. Currently considered **Near Threatened** globally. In Madagascar it occurs in the east and on the high plateau but is uncommon throughout. Numbers are declining, possibly due in part to hunting. Found from sea level to 2,000m.
WHERE TO SEE Largest numbers are likely to be found in wetland habitats around Lake Alaotra. More accessible sites where small numbers may be encountered include Lake Alarobia (near Antananarivo), Torotorofotsy marsh and marshes and the river at Vohiparara.
SIMILAR SPECIES Large size, dark coloration (particularly on the head), long, heavy grey bill and dark greenish speculum give this dabbling duck a very distinctive appearance unlike any other species in Madagascar.

50 Madagascar Teal *Anas bernieri*

DESCRIPTION Size: 40-45cm. A small to medium-sized dabbling duck. Sexes alike, plumage variations with age unknown. Males slightly larger than females. Head buff with darker feather centres. Upperparts dark brown with narrow buff feather edges, underparts warm buff with darker brown feather centres. Upperwing-coverts brown with white tips forming a white bar above the black speculum, which has broad white tips forming a second, narrower, white bar. Underwing grey with white axillaries. Iris chestnut pink, bill reddish, legs and feet dull reddish-orange. Immature poorly known, though very similar to the adult.
VOICE Not well known, the male gives a whistle, the female a croaking *quak*.
HABITAT/BEHAVIOUR Shallow fresh and brackish water with emergent vegetation including marshes, river mouths, small lakes and mangroves. Usually in pairs or small groups. Feeds actively throughout the day by dabbling and filtering mud. Exact diet unknown. Breeds during and after the wet season. Nests in tree cavities.
RANGE/STATUS Endemic to Madagascar, poorly known. **Globally Threatened** and currently classified as **Endangered**. Monotypic. Sub-fossil analysis suggests that this species was previously widespread over much of Madagascar. Now confined to a few sites on the west coast between Morombe and Ambilobe. Only observed around sea level.
WHERE TO SEE Due to the scarcity of this species and the inaccessibility of many of its sites (such as Lake Bemamba) it is difficult to find. It is occasionally encountered at Lake Amboromalandy near to Ampijoroa and in the Bombetoka Estuary south of Mahajanga which is accessible by boat from Boanamary.
SIMILAR SPECIES A small, elegant, long-necked duck usually found wading at the edge of shallow water. The small size, uniform warm brown plumage, red bill and diagnostic wing pattern make the identification of this species relatively straightforward. Red-billed Teal differs by its contrasting head pattern and whitish speculum while Meller's Duck is much larger and darker with a long grey bill and lacks the white wing-bars of Madagascar Teal. Garganey (*Anas querquedula*), a small dabbling duck which has occurred on Réunion, may occur in Madagascar as a vagrant in the future. This species lacks the red bill and white wing patch of Madagascar Teal and shows a strongly contrasting face pattern and, in flight, a grey-blue forewing.

49a. Meller's Duck, adult. 49b (inset) Meller's Duck, adult.

50a. Madagascar Teal, adult. 50b (inset) Madagascar Teal, adult.

51 Red-billed Teal *Anas erythrorhyncha*

DESCRIPTION Size: 43-48cm. A medium-sized dabbling duck. Sexes alike, plumage varies slightly with age. **Adult:** Crown and hindneck dark brown, rest of head from below the eye buff-white. Upperparts dark brown with buff feather fringes. Lower neck buff-white, speckled brown. Underparts buff-white with dark brown feather centres giving scalloped appearance. Upperwing dark brown with buff-white secondaries and tips to greater coverts, which are separated by a narrow black line. Underwing dark grey-brown with a paler trailing edge. Iris dark brown, bill red with the culmen and nail darker brown, legs and feet dark grey. **Immature:** As adult but duller, underparts more buffy and bill brownish-pink.
VOICE Generally silent, though the male may give a soft *whizz* and the female a weak series of quacks during display.
HABITAT/BEHAVIOUR Open shallow freshwater with much emergent vegetation, including lakes, marshes and flooded land. Usually feeds in pairs or small groups on seeds, fruit, aquatic vegetation and aquatic invertebrates. May also graze on land and in rice paddies at night. Nests on the ground among dense vegetation near water, though there are few breeding records in Madagascar.
RANGE/STATUS Occurs in eastern and southern Africa. Not globally threatened. Monotypic. In Madagascar uncommon in the east but common throughout the rest of the island from sea level to 2,000m.
WHERE TO SEE Easily seen at many wetlands including Lake Alarobia (near Antananarivo), wetlands around Ampijoroa, wetlands around Maroantsetra and marshes at Vohiparara.
SIMILAR SPECIES Combination of the white wing-patch, pale cheeks, contrasting dark cap and red bill make this species unmistakable. The smaller Hottentot Teal shows a dark cap but has a dark patch on the cheeks, a blue bill and a green speculum.

52 Hottentot Teal *Anas hottentota*

DESCRIPTION Size: 30-35cm. A small dabbling duck. Plumage varies slightly with sex and age. **Adult male:** Crown to below the eye and hindneck blackish-brown. Rest of head and upper neck buff with a large dusky patch from the ear-coverts to the hindneck. Upperparts dark brown with feathers fringed buff but for the long scapulars which are metallic greenish-black. Underparts pale brown with dark brown centres to the feathers on the breast and flanks, becoming barred on the belly. Upperwing blackish-brown, speculum metallic green with a black subterminal line and white trailing edge. White underwing-coverts show in flight. Iris dark brown, bill blue with the culmen, cutting-edge and nail black and the lower mandible darker grey. Legs and feet blue-grey. **Adult female:** As male but duller, belly not barred, scapulars shorter, speculum browner and bill dull blue-grey. **Immature:** As adult female but duller.
VOICE Generally silent, though gives soft clicking calls and a harsh *ke-ke* in flight.
HABITAT/BEHAVIOUR Shallow freshwater with much emergent vegetation, including lakes, marshes and ponds. Mainly a crepuscular feeder, feeding on aquatic invertebrates, seeds, fruits and aquatic plants. Unobtrusive and usually seen in pairs or small groups.
RANGE/STATUS Occurs in sub-Saharan Africa. Not globally threatened. Monotypic. Common in west Madagascar but uncommon over the rest of the island from sea level to 1,500m.
WHERE TO SEE Fairly common and may be found at wetlands such as Lake Alarobia (near Antananarivo), Lake Ranobe (north of Toliara/Ifaty), and in wetlands around Ampijoroa including Lake Amboromalandy.
SIMILAR SPECIES This small duck is highly distinctive. May possibly be mistaken for Red-billed Teal, which see for identification discussion.

a. Red-billed Teal, adult.

b. Hottentot Teal, adult.

53 Madagascar Pochard *Aythya innotata*

DESCRIPTION Size: 45-56cm. A medium-sized diving duck. Sexes differ and plumage varies with season. **Adult male breeding:** Head, chin, throat and neck dark chestnut. Upperparts blackish-brown, wings dark brown with a broad white wing-bar across the flight feathers. Breast dark chestnut, belly and undertail-coverts white diffusing to brown on the flanks. Underwing-coverts white. Iris white, bill dark grey with nail black, legs and feet dark grey. **Adult male eclipse:** Head, neck and breast duller brownish-chestnut, belly browner, iris remains white. **Adult female:** As male eclipse but iris brown. **Immature:** As female but paler brown, iris of young male whitens during the first winter.
VOICE Generally not well known but thought to be generally silent except in display when the male utters a cat-like *wee-oow* and a rolling *rrr*, while the female gives a harsh *squak*.
HABITAT/BEHAVIOUR Freshwater lakes and marshes combining open water with areas of dense vegetation. Secretive and little known. Feeds on aquatic invertebrates and seeds of aquatic plants. In past seen alone or in pairs. Nests on a tuft of vegetation on a bank.
RANGE/STATUS Endemic to Madagascar and largely restricted to the Lake Alaotra region. **Globally Threatened** and currently classified as **Critically Endangered**. Monotypic. Numbers have declined sharply since 1930 due to hunting, trapping, loss of habitat and introduction of non-native fish which have reduced aquatic flora. Only recent observations are of a pair in 1970 and a male caught in fishing gear in 1991. The species is now on the brink of extinction. Previously found from 750m to 1,500m.
WHERE TO SEE Although possibly extinct it may be worth searching any wetland habitats around Lake Alaotra.
SIMILAR SPECIES Uniform dark chestnut plumage, thickset diving duck shape and broad white wing-bar combined with its diving behaviour render this species unmistakable.

54 Osprey *Pandion haliaetus*

DESCRIPTION Size: 55-61cm. Wingspan: 145-165cm. A medium-large fish-eating raptor. Sexes alike, plumage varies with age. **Adult:** Head white with some dark streaking on the crown and a thick dark brown eye-stripe which joins the dark brown nape. Upperparts uniform dark brown except for the tail which shows some indistinct darker barring. Underparts white with a buff suffusion and some dark streaking on the breast. In flight shows long, narrow, angled wing. The underwing is white with a contrasting dark carpal patch, dark primary tips and a dark band across the centre of the wing. The undersides of the flight feathers are variably barred with dark brown. Iris pale yellow, cere and bill blackish, legs and feet pale grey. **Immature:** As adult but shows conspicuous pale buff fringes to the upperparts.
VOICE Typical call is a loud mournful *yeeelp yeeelp*.
HABITAT/BEHAVIOUR Usually seen close to shallow water including lakes, rivers, estuaries and marine habitats. Usually seen alone or in pairs, often perching prominently overlooking water. Feeds almost exclusively on live fish.
RANGE/STATUS Cosmopolitan, distributed widely in all continents except Antarctica. Not globally threatened. In Madagascar, represented by the nominate subspecies which is a rare visitor with at least three recent records.
WHERE TO SEE A rare vagrant, most likely to be encountered in coastal wetlands in the south and west.
SIMILAR SPECIES The long, narrow, angled wings, distinctive head and underwing pattern and preference for wetland habitats render this species unmistakable.

Madagascar Pochard, adult.

54. Osprey. 54a (inset) adult in flight. 54b. Adult.

55 Madagascar Cuckoo-Hawk *Aviceda madagascariensis*

DESCRIPTION Size: 40-45cm. Elusive, small to medium-sized raptor. Sexes alike, plumage variations with age unknown. **Adult:** Head brown, short crest on nape not usually visible. Upperparts uniform dark brown. Throat usually brown with darker mesial stripe. Rest of underparts bright white with rufous mottling on breast and flanks, often forming an irregular broad dark band across breast. Tail brown with three broad dark bands visible from the underside. In flight, shows relatively short broad wings held forward with noticeably bulging secondaries. Upperparts uniform dark brown with three broad dark bars in tail and, when spread, often two white bands formed by white in inner webs of the tail feathers. Undersides of wings are barred with dark brown across coverts. Iris yellowish, darker in the immature. Bill dark brown, legs and feet yellowish-grey.
VOICE Unknown, though a weak two-note whistle is thought to be given by this species.
HABITAT/BEHAVIOUR All types of forest. Often crepuscular. Stays below and hunts from perch within the canopy. Rarely soars; seen flying between forest blocks over open country with wavering flight. Display consists of three or four flickering wing-beats given while bird turns with its wings held vertically. Feeds on small reptiles and insects; may rob nests. Usually seen at forest edge and around clearings. Nest built in the canopy.
RANGE/STATUS Endemic to Madagascar. Currently considered **Near Threatened**. Monotypic. Most common in southern forests, rare in evergreen humid forest. Found from sea level to 1,600m.
WHERE TO SEE This species' scarcity and secretive nature make it difficult to locate. It is widespread and may be encountered at any forested area. Regularly reported from Ifaty, Berenty and Zombitse Forest: also present at Tsimbazaza Park and Lake Alarobia in Antananarivo.
SIMILAR SPECIES Madagascar Cuckoo-Hawk is smaller, slimmer and longer tailed than Madagascar Buzzard. When perched the rounded head and large, bulging eyes identify it. In flight, underwings, especially the flight feathers, heavily barred (blackish and white) lacking the darker tip to the primaries often shown by Madagascar Buzzard and the lesser and median underwing-coverts lack the dark bar. Underparts show band of rufous mottling across the breast and white belly; the tail shows three bands from below. By contrast, Madagascar Buzzard typically shows more dark markings on the belly, and underside of tail shows fine bars. In addition, Madagascar Buzzard is longer winged and shorter tailed.

56 Bat Hawk *Macheiramphus alcinus*

DESCRIPTION Size: 45cm. A medium-sized falcon-like raptor. Sexes alike, plumage varies slightly with age. **Adult:** Head dark brown with narrow white marks above and below eyes, throat white with dark brown mesial streak. May show slight crest on nape. Upperparts uniformly dark brown. Underparts dark brown with variable patches of white on the throat, breast and abdomen. Tail dark brown with indistinct pale bars. In flight shows long pointed wings giving the species falcon like shape. Underside of the flight feathers may show indistinct barring. Iris large and bright yellow, bill blackish, cere blue-grey, legs and feet grey. **Immature:** Plumage browner, shows more white on the underparts, and iris is dark brown.
VOICE Generally quiet, though occasionally gives a series of piercing whistled calls.
HABITAT/BEHAVIOUR Woodland near bat colonies with open spaces for hunting, especially near cliffs. Difficult to observe due to its secretive nature and crepuscular activity. Hunts at dawn and, in particular, dusk, catching emerging bats but may also hunt during moonlit nights. Spends the day concealed in foliage where it perches almost horizontally. Feeds on small bats, birds and large flying insects. Constructs a fairly large nest in the tree canopy.
RANGE/STATUS Occurs in sub-Saharan Africa, south-east Asia and New Guinea. Not globally threatened. In Madagascar, represented by the subspecies *M. a. anderssoni* which occurs widely in sub-Saharan Africa. Apparently rare in Madagascar where its status is uncertain. It is probably a localised resident throughout, though may also occur as migrant. Found from sea level to 1,500m.
WHERE TO SEE Elusive. Recent sightings have been made from Ampijoroa, Isalo and near Maroantsetra. Occasionally winters in Antananarivo.
SIMILAR SPECIES A slim, dark, medium-sized raptor. If seen well, the uniformly dark plumage with whitish throat and bright yellow iris are diagnostic. In flight, may be mistaken for a falcon but larger than Sooty or Eleonora's Falcons. Peregrine is closer in bulk, though Bat Hawk appears heavier, longer winged, is much darker and has a more leisurely and buoyant flight.

61. Madagascar Harrier-Hawk. 61a (inset left) and 61b (left) adults. 61c (inset right) and 61d (right) immatures.

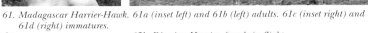. Réunion Harrier, male in flight.

62b. Réunion Harrier, female in flight.

63 Henst's Goshawk *Accipiter henstii*

DESCRIPTION Size: 52-62cm. Large, powerful accipiter. Sexes alike, plumage varies with age. Female larger than male. **Adult:** Head and nape dark brown with a narrow, white supercilium (sometimes poorly marked) and mottled ear-coverts. Upperparts uniformly dark grey-brown with slightly darker flight feathers and six dark bars on the tail. Throat white, prominently marked with brown streaks and bars giving a mottled effect. Rest of underparts white with fine dark brown barring. Undertail-coverts barred, though barring wider-spaced and fainter towards tips. Underside of tail grey-brown with inconspicuous darker barring. In flight shows characteristic short-winged, long-tailed accipiter shape, underwings barred and whitish (lightly barred) undertail-coverts are conspicuous. Iris and cere yellow, bill black, legs and feet yellow. **Immature:** As adult, though upperparts duller, paler brown and underparts pale brown with irregular dark streaking and spotting.
VOICE Gives a long, descending, mewing *weeeeeeooo*, a short squeaking *squip* and a typical accipiter call which consists of a long series of short 'angry' notes. Has a similar quality to the yapping of a small dog, *angk-angk-angk-angk-angk-angk-angk-angk*. The latter call distinctive and sometimes given by flying birds, making the species easy to detect.
HABITAT/BEHAVIOUR Primary evergreen humid forest, dry forest and sometimes secondary forest. Solitary and secretive, usually in the sub-canopy. Feeds on birds and small mammals probably including some species of lemur. Builds a stick nest in the main fork of a large tree.
RANGE/STATUS Endemic to Madagascar. Currently considered **Near Threatened** globally. Monotypic. Generally rare and present in low densities in eastern and western forests, though absent from the far south. Found from sea level to 1,800m, though rare over 1,200m.
WHERE TO SEE: Widespread, though generally scarce. Sites where it is most frequently seen include Ampijoroa, Ranomafana and Kirindy Forest north of Morondava.
SIMILAR SPECIES: Surprisingly similar to the rare Madagascar Serpent Eagle (see that species). May also be confused with the similar female Madagascar Sparrowhawk from which it differs chiefly in its larger size, stronger build and browner plumage. Heavy markings on the throat and barring on the undertail-coverts are absent in Madagascar Sparrowhawk.

64 Madagascar Sparrowhawk *Accipiter madagascariensis*

DESCRIPTION Size: 29-40cm. A seldom seen, small to medium-sized Accipiter. Plumage varies with sex and age. Female substantially larger than male. **Adult male:** Head and upperparts uniformly dark grey-brown to slate-grey. Throat white with fine dark grey streaking, rest of underparts white with fine, dark, cold-brown barring except for white undertail-coverts. The dark barring extends slightly down each feather vein appearing as arrow-mark. Tail grey-brown with darker bands, though the uppertail appears uniformly dark. Iris and cere yellow, bill black, legs and feet yellow. The legs and in particular the toes are very long. In flight shows a typical accipiter shape and in all plumages shows prominent barring on the underwings. Longer outer primaries produce a more pointed wing shape than Frances's Sparrowhawk. **Adult female:** As male but much larger, slightly browner and underparts more broadly barred with brown. **Immature:** Similar to the adult but upperparts browner with narrow pale fringes, underparts white with dark brown streaks and tear-shaped spots.
VOICE Said to give a typical accipiter *kee-kee-kee-kee-kee-kee-kee-kee.*
HABITAT/BEHAVIOUR Primary evergreen humid forest, dry forest and thorn scrub. Rarely in degraded habitats. A solitary, sub-canopy species, preys mainly on birds but also insects, reptiles and amphibians. Builds a stick nest in the canopy.
RANGE/STATUS Endemic to Madagascar. Considered **Near Threatened** globally. Monotypic. Distributed thinly and is uncommon. Rare on high plateau. Found from sea level to 1,500m.
WHERE TO SEE A scarce and seldom-seen species which is easily confused with Frances's Sparrowhawk. It is best looked for at Ampijoroa Forest Station, Berenty and in forests on the Masoala Peninsula.
SIMILAR SPECIES Similar to both larger Henst's Goshawk, which see, and smaller Frances's Sparrowhawk. Difficult to separate this species from much commoner and similar Frances's Sparrowhawk. Madagascar Sparrowhawk tends to show a white throat with fine grey streaks and white undertail-coverts; Frances's Sparrowhawk shows more heavily marked throat with prominent mesial throat-stripe and some barring on the undertail-coverts. Madagascar Sparrowhawk is colder and greyer in colour, especially on the underparts, and on average shows less conspicuous tail-barring than Frances's Sparrowhawk. In flight, Madagascar Sparrowhawk may appear to have more pointed wings due to the longer outer primaries. Immature birds are easily separated by their spotted and streaked as opposed to barred underparts.

. *Henst's Goshawk, adult.*   63b. *Henst's Goshawk, adult.*

Madagascar Sparrowhawk. 64a (inset left) adult female. 64b (inset right) adult female. 64c (centre) immature.

65 Frances's Sparrowhawk *Accipiter francesii*

DESCRIPTION Size: 28-35cm. A small accipiter. Plumage varies with sex and age. Female larger than male. **Adult male:** Head, nape and upperparts pale slate-grey. Throat and underparts including undertail-coverts white with variable amounts of rufous-orange barring on the breast and flanks, though typically appearing very pale. Upperwing and tail dark grey, underwing whitish. Iris and cere yellow, bill black, legs and feet yellow. **Adult female:** Head brown, tinged blue-grey, upperparts and wings brown, the cheeks often tinged grey. Throat whitish, typically barred at the sides and with a dark mesial stripe. Rest of the underparts whitish with widely spaced brown bars from the throat to the undertail-coverts. Tail brown with darker bands. Bare parts as male. **Immature:** Similar to the adult female, though upperparts paler brown, there are pale patches on the nape and lores and the plumage is overall warmer. In addition, the bars on the underparts are typically broader, more rufous and finely bordered darker.
VOICE A single, repeated, high-pitched *keek* or *kwik* repeated at 1 to 10-second intervals.
HABITAT/BEHAVIOUR Primary and secondary forest, wooded areas in parks and large gardens and plantations. Usually perches in the sub-canopy and preys on large insects, reptiles, amphibians, rodents and small birds. Often very tame. Male has a display flight where it flies with slow, deep exaggerated wingbeats like a Cuckoo-Roller. Builds a stick nest in the dense foliage of a tree.
RANGE/STATUS Regional Endemic. Occurs in Madagascar and the Comoros. Not globally threatened. In Madagascar represented by the endemic nominate subspecies which occurs commonly throughout. Found from sea level to 2,000m.
WHERE TO SEE Common and widespread. By far the most frequently encountered accipiter, may be found in fairly degraded habitats and in rural areas with large trees and even in Antananarivo.
SIMILAR SPECIES The smallest accipiter in Madagascar, though male Madagascar Sparrowhawk is almost as small as male Frances's Sparrowhawk. The small size and pale underparts of the male make it unmistakable. The female may easily be confused with the similar Madagascar Sparrowhawk. For differences see that species. Can easily be distinguished from Banded Kestrel by the short wings (falling well short of the tail tip) and the lack of bare yellow skin around the eye.

66 Madagascar Buzzard *Buteo brachypterus*

DESCRIPTION Size: 48-51cm. A medium-large, broad-winged and short-tailed raptor. Sexes alike, plumage varies slightly with age. Extensive plumage variation between individuals. **Typical adult:** Head grey-brown, upperparts and wings uniformly brown. Rump white or brown, tail grey-brown with around six narrow and indistinct darker bands. Individuals with typical underparts show a white throat streaked with brown, white breast irregularly marked with brown, brown lower breast and belly with some white on the lower belly and vent. When soaring, the wings are held above the horizontal in typical buzzard fashion. The underwings show weak barring on the flight feathers which show a markedly darker tip and more prominent barring on the greater coverts, a dark mark on the carpal and brown lesser coverts which usually appear as a band, the latter striking in flight. Iris pale yellow, cere bluish-grey, bill black, legs and feet yellowish-white. **Immature:** As adult but iris grey-brown and the head often shows a slightly darker mask. There is wide individual variation in plumage in both adults and immatures and atypical individuals may be substantially paler or darker than the above description.
VOICE: A loud mewing call, *meee-uuw*, is often given, especially when soaring, like Madagascar Harrier-Hawk, though lower and less whining.
HABITAT/BEHAVIOUR Primary and secondary forest, areas of woodland and high rocky slopes. Usually seen alone or in pairs, often perching prominently and soaring over the forest. Feeds mainly on small vertebrates including reptiles, amphibians, rodents and small and medium-sized birds. Builds a stick nest in a high fork of a large tree.
RANGE/STATUS Endemic to Madagascar. Not globally threatened. Monotypic. Occurs commonly throughout the island except on the largely deforested high plateau where it is rare. Found from sea level to 2,300m.
WHERE TO SEE Common and widespread, likely to be encountered at most forested sites including the spiny desert in the south-west.
SIMILAR SPECIES The broad wings, short rounded tail and stocky silhouette are distinctive. It is most likely to be mistaken for the much scarcer Madagascar Cuckoo-Hawk, which see for identification discussion.

Frances's Sparrowhawk. 65a (left) adult male. 65b (right) adult female. 65c (inset) adult in flight.

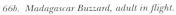

66a. Madagascar Buzzard, adult.   *66b. Madagascar Buzzard, adult in flight.*

67 Madagascar Kestrel *Falco newtoni*

DESCRIPTION Size: 25-30cm. A small, typical kestrel. Plumage varies slightly with sex and age. Occurs in two colour phases. Female averages larger. **Adult male pale phase:** Head greyish with darker streaking and moustachial stripe. Upperparts and upperwing-coverts chestnut with irregular, small black spots. Flight feathers dark grey and tail grey with blackish bands including a broad subterminal band. Underparts white with limited black spotting mostly on the breast. Iris dark brown, cere yellow, bill black, legs and feet yellow. **Adult female pale phase:** As male but head and tail browner, upperparts and underparts more heavily spotted. **Adult male dark phase:** Head and nape dark slate grey, upperparts and underparts chestnut with heavy black streaks and bars. Undertail-coverts whitish, heavily barred darker. Tail dark grey with blackish bands. Bare parts as pale phase. **Adult female dark phase:** As male but browner overall and more heavily streaked. **Immature:** As female phases.
VOICE Call is frequently heard, a shrill and high-pitched *kiti-kiti-kiti-kiti-kiti.*
HABITAT/BEHAVIOUR Open country, grasslands, cultivated land, forest edge, towns and road verges. Usually seen alone or in pairs hovering or sitting on a prominent perch. Feeds mainly on insects but also small vertebrates. Often soars and pursues insects aerially. Nests in crevices in cliffs, buildings and tree hollows.
RANGE/STATUS Regional Endemic. Occurs in Madagascar and Aldabra. Not globally threatened. Represented in Madagascar by the nominate subspecies which is common throughout the island. Dark-phase birds are commoner in the east. Found from sea level to 2,000m.
WHERE TO SEE Very common and widespread, likely to be encountered almost daily. Even common in and around Antananarivo.
SIMILAR SPECIES The smallest falcon in Madagascar and easily recognised by its typical kestrel patterning and distinctive rufous-chestnut upperparts.

68 Banded Kestrel *Falco zoniventris*

DESCRIPTION Size: 25-35cm. A small, atypical falcon. Sexes alike, plumage varies slightly with age. **Adult:** Head grey and lightly streaked, lacking the darker moustachial stripe of many falcons, upperparts and wings blue-grey with darker barring. Flight feathers blackish with pale spots on the inner webs which form conspicuous bars in flight. Throat and upper breast white with diffuse grey-brown streaking, rest of underparts white with conspicuous dark grey to rufous-brown barring. Tail grey with darker bands. In flight, shows conspicuous barring on the underside of the long wings. Iris pale yellow, broad and conspicuous orbital-ring yellow, cere yellow, bill stout and black, legs and feet yellow. **Immature:** As adult but overall much browner with clearer streaking and barring on the underparts, darker iris and reduced orbital-ring.
VOICE Calls include a repeated *wick-it* and a short, weak *kikikikikik* which is similar to Madagascar Kestrel, though shorter and weaker.
HABITAT/BEHAVIOUR Primary and secondary forest including dry forest in the south and south-west. Favours forest edge and clearings. Usually seen perched alone on lower branches of a tree, though may perch conspicuously when actively hunting. Tame and often inactive for long periods. Hunts from a perch, feeding mainly on reptiles, also insects and small vertebrates. Nests in old nests, particularly of Sickle-billed Vanga and among epiphytes on forest trees.
RANGE/STATUS Endemic to Madagascar. Not globally threatened. Monotypic. Uncommon in the south and west, rare in the north and east, absent from the high plateau. Possibly overlooked due to its inconspicuous behaviour. Found from sea level and reported up to 2,000m.
WHERE TO SEE Scarce and difficult to find. Lone individuals may be seen at any forested site. It is perhaps most likely to be encountered in the arid south-west where it is frequently seen in the spiny forest north of Toliara. It is occasionally seen at most other forest sites.
SIMILAR SPECIES Unlikely to be confused with any of the other falcons in Madagascar. The dark upperparts and barred underparts may recall an accipiter but the conspicuous bare yellow orbital skin, stout bill and long wings reaching almost to the tail-tip easily distinguish this species.

7. *Madagascar Kestrel. 67a (inset) adult male pale phase. 67b (left) adult dark phase. 67c (right) juvenile.*

8a. Banded Kestrel, adult.   *68b. Banded Kestrel, adult.*

69 Eleonora's Falcon *Falco eleonorae*

DESCRIPTION Size: 36-42cm. Wingspan: 90-105cm. A medium-large falcon with very long wings and tail. Sexes alike, plumage varies slightly with age. Females average slightly larger. Two colour phases with some intermediates, pale phase is commonest. **Adult pale phase:** Head sooty brown except for white cheeks and throat which isolate the dark moustachial stripe. Upperparts and upperwings uniformly sooty brown tinged slate. Underparts pale rufous becoming darker rufous towards the vent with black streaks on the breast, belly and flanks. Underwings grey with contrasting darker underwing-coverts. Tail dark grey with indistinct barring. Iris dark brown, bill black, cere and orbital-ring yellow, legs and feet yellow. In the female, the cere and orbital-ring may be greyish. **Immature pale phase:** As adult but upperparts browner and underparts paler with brown streaking. Flight feathers barred rufous. Underwing finely barred but still shows contrasting darker underwing-coverts. **Adult dark phase:** Entirely blackish-brown. Bare parts as in pale phase. **Immature dark phase:** As adult dark phase but with indistinct rufous barring on the body, wings and tail.
VOICE Generally silent in Madagascar. Gives a *kee-kee-kee-kee* on the breeding grounds.
HABITAT/BEHAVIOUR Often found adjacent to water, including lakes, rivers and rice paddies, also open woodland and evergreen humid forest. Often in small groups sometimes with Sooty Falcons. Feeds mainly crepuscularly by hawking insects and eating them while in flight.
RANGE/STATUS A migratory species which breeds in the Mediterranean region, the Canary Islands and north-west Morocco and winters mainly in Madagascar. A little-known small population winters in East Africa and the Mascarenes. Not globally threatened. Monotypic. In Madagascar it occurs mainly in the east and on the high plateau from late October to late April. Found from sea level to 2,000m.
WHERE TO SEE Can be encountered anywhere, but most common in the eastern part of the high plateau and scarce in the west. Locally distributed according to food availability. May be more conspicuous after rain and during insect emergences.
SIMILAR SPECIES An extremely agile and acrobatic flier. The similarly plumaged Peregrine Falcon is much stockier with shorter broader wings and a shorter tail. It also lacks the contrastingly dark underwing-coverts of Eleonora's, has whiter underparts and has a more powerful direct flight. Pale phase Eleonora's Falcon is the only falcon in Madagascar to show rufous underparts and undertail-coverts. May also be confused with the smaller Sooty Falcon. Adult dark phase is much darker sooty-black than the slate-grey adult Sooty Falcon and lacks the contrast between the paler upperwing-coverts and darker flight feathers shown by that species. Juvenile Sooty Falcon is very similar to juvenile Eleonora's but is typically washed ochre-brown on the face (as opposed to off-white), is more heavily streaked on the underparts and shows a dark extension on the rear end of the ear-coverts. In addition, juvenile Sooty Falcons lack contrast between the underwing-coverts and the flight feathers and show a fairly conspicuous pale tip to the tail.

70 Sooty Falcon *Falco concolor*

DESCRIPTION Size: 31-38cm. Wingspan 78-100cm. A medium-sized falcon with an elegant, slender silhouette. Sexes alike, plumage varies with age. **Adult:** Entirely mid-grey with darker primaries and tail-tip. Iris dark brown, cere and eye-ring yellow, tinged orange, legs and feet orange-yellow. **Immature:** Head dark brown with a broad moustachial stripe and dark extension on the rear end of the ear-coverts, nape buff, upperparts grey-brown with feathers fringed buff. Underparts pale ochre-brown with heavy blackish streaking. Bare parts as adult.
VOICE Generally silent in Madagascar, though gives a slow *keee-keee-keee-keee* on the breeding grounds.
HABITAT/BEHAVIOUR As for Eleonora's Falcon.
RANGE/STATUS A migratory species which breeds in north-east Africa, the Red Sea, the Middle East and south-west Pakistan. Winters mainly in Madagascar but also in south-east Africa. Not globally threatened. In Madagascar fairly common throughout the island from late October to early May. Most common in the south and west and may migrate in large loose groups over the high plateau in April. Found from sea level to 2,000m.
WHERE TO SEE Can be encountered anywhere. Seen regularly at Berenty, Ampijoroa and around Antananarivo where they are regularly seen at the airport, particularly late in the afternoon. Abundant to the north of Morondava, near Andranomena where hundreds may be seen together.
SIMILAR SPECIES Adults with their grey plumage and darker flight feathers are highly distinctive. Immatures must be separated from Eleonora's Falcon with care. For differences between these species see Eleonora's Falcon.

. Eleonora's Falcon, adult pale phase in flight.

a. Sooty Falcon, adult.   70b. Sooty Falcon, adult in flight.

71 Peregrine Falcon *Falco peregrinus*

DESCRIPTION Size: 34-45cm. Wingspan: 75-105cm. A medium-large, powerful falcon. Sexes alike, plumage varies with age. Females average larger and paler. **Adult:** Head blackish except for white cheek and throat which contrast with the broad black moustachial stripe. Upperparts and wings dark grey, lightly barred darker, flight feathers blackish. Underparts white with narrow, dark grey barring from the breast downwards. Tail dark grey with blackish bands. Iris dark brown, bill black, cere, eye-ring, legs and feet yellow. **Immature:** Crown and narrower moustachial streak dark brown, upperparts, wings and tail dark brown with feathers edged rufous on the upperwing-coverts. Underparts creamy white with dark brown streaking on the breast and belly and barring on the undertail-coverts. Bare parts as adult.
VOICE A loud, repeated *keh-keh-keh-keh-keh*.
HABITAT/BEHAVIOUR Very varied including cliffs, secondary woodland and lake shores. Usually seen alone, most active in the morning and late afternoon. Feeds mainly on birds which are chased at high speed and then eaten on a nearby perch. Nests on inland or coastal rocky cliffs and occasionally even on buildings in urban areas, though this behaviour has not been recorded in Madagascar. No nest is constructed but eggs are laid on a bare ledge.
RANGE/STATUS Widespread throughout much of the world. Not globally threatened. In Madagascar represented by the small subspecies *F. p. radama* which also occurs in the Comoros. It is smaller and darker than the African race *F. p. minor*, and more heavily barred below. In Madagascar it is scarce and occurs patchily throughout the island. Found from sea level to 2,000m.
WHERE TO SEE A scarce and difficult species to find in Madagascar. May be encountered anywhere, though most likely in rocky areas particularly near Cap Ste. Marie, near Nosy Be and in Ankarana.
SIMILAR SPECIES Powerful, stocky build with broad-based short wings and short tail. Combination of slate-grey upperparts, broad black moustachial stripes contrasting with white cheeks and lightly barred white underparts is distinctive. May be confused with Eleonora's Falcon, which see for differences.

72 Madagascar Partridge *Margaroperdix madagascarensis*

DESCRIPTION Size: 24-30cm. A large, distinctive partridge. Sexes differ, plumage varies with age. Males average slightly larger. **Adult male:** Forehead and crown rufous brown with a narrow white crown-stripe. Head pattern distinctive - black eye-stripe, lores and throat, white supercilium and submoustachial-stripe, grey cheeks. Upperparts, wings and tail brown, intricately marked with black and white bars and white striations. Flight feathers browner with black barring on the secondaries. Centre of breast rufous surrounded by blue-grey. Lower breast and belly blackish with large white spots. Flanks and undertail-coverts rufous with white streaks. Iris dark brown, bill black, legs and feet grey. **Adult female:** Head and upperparts dull brown intricately marked with black and buff. Underparts paler brown with blackish scallops. Bare parts as male. **Immature:** As adult female.
VOICE Little known. Generally quiet, though utters various alarm calls, including a loud *trao trao*, especially when disturbed.
HABITAT/BEHAVIOUR Wooded areas, secondary habitats, bushy areas and grassland. Secretive, usually seen in pairs or family groups. Runs or flies briefly when startled. Probably feeds on seeds, berries, roots and insects. Nests on the ground concealed by vegetation.
RANGE/STATUS **Endemic to Madagascar**, introduced to Réunion. Not globally threatened. Monotypic. Uncommon throughout the island except in the far south where it is largely absent. Found from sea level to 2,700m.
WHERE TO SEE Could be encountered in any suitable habitat. Frequently seen in open areas near to Perinet-Analamazaotra but probably best searched for between Toliara and Ihosy where it is often seen from the road between Ihosy and Ranohira. The Oasis and Zombitse are regular sites for this species on this route.
SIMILAR SPECIES Unmistakable, far larger than the quail species and the only medium-sized gamebird in Madagascar.

. Peregrine Falcon, adult in flight.

72a. Madagascar Partridge, male.

2b. Madagascar Partridge, male.

72c. Madagascar Partridge, female.

73 Common Quail *Coturnix coturnix*

DESCRIPTION Size: 16-18cm. A typical quail. Plumage varies with sex and age. **Adult male:** Forehead and crown brown with a narrow yellowish crown-stripe. Broad yellowish supercilium extending to the nape and a short, narrow, dark brown submoustachial stripe. Rest of the face pale brown. Upperparts, wings and tail brown, intricately marked with blackish, buff and white streaks. Flight feathers grey-brown mottled buff. A blackish line down the centre of the throat joins a blackish band across the lower throat. Rest of the throat, breast and flanks rufous with broad black and buff streaking on the flanks. Belly and undertail-coverts greyish-white. Iris brown, bill grey, legs and feet yellowish-brown. **Adult female:** As adult male but generally duller brown, lacks the blackish 'anchor' mark on the throat and has dark spotting on the breast. **Immature:** As adult female but paler and with more spotting on the underparts.
VOICE Distinctive and well-known call *whet-wor-wit* with a liquid quality. Often transcribed as 'wet my lips'. The middle syllable is slightly shorter and less well-emphasised than the other two.
HABITAT/BEHAVIOUR Semi-arid grasslands and sometimes dense cultivated vegetation. Terrestrial and shy, usually runs when disturbed. Feeds mainly on seeds but also insects and spiders. Nests on the ground concealed by vegetation.
RANGE/STATUS Occurs in Africa, Europe and Asia. Not globally threatened. In Madagascar, represented by the subspecies *C. c. africana* common to sub-Saharan Africa and the Comoros. It is uncommon on the high plateau, the north and the west and rare in the south. Possibly under-recorded due to the difficulties of observing the species. May breed in Madagascar and is apparently present all year. Found from sea level to 2,000m, and commoner at higher altitudes.
WHERE TO SEE Difficult to find in Madagascar. Most likely to be found by searching suitable habitat near Antananarivo and in the vicinity of Lake Alaotra.
SIMILAR SPECIES Most likely to be confused with Harlequin Quail and perhaps Madagascar Buttonquail. Male Harlequin Quail with its dark rufous and black underparts is far darker than Common Quail and shows a distinctive white throat. Female Harlequin Quail is similar to Common Quail and is difficult to distinguish in the field. It is however darker than Common Quail and shows browner underparts with heavier streaking on the breast. Distinguished from Madagascar Buttonquail by its larger size, powerful direct flight and dull straw-brown plumage. If seen on the ground, Madagascar Buttonquail shows a pale iris, slender grey bill and distinctive plumage, especially the attractively patterned female.

74 Harlequin Quail *Coturnix delegorguei*

DESCRIPTION Size: 16-19cm. A typical quail. Plumage varies with sex and age. **Adult male:** Forehead, crown and nape grey-brown with a narrow white crown-stripe. Long white supercilium extends to the nape. Eye-stripe and ear-coverts grey-brown and moustachial stripe black. Throat white with black 'anchor' pattern. Upperparts, wings and tail grey-brown with fine cream streaks and bars. Flight feathers grey-brown and unbarred. Centre of the breast black, rest of the underparts chestnut with broad black streaks particularly on the flanks. Iris brown, bill black, legs and feet yellowish-brown. **Adult female:** As female Common Quail but upperparts more buff and underparts browner and more heavily marked. **Immature:** As adult female but paler overall.
VOICE A high-pitched *wit-wit-wit, wit-wit-wit,* similar to Common Quail, though with a more metallic quality and all notes with the same emphasis.
HABITAT/BEHAVIOUR Open grassland with scattered bush cover, cultivated areas and grass along watercourses. Terrestrial and shy, usually seen in pairs or small groups. Runs or flies briefly when disturbed. Feeds on seeds, green shoots and insects. Nests on ground concealed by vegetation.
RANGE/STATUS Occurs in sub-Saharan Africa, Madagascar and southern Arabia. Not globally threatened. In Madagascar represented by the nominate subspecies which is common to Africa. An infrequent visitor to Madagascar, most regular in the austral summer and may also breed sporadically. Found from sea level to 1,600m. Seems to prefer lower altitudes than Common Quail.
WHERE TO SEE A scarce and erratic visitor, recorded most frequently in the Toliara area.
SIMILAR SPECIES Most similar to Common Quail, especially the female which is extremely difficult to separate under normal viewing conditions. Differs from Madagascar Buttonquail in the same ways as Common Quail. See Common Quail for discussion of similar species.

Common Quail, adult.

Harlequin Quail; male left, female right.

75   Helmeted Guineafowl   *Numida meleagris*

DESCRIPTION Size: 53-65cm. A large and unmistakable gamebird. Sexes alike, plumage varies with age. Males average larger. **Adult:** Bare blue skin covers the head, throat and neck, with a triangular, red casque on top of the head and red wattles on the face. Short, bristly, dark grey feathers on the hindneck. Rest of the plumage dark grey with white spots and vermiculations. Iris dark brown, bill grey-brown, legs and feet dark grey. **Immature:** Plumage dull grey-brown with buff and black spotting. Down retained on the head, casque and wattles reduced.
VOICE A loud, repeated *kurdi-kurdi-kurdi-kurdi* which is very distinctive. Also has a *kek-kek-kek* alarm call.
HABITAT/BEHAVIOUR Open country with nearby trees or bushes for roosting. Suitable areas include woodland edges, grassland and cultivated land. Terrestrial and usually seen in groups. Feeds on seeds, roots, berries, and insects. Nests on the ground concealed by vegetation.
RANGE/STATUS Native to Africa, probably introduced to Madagascar. Not globally threatened. Represented in Madagascar by the subspecies *N. m. mitrata* common to south-east Africa. Occurs commonly throughout Madagascar except on the high plateau and is uncommon in the east. Numbers are under pressure due to hunting and trapping. Found from sea level to 1,500m.
WHERE TO SEE Most likely to be seen from the road when travelling or in degraded or dense secondary forest.
SIMILAR SPECIES Unmistakable.

76   White-breasted Mesite   *Mesitornis variegata*

DESCRIPTION Size: 31cm. A long-tailed, terrestrial, rail-like species. Sexes alike, plumage varies slightly with age. **Adult:** Crown and broad eye-stripe dark rufous, moustachial stripe blackish. Rest of the head including the throat white or creamy white. Mantle grey, rest of the upperparts, wings and tail chestnut with a maroon hue. Breast white with black crescents on the sides and a variable buff to rufous breast-band which joins the moustachial stripes. Belly and undertail-coverts pale brown darkening towards the vent and narrowly barred darker. Iris brown, orbital-ring blue, bill black, legs and feet brownish-yellow. **Immature:** As adult but throat and supercilium buffy with blackish streaking.
VOICE A vocal species, often duetting. Typical song is a loud, whistled duet, *weeeeee titititi .... weee titititi ..... titit wee titit weee .... weee titititi*, typically accelerating and becoming more excited before dropping off again. Also gives clipped *shik* notes in alarm.
HABITAT/BEHAVIOUR Dry deciduous forest on sandy soils with deep leaf litter and little herbaceous growth. Recent records also from lowland evergreen humid forest. Diurnal, terrestrial, fairly secretive and usually in family groups consisting of a breeding pair and their most recent young. Forages on the forest floor feeding mainly on insects, insect larvae, spiders and seeds. Roosts and nests in the shrub layer, the nest consists of a flat, stick platform around 1 to 2m from the ground.
RANGE/STATUS **Endemic to Madagascar**. **Globally Threatened** and currently classified as **Vulnerable**. Monotypic. Locally frequent at a small number of sites in west Madagascar and rare in lowland evergreen humid forest in the east at Ambatovaky. Threatened by forest degradation, habitat loss and hunting. Found from sea level to 150m.
WHERE TO SEE Relatively common and easy to see at Ampijoroa Forest Station, less common at Kirindy and Ankarana.
SIMILAR SPECIES The distinctive elongated shape, terrestrial habits and striking plumage render the species unmistakable. In the areas where the species seems to be sympatric with Brown Mesite (Ambatovaky), this species may be readily separated by its distinctive calls, striking head pattern and white, spotted underparts.

75. Helmeted Guineafowl, adult.

76a (inset left) White-breasted Mesite, adults.

76b. White-breasted Mesite, adult.

77 Brown Mesite *Mesitornis unicolor*

DESCRIPTION Size: 30cm. A long-tailed, terrestrial, rail-like species. Sexes alike. **Adult:** Upperparts chestnut, darkest on the wings and tail, except for a white streak behind the eye which varies in intensity and extent. Head typically shows a grey tinge to the crown. The chin and throat may be whitish or pale rufous, the rest of the underparts paler than the upperparts, a peachy rufous colour. Iris dark brown, bill blackish, legs greyish, feet yellow. **Immature:** Not well known, probably as adult but duller.

VOICE Vocal, especially in the mornings. Song is typically a long series of phrases beginning with a short series of gruff 'chucking' notes and ending in a series of discordant whistles: *chok-chok-chok-chok chooil-woop chooil-woop chooil-woop chooil-woop*. This is often immediately followed by the next series of phrases. When disturbed may utter hissing and clicking notes similar to White-breasted Mesite.

HABITAT/BEHAVIOUR Primary evergreen humid forest. Seems to like steep slopes and dark areas with much leaf litter and little herbaceous growth. Terrestrial and secretive. Forages on the forest floor usually in family groups. Feeds mainly on invertebrates. Nests on a stick platform in the fork of a sloping tree 1 to 2m from the ground, which is usually accessible without flying.

RANGE/STATUS Endemic to Madagascar. Globally Threatened and currently classified as **Vulnerable**. Monotypic. Distributed patchily in forests in east Madagascar. Threatened mainly by habitat loss but also from hunting in some areas. Found from sea level to 1,200m. Possible seasonal altitudinal movement.

WHERE TO SEE This secretive species is more easily heard than seen. Best looked for in forest on the Masoala Peninsula including Ambanizana and at Ranomafana. Also occurs at Perinet-Analamazaotra where it seems to be scarce.

SIMILAR SPECIES The long slender shape and terrestrial habits are unlike any other species in most of its range. Overlaps marginally with White-breasted Mesite, which see for differences. Madagascar Wood Rail which also occurs in eastern evergreen humid forests is larger bodied, more upright and shorter tailed.

78 Subdesert Mesite *Mesitornis benschi*

DESCRIPTION Size: 32cm. A long-tailed, terrestrial, rail-like species. Plumage varies with sex and age. **Adult male:** Forehead, crown, broad eye-stripe and nape grey brown. Long white supercilium, rest of head including the throat white with narrow black moustachial stripes. Upperparts, wings and tail grey brown. Breast white marked with black crescents, belly whitish, flanks and undertail-coverts brown. Iris reddish, bill long and decurved, black with an extensive reddish base, legs and feet red. **Adult female:** Upperparts as male, supercilium in front of the eye buff. Underparts buff with heavy dark rufous spotting on the breast and brown flanks and undertail-coverts, sometimes with dark spotting on the flanks. Iris orange to brown, bill black with a variable amount of red at the base, legs and feet red. **Immature:** As adult but plumage generally browner with dark spotting on the breast. Bill dark grey, legs and feet pinkish.

VOICE Song is a long series of repeated whistled phrases ending in a short trill, *chi-chi-chi-chip-chip-chip-chip-chip-irrrrr*, which may last for nearly a minute and is audible at some distance. This call may be given by several members of a group. Also groups frequently call when foraging, an agitated nasal clucking *chek chek chek*.

HABITAT/BEHAVIOUR Dry, spiny forest with much leaf litter and little herbaceous growth. Can tolerate more open, slightly degraded forest providing there are areas of shade and leaf litter. Terrestrial and usually in small groups. Forages on the ground and probes its bill into sand. Feeds mainly on invertebrates but also seeds and small fruits. To escape danger, birds fly up and perch motionless a few metres off the ground with their head down and their tail cocked up. Roosts and nests on a low branch which is accessible without flying to it. The nest is a flat platform built of twigs, leaves and bark.

RANGE/STATUS Endemic to Madagascar. Globally Threatened and currently classified as **Vulnerable**. Monotypic. Uncommon and restricted to a coastal strip *c.* 70km wide and *c.* 200km long between the Mangoky and Fiherenana rivers in south-west Madagascar, none of which is protected at present. Threatened primarily by habitat loss and to a lesser degree, hunting. Found from sea level to 130m.

WHERE TO SEE Most readily seen in the spiny forest north of Toliara in the vicinity of Ifaty. Without local assistance the species can be difficult to find.

SIMILAR SPECIES Distinctive shape and plumage and terrestrial habits make this species unmistakable within its restricted range.

77. Brown Mesite, adult.

78a. Subdesert Mesite, adult male.

78b. Subdesert Mesite, adult female.

79 Madagascar Buttonquail *Turnix nigricollis*

DESCRIPTION Size: 14-16cm. A tiny, plump, terrestrial species, similar to the true quails. Sexes differ. Females average larger and are brighter. **Adult male:** Crown dark grey with a narrow central crown-stripe, face grey and heavily mottled, upperparts brown intricately marked with black barring and black and white streaks. Wing-coverts rufous brown with white spotting. Flight feathers greyish-brown. Underparts white with narrow black bars on the throat becoming heavier across the breast. Iris white, bill fine and grey, legs and feet fleshy grey. **Adult female:** Crown chestnut streaked with black, face and upperparts similar to male, though brighter and more rufous with an obvious white moustachial area. Throat and upper breast black, breast and flanks grey, belly white, undertail-coverts rufous. There is a bright rufous-orange patch on the sides of the breast extending to the upper flanks. Bare parts as male.
VOICE Usually quiet, though the female gives a prolonged, deep, humming boom which lasts for about 3 seconds and ends abruptly.
HABITAT/BEHAVIOUR Grassland, dry forest, disturbed woodland and dry cultivated areas. Terrestrial and usually seen in pairs or small groups. Forages in the leaf litter, clearing circular areas by kicking debris away with its feet. Feeds on insects and seeds. When disturbed, runs or flies a short distance, and then runs. Nests on the ground under a grass tussock or bush.
RANGE/STATUS Endemic to Madagascar and introduced to Réunion and Glorieuses Island. Not globally threatened. Monotypic. Distributed throughout Madagascar, common in the north, west and south, uncommon on the high plateau and in the east. Found from sea level to 1,900m.
WHERE TO SEE Uncommon in the east, though may be seen in disturbed dry areas around Vohiparara. Common in the west and south-west where it is easily found around Toliara, Zombitse and in the dry forest at Ampijoroa Forest Station.
SIMILAR SPECIES In Madagascar, only likely to be confused with the two quail *Coturnix* species, which see for differences.

80 Madagascar Flufftail *Sarothrura insularis*

DESCRIPTION Size: 14cm. A tiny crake. Sexes differ. **Adult male:** Head, neck, breast and fluffy tail bright chestnut. Rest of the body black with golden-buff streaks on the upperparts and wings and bold white streaks on the underparts. Iris dark brown, bill dark grey, legs and feet greyish-brown. **Adult female:** Entirely brown except for the whitish throat. Black streaking on the upperparts, spotting on the breast and barring on the belly. Tail dark chestnut barred with black. Bare parts as adult male. **Immature:** As adults but possibly duller. Young juveniles are small and all-black.
VOICE Typical call is a long series of squeaking notes which both accelerate and decrease in volume and may last for 30 seconds or more. Often introduced by double notes, hence *eek-eek eek-eek eek-eek eek eek eek,* etc.
HABITAT/BEHAVIOUR Grassland at forest edges, secondary habitats including dense bracken, marshes, dense cultivation and even evergreen humid forest. Secretive, usually solitary or in pairs, feeds mainly on insects and seeds. Builds a domed nest of interwoven grass on the ground.
RANGE/STATUS Endemic to Madagascar. Not globally threatened. Monotypic. Widespread and common throughout the east and on the high plateau. Found from sea level to 2,300m.
WHERE TO SEE Fairly common at Perinet-Analamazaotra and Ranomafana (including Vohiparara). However, it may be difficult to see due to its skulking nature.
SIMILAR SPECIES The distinctive plumage of the male renders it unmistakable. The female is somewhat similar to Slender-billed Flufftail and juvenile Baillon's Crake, which see for differences. Confusion is, however, unlikely.

. *Madagascar Buttonquail. 79a (inset) adult female. 79b. Adult female.*

a. Madagascar Flufftail, adult male. 80b. *Madagascar Flufftail, adult male.*

81 Slender-billed Flufftail *Sarothrura watersi*

DESCRIPTION Size: 14-17cm. A tiny, secretive crake. Sexes differ. **Adult male:** Head, neck, breast and upper mantle chestnut. Throat whitish-buff. Upperparts and wings olive-brown with indistinct darker streaks. Belly and undertail-coverts grey-brown. Tail chestnut with blackish feather tips. Iris dark brown, bill grey, legs and feet greenish-brown. **Adult female:** Head light brown with an indistinct pale buff supercilium and throat. Upperparts and wings dark brown and may show indistinct buff spots. Breast buff-brown, rest of the underparts grey-brown, paler on the centre of the belly. Tail chestnut with blackish bars becoming broader towards the tip which is white.
VOICE A rhythmical and rapidly repeated *chong-cha-chonk chong-chonk* and similar variations.
HABITAT/BEHAVIOUR Small wetlands with *Cyperus* sedges near mid-altitude and montane and disused rice paddies. Secretive. Feeding and nesting habits unknown.
RANGE/STATUS Endemic to Madagascar. Globally Threatened and currently classified as **Endangered**. Monotypic. Known from only a handful of localities in east Madagascar from Andapa south to Ranomafana where it appears to be restricted to high altitude marshlands within or adjacent to evergreen humid forest. Records in rice paddies near Antananarivo are now considered doubtful. It may occur at other sites and may have been overlooked due to its extremely secretive behaviour. Found from 700m to 1,800m.
WHERE TO SEE Recent records from marshes at Vohiparara and Torotorofotsy near Perinet-Analamazaotra suggest that these are the most likely places to see this extremely difficult species.
SIMILAR SPECIES Most similar to Madagascar Flufftail from which it differs in its longer, finer bill, much longer toes and drabber, plainer plumage. The male is browner and lacks the conspicuous streaking and overall brightness of male Madagascar while the plain plumage of the female is different from the brown, heavily and intricately barred with black, plumage of female Madagascar.

82 Madagascar Wood Rail *Canirallus kioloides*

DESCRIPTION Size: 28cm. A large, short-billed forest rail. Sexes alike, plumage varies slightly with age. Two subspecies currently recognised. **Nominate adult:** Head shows a conspicuous area of naked, pale grey skin which is variable in extent. Chin and throat white bordered by chestnut moustachial stripes. Crown and upperparts dark chestnut tinged olive on the wings, underparts bright chestnut except for the belly and undertail-coverts which are dark brown with rufous bars. Iris brown, bill pale yellowish-grey, legs and feet dark grey. **C. k. berliozi adult:** As Nominate subspecies but plumage generally paler with more extensive grey on the head and white on the throat. **Immatures of both races:** As adult but generally duller with less extensive grey on the head and yellow spots on the undertail-coverts. Birds from Bemaraha in the central west show less grey on the head.
VOICE Usual call is a loud rapid *chyut-chyut-chyut-chyut-chyut-chyut* lasting for several seconds and typically speeding up towards the end. Also call constantly when feeding: a variety of pig-like grunts and a loud *snick* which sounds like a sneeze.
HABITAT/BEHAVIOUR Primary evergreen humid forest, woodland watercourses, pond and marsh edges and secondary forest with little herbaceous growth. More rarely in dry deciduous forest. Secretive, usually in pairs or small groups. Feeds on insects, amphibians and seeds. Nests in a bowl of grass and leaves concealed 2-3m above the ground in a bush or tangle of vegetation.
RANGE/STATUS Endemic to Madagascar. Not globally threatened. Race *kioloides* occurs in the east and on the high plateau. Race *berliozi* occurs in Sambirano area in the north-west. Birds have also been recorded from Bemaraha but their subspecific identity is unclear. Both subspecies are locally common. Found from sea level to 2,000m.
WHERE TO SEE Common at evergreen humid forest sites in the east such as Ambanizana, Perinet-Analamazaotra and Ranomafana. Shy and sometimes difficult to observe, best located by VOICE.
SIMILAR SPECIES The characteristic dark chestnut plumage and grey head make this species unlikely to be confused with other species, but see Madagascar and White-throated Rails for summaries of differences.

1. *Slender-billed Flufftail. 81a (left) male in hand. 81b. Illustration showing female, left, and male, right.*

2. *Madagascar Wood Rail.*

83 Madagascar Rail *Rallus madagascariensis*

DESCRIPTION Size: 25cm. A medium-sized long-billed rail of marshy habitats. Sexes alike, plumage varies slightly with age. **Adult:** Face and throat dark ashy grey. Nape and neck brown tinged pink and streaked with black. Rest of upperparts, wings and tail dull olive-brown with prominent black feather centres giving a streaked appearance. Underparts dull brown, darker on the belly and vent. The breast has black streaks and a pinkish-orange hue. Undertail-coverts white. Iris bright red, bill long and slightly decurved, pinkish red, darker and more purple at the base with a blackish culmen and tip. Legs and feet dull straw to fleshy grey. **Immature:** As adult but duller, iris brown and bill brownish.

VOICE Has a variety of calls including a short, sharp, squeaking *eak eak eak*, a croaking grunt *grrr grrrek*, a loud whinnying which drops in pitch and is reminiscent of Little Grebe, a call reminiscent of a car alarm, *eeoo-eeoo-eeoo-eeoo*, and a high-pitched, metallic clicking *tsick*.

HABITAT/BEHAVIOUR Dense aquatic vegetation of marshes, wet woodlands and river margins. Secretive, usually alone or in pairs. Feeds on invertebrates by probing in mud. Nests among dense aquatic vegetation.

RANGE/STATUS Endemic to Madagascar. Not globally threatened. Monotypic. Occurs in east Madagascar where it is locally frequent in suitable areas but is becoming rare due to habitat loss. Found from sea level to 1,800m, more frequent at mid-altitudes.

WHERE TO SEE A rare and difficult species to find. Most frequently seen in marshes near to Perinet-Analamazaotra including the large Torotorofotsy Marsh.

SIMILAR SPECIES Unlikely to be mistaken for any other species. The larger White-throated Rail has a shorter, stouter bill and a conspicuous white throat which contrasts with its dark chestnut head. Madagascar Wood Rail is larger, uniformly rufescent brown with a grey head and a small white throat patch, has a short bill, lacks the white undertail-coverts of Madagascar Rail and inhabits forested areas.

84 White-throated Rail *Dryolimnas cuvieri*

DESCRIPTION Size: 30-33cm. A large rail with a stout straight bill. Sexes alike, plumage varies slightly with age. **Adult:** Head, neck and breast dark chestnut; chin, throat and upper foreneck white. Upperparts, upperwings and tail dark olive-green with black streaks on the mantle. Belly and flanks olive-brown narrowly barred with white. Undertail-coverts white. Iris red, bill red tipped with black, longish, straight and stout. Legs and feet greenish-grey. **Immature:** As adult but duller, iris and bill brown.

VOICE Typical call is a long series of loud curlew-like whistles which become louder and more intense: *kreee-eik kreee-eik kree-eik*. Sometimes given as a discordant duet. Also utters grunting calls when feeding.

HABITAT/BEHAVIOUR Variety of wetland habitats with dense herbaceous growth including marshes, stream edges, woodland water courses, rice paddies, mangroves and beaches. Usually found in pairs. Feeds on insects, insect larvae, termites and small molluscs. Builds a nest of leaves and grass on ground in dense aquatic vegetation.

RANGE/STATUS Regional Endemic, occurring in Madagascar and Aldabra. Not globally threatened. Represented in Madagascar by the endemic nominate subspecies. Common throughout Madagascar although rarer on the high plateau and in the south. Found from sea level to 1,600m.

WHERE TO SEE Fairly common in suitable habitats. Good areas include wetlands and river margins at Perinet-Analamazaotra, Berenty and Ampijoroa as well as Lake Alarobia in Antananarivo.

SIMILAR SPECIES Unlikely to be confused with any other species. There is a slight chance of confusion with Madagascar Rail (which see) and Madagascar Wood Rail. The latter differs in its stockier shape, shorter bill and drabber plumage. Also differs in its grey head, indistinct white throat and lack of white undertail-coverts

83. *Madagascar Rail, adult.*

84a. *White-throated Rail, adult.*

84b. *White-throated Rail, adult.*

85 Sakalava Rail *Amaurornis olivieri*

DESCRIPTION Size: 19cm. A small, dark and little-known rail. Sexes alike. **Adult:** Plumage entirely dark sooty grey except for dark brown mantle, rump and upperwing-coverts. Iris and eye-ring red, bill yellow, legs and feet pinkish-red. **Immature:** Plumage undescribed but thought to be browner overall than the adult.

VOICE Unknown.

HABITAT/BEHAVIOUR Streams and marshes with adjacent reedbeds, stretches of open water and patches of floating vegetation, in particular, waterlilies. Not very shy. Thought to forage on floating vegetation near cover but diet unknown. Builds a nest *c.* 50cm above ground in dense vegetation near water.

RANGE/STATUS Endemic to Madagascar. Globally Threatened and currently classified as **Critically Endangered.** Monotypic. Known from only three widely separated areas in the west between Mahajanga and Morombe. Had not been recorded since 1962 until it was observed in 1995 at Lake Bemamba in the central west. Decline possibly due to human predation, loss of lilypad habitat and impact of introduced fish.

WHERE TO SEE Most likely to be seen by searching wetlands around Lake Bemamba, though it may be worth searching any suitable western wetland.

SIMILAR SPECIES Small rail with dark plumage, yellow bill and red legs which is distinctive and easily separated from Allen's Gallinule by the yellow bill and dark brown back.

86 Baillon's Crake *Porzana pusilla*

DESCRIPTION Size: 17-19cm. A small, short-billed aquatic crake. Sexes alike, plumage varies with age. **Adult:** Crown and nape rufous with indistinct black streaks. Rest of the head, throat and breast bluish-grey. Upperparts rufous with black and white streaks. Flight feathers dark grey. Belly, flanks and undertail-coverts barred black and white. Iris red, bill greenish, legs and feet dull green. **Adult female:** May show a whitish chin. **Immature:** Upperparts as adult but paler. Brown ear-coverts, greyish supercilium, throat and breast whitish with brown mottling. Belly and flanks as adult, though duller. Bare parts brownish.

VOICE Fairly quiet, calling mostly at night. Typical call is a scratchy rattle which varies in intensity and lasts for 2 to 3 seconds and is repeated every few seconds. Alarm call is a sharp *tak.*

HABITAT/BEHAVIOUR Dense vegetation bordering freshwater or brackish lakes and streams, marshes and flooded grassland. Shy, skulking and solitary although in pairs when breeding. Feeds mainly on aquatic insects and their larvae, (but also small crustaceans, fish and seeds.) Nests in thick vegetation near water. Builds a shallow bowl-shaped nest from a variety of aquatic plants.

RANGE/STATUS Occurs in Africa, Europe, Asia and Australasia. Not globally threatened. Represented in Madagascar by the subspecies *P. p. intermedia* which is common to Europe, Asia Minor and Africa. Distributed locally in suitable habitat throughout Madagascar. Found from sea level to 1,500m.

WHERE TO SEE Seldom seen due to its skulking nature. Areas where the species may be seen include the marshes around Vohiparara, Lake Alaotra and Torotorofotsy marsh near Perinet-Analamazaotra.

SIMILAR SPECIES Bluish-grey and rufous plumage of the adult is distinctive and unmistakable. Juveniles may be confused with Slender-billed Flufftail which may occur in the same areas. The flufftail is smaller and lacks the heavily marked upperparts and barred flanks of the crake. Female Madagascar Flufftail is smaller, darker and lacks the white barring on the flanks of Baillon's Crake.

. *Sakalava Rail, adults.*

. *Baillon's Crake, adult male.*

87 Purple Swamphen *Porphyrio porphyrio*

DESCRIPTION Size: 42-48cm. A very large moorhen-like species. Sexes alike, plumage varies with age. Females average smaller. **Adult:** Crown, hindneck and upper mantle dark purplish-blue. Face, throat and upper breast pale blue. Upperparts, scapulars and tertials bronze-green becoming darker towards the tail. Wing-coverts dark purplish-blue and flight feathers black. Underparts dark purplish-blue, belly black, undertail-coverts white. Iris, bill, frontal shield, legs and feet red. **Immature:** As adult but much greyer, throat whitish and underparts paler. Bill and frontal shield smaller and dark grey.
VOICE Very vocal and has a large variety of loud trumpeting, booming, shrieking and wailing notes.
HABITAT/BEHAVIOUR Freshwater and brackish wetlands with dense emergent and floating vegetation. Preferred areas include marshes, reedbeds, flooded grasslands and lakes. May wander into open habitat adjacent to wetlands. Fairly shy, usually in pairs or small groups. Feeds mainly on aquatic plants but also small vertebrates and invertebrates including insects, spiders, molluscs and leeches. Builds a large nest just above water in dense emergent vegetation.
RANGE/STATUS Occurs in Africa, Europe, Asia and Australasia. Not globally threatened. Represented in Madagascar by the subspecies *P. p. madagascariensis* which is common to Egypt and sub-Saharan Africa. Occurs throughout Madagascar except on the high plateau. Locally common but heavily hunted. Rare in the south. Found from sea level to 800m.
WHERE TO SEE Its preference for dense wetland habitats and its retiring nature mean that it is seldom seen, though is present and common in many wetlands. It is seen regularly in the wetlands and marshes in the vicinity of Lake Amboromalandy, north west of Ampijoroa and at Lake Ranobe, north of Toliara/Ifaty.
SIMILAR SPECIES Easily recognised by its large size and purple plumage with red bare parts. There is a slight chance of confusion with the smaller Allen's Gallinule, which see.

88 Allen's Gallinule *Porphyrula alleni*

DESCRIPTION Size: 22-26cm. A small, moorhen-like species. Sexes alike, plumage varies with age. Females average smaller. **Adult:** Head and neck black grading to purplish-blue on the hindneck. Upperparts, wings and tail dark green with a bronze wash. Underparts dark purplish-blue becoming blackish on the belly. Undertail-coverts white. Iris red when breeding, brown when non-breeding. Bill red, frontal shield pale blue, legs and feet red. **Immature:** Crown and hindneck brown, rest of head light brown. Upperparts dark brown with pale feather fringes. Underparts buff with a whitish throat and belly. Iris brown, bill brown with a red base, frontal shield grey-brown, legs and feet brown.
VOICE Gives a variety of harsh and often nasal calls. Calls include a series of sharp clicks, *kuk-kuk-kuk-kuk-kuk*, a dry *kek*, a sharp *kik* and various quacking notes.
HABITAT/BEHAVIOUR Freshwater wetlands with dense emergent and floating vegetation. Preferred areas include marshes, reedbeds, flooded grasslands and lakes. Fairly shy, usually alone, in pairs or small family groups. Most active early morning and late afternoon. Feeds on aquatic plants and their seeds, insects, crustaceans, molluscs, spiders, earthworms and fish eggs. Nests in dense vegetation just above water.
RANGE/STATUS Occurs in sub-Saharan Africa and Madagascar. Not globally threatened. Monotypic. Distributed throughout Madagascar except on the high plateau. Uncommon throughout and rare in the south. Found from sea level to 800m.
WHERE TO SEE Its preference for dense wetland habitats and its retiring nature make this species difficult to find. It is seen with some regularity in the wetlands and marshes in the vicinity of Lake Amboromalandy west of Ampijoroa.
SIMILAR SPECIES Could possibly be confused with Purple Swamphen from which it is best distinguished by its much smaller size and pale blue frontal shield. The immature may be confused with immature Moorhen, which see for differences.

89 Common Moorhen *Gallinula chloropus*

DESCRIPTION Size: 30-38cm. A typical moorhen. Sexes alike, plumage varies with age. **Adult:** Head and neck dull black grading into the sooty mantle. Upperparts and wings dark olive-brown. Underparts sooty black with broad white streaks on the flanks, which form a line, and pale buff undertail-coverts. Tail sooty brown. Iris reddish, bill red with a yellow tip and a red frontal shield. Legs and feet yellowish-green with a reddish patch on the tibia. **Immature:** Generally greyish-brown. Face light brown, throat white. Upperwing-coverts dark brown, flight feathers and tail blackish and undertail-coverts whitish. Iris dark brown, bill black, legs and feet olive.

VOICE Very varied calls including a gurgling *kurrruk*, a repeated *kek* and a piercing *kree-eck* as well as various muffled grunts.

HABITAT/BEHAVIOUR Freshwater wetlands with fringing emergent vegetation including lakes, ponds, reservoirs, rivers and marshes. Usually seen alone or in pairs along wetland margins. Feeds on aquatic plants and a variety of small vertebrates and invertebrates which it takes while walking or swimming. Nests in dense aquatic vegetation. The nest is saucer-shaped and usually built just above the water.

RANGE/STATUS Occurs in Africa, Europe, Asia, Australasia and the Americas. Not globally threatened. Represented in Madagascar by the subspecies *G. c. pyrrhorhoa* which is common to Réunion, Mauritius and the Comoros. Occurs commonly throughout Madagascar. Found from sea level to 2,300m.

WHERE TO SEE Common in wetlands. Easily seen at Lake Alarobia and in marshes at Perinet-Analamazaotra and Ampijoroa.

SIMILAR SPECIES The dark plumage, white flank line and red frontal shield of the adult mean that this species should not be confused with any other species. The juvenile is similar to the smaller juvenile Allen's Gallinule but shows uniform upperparts (darker feather centres in Allen's Gallinule) and shows some white streaking on the flanks as in the adult.

90 Red-knobbed Coot *Fulica cristata*

DESCRIPTION Size: 35-42cm. A typical coot. Sexes alike, plumage varies with age. **Adult:** Head and neck black, rest of plumage dark sooty grey. Iris red, bill and frontal shield white, tinged pale blue with two red knobs at the top, legs and lobed feet greenish-grey. In non-breeding plumage, the bare parts are duller and the red knobs are much smaller or absent. **Immature:** Upperparts dark grey-brown with white flecking on face and neck. Throat whitish, rest of underparts pale grey. Iris brown, bill, legs and feet dark grey, frontal shield very small.

VOICE Fairly vocal. Calls include a sharp *kik* and a deep and distinctive *hoo.*

HABITAT/BEHAVIOUR Open freshwater lakes, ponds, floodplains and swamps. Prefers still water. Gregarious when not breeding. Feeds on aquatic plants and invertebrates. Breeds on waters with emergent vegetation to which the large nest is anchored.

RANGE/STATUS Occurs in southern Spain, northern Morocco and eastern and southern Africa. Not globally threatened. Monotypic. In Madagascar, common in suitable habitat in the west and south, uncommon in the east and rare in the north and the high plateau. Found from sea level to 1,500m.

WHERE TO SEE Most likely to be encountered in wetlands in the west. Regularly recorded at Lake Ranobe north of Toliara/Ifaty.

SIMILAR SPECIES The only coot found on Madagascar, unlikely to be confused with any other species.

9a. Common Moorhen, adult.

9b. Common Moorhen, juvenile.

90. Red-knobbed Coot, adult breeding.

91 Madagascar Jacana *Actophilornis albinucha*

DESCRIPTION Size: 30-31cm. A medium-sized rail-like wader. Sexes alike, females average slightly larger. Plumage varies with age. **Adult:** Crown and hindneck white with yellowish patches at the base of the neck. Chin, face, throat and foreneck black. Upperparts, wings and tail rufous, primaries black. Uppertail-coverts white extending round on to the thighs. Upper breast black, rest of the underparts rufous, Iris brown, bill and frontal shield pale blue, legs and feet blue-grey. **Immature:** Crown and hindneck black extending to the yellowish patches at the base of the neck. Face, chin, throat and foreneck white. Upperparts and wings rufous-brown except for black primaries and brighter rufous rump. Underparts whitish with rufous thighs and undertail-coverts. Bare parts as adult but duller and frontal shield much reduced or absent.
VOICE Calls include a sharp *kreeee-kreee-kreee* which diminishes in volume and a whinnying call.
HABITAT/BEHAVIOUR Floating vegetation on freshwater marshes, lakes, ponds and slow-flowing river margins. Not shy, usually alone or in pairs. Forages from floating vegetation, feeding mainly on insects, insect larvae, other invertebrates and aquatic plant seeds. Nests on a floating pile of aquatic plants.
RANGE/STATUS Endemic to Madagascar. Not globally threatened. Monotypic. Common in suitable habitat in the north and west but rare in the east and south. Found from sea level to 750m.
WHERE TO SEE Easily seen in wetlands in the west including the lake at Ampijoroa Forest Station, Lake Amboromalandy and adjacent marshes and around Morondava.
SIMILAR SPECIES A long-legged wetland species with exceptionally large feet. The only jacana found in Madagascar, unlikely to be confused with any other species.

92 Greater Painted-snipe *Rostratula benghalensis*

DESCRIPTION Size: 23-26cm. A medium-sized rail-like wader. Plumage varies with sex and age. **Adult male:** Head, neck and upper breast olive-brown streaked paler on the chin and throat. A golden-buff patch extends around and behind the eye and there is a narrow golden-buff crown-stripe. Rest of underparts white with a whitish band which extends around the sides of the breast and joins the conspicuous golden-buff mantle lines which form an obvious 'V'. Rest of the upperparts olive-grey with black bars and golden-buff spots, particularly on the wing-coverts. Tail olive-grey with golden-buff bars. Iris brown, bill slightly decurved, pinkish-brown with a darker tip, legs and feet pale olive. **Adult female:** Similar to male, though brighter and more boldly marked. Differs in head, neck and upper breast chestnut becoming black on the lower breast, eye-patch white, upperparts glossy greyish-green with narrow black bars. **Juvenile:** Very similar to adult male, though the patterning on the wing-coverts is slightly different.
VOICE The song, mostly heard at night and given by the female is a soft *hoo hoo hoo*, similar to the sound made by blowing across the top of an empty bottle. May also give a loud *kek* when flushed, though usually silent.
HABITAT/BEHAVIOUR Wetlands including swamps, overgrown rice paddies and muddy edges to pools. Secretive and chiefly crepuscular. Usually found singly or in pairs. Feeds on invertebrates and seeds. Nests in dense grass close to water. Female is polyandrous and the males carries out all the incubation.
RANGE/STATUS Occurs over large areas of Africa, Asia and Australasia. Not globally threatened. Represented in Madagascar by the nominate subspecies which is common to Africa and Asia. Patchily distributed in suitable habitat throughout, though is rather scarce in the south. Found from sea level to 1,500m.
WHERE TO SEE Its secretive nature and preference for dense wetland habitats make this species difficult to find. It may be seen in wetland areas around Antananarivo, in swampy areas at the Onilahy River mouth at St. Augustin south of Toliara, at Lake Amboromalandy near to Ampijoroa and in small lakes near Morondava.
SIMILAR SPECIES A bulky wader with contrasting plumage and a longish decurved bill. The distinctive plumage pattern and shorter bill readily separate this species from the larger Madagascar Snipe. In flight, the broad wings and slow flight are distinctive.

z (inset) Madagascar Jacana, adult in flight.

91b. Madagascar Jacana, adult.

Greater Painted-snipe, adult male.

93 Crab Plover *Dromas ardeola*

DESCRIPTION Size: 36-41cm. A large, coastal wader. Sexes alike, plumage varies slightly with age. **Adult:** All-white but for the short black eye-stripes, variable black streaking on the crown which is heavier in the non-breeding season, black mantle and upper scapulars and black greater coverts, primaries and secondaries. Iris dark brown, bill black, relatively short and powerful, deep-based with both mandibles tapering to a point. Long legs and feet greyish-blue. **Juvenile:** Similar to the adult, though head streaking more extensive and the white of the upperparts is sullied with grey-brown.
VOICE Typical call is a sharp *ka*. Often vocal at night.
HABITAT/BEHAVIOUR Sandy coastlines and islands, mudflats, estuaries and mangroves. Gregarious, most active at dusk and at night. Feeds mainly on crabs. Not known to nest in Madagascar.
RANGE/STATUS Occurs on coasts of the western Indian Ocean, from East Africa east to India, Sri Lanka and Thailand. Only known to breed in the Gulf of Oman, Gulf of Aden and the southern Red Sea. Not globally threatened. Monotypic. A common visitor to the west coast which may be seen at all seasons. Observed at sea level.
WHERE TO SEE Most easily seen in the Toliara and Nosy Be regions. Good areas include the mudflats at Toliara itself, the coast between Toliara and Anakao and the island of Nosy Ve.
SIMILAR SPECIES The pied plumage and massive bill render this species unmistakable. In flight, may be mistaken for Avocet, which see for differences.

94 Black-winged Stilt *Himantopus himantopus*

DESCRIPTION Size: 35-40cm. A large, slim, exceptionally long-legged wader. Plumage varies slightly with sex and age. **Adult male:** Head, neck, tail, back, underparts and axillaries white. Wings and mantle glossy black. May show variable dark patterning on the crown and hindneck, though this is absent on most birds in Madagascar. Iris dark red, bill fine and black. Very long legs and feet bright pink. **Adult female:** Similar to male, though black of plumage less glossy, often tinged brown. **Juvenile:** Similar to adult, though upperparts paler brown with narrow buff feather fringes. Legs duller pink.
VOICE Vocal, with typical calls including a sharp *kek* and a continuous high-pitched *kekekekek*, especially when alarmed.
HABITAT/BEHAVIOUR Fresh water and brackish wetlands including lakes, rivers, estuaries and rice paddies. Gregarious. Feeds mainly on aquatic invertebrates which are caught in shallow water. Nest is a simple scrape built up with twigs either on open bare ground or in vegetation adjacent to wetlands.
RANGE/STATUS Occurs over large areas of Africa, Europe, the Americas, Asia and Australasia. Not globally threatened. Represented in Madagascar by the nominate subspecies which is common to Africa and Europe. Fairly common in suitable habitat throughout, though absent from the high plateau. Found from sea level to 750m.
WHERE TO SEE Most likely to be seen at wetlands in the west such as pools near Toliara and wetlands around Ampijoroa.
SIMILAR SPECIES The exceptionally long pink legs and contrasting black and white plumage make this species easy to identify.

93a. Crab Plover, adult.

93b. Crab Plover, adult in flight.

94. Black-winged Stilt, adult male.

95　Pied Avocet　*Recurvirostra avosetta*

DESCRIPTION Size: 42-45cm. A large wader with a distinctive upturned bill. Sexes alike, plumage varies slightly with age. **Adult:** All-white but for crown, nape and hindneck, edges of mantle and upper scapulars, lesser and median coverts and primaries which are all-black. Iris brown, bill fine, strongly upturned and black, long legs and feet greyish-blue. **Juvenile:** Similar to the adult, though the black plumage is replaced with brown and the white in the upperparts is mottled with brown. Legs duller than the adult.
VOICE Typical call is a clear *kluit* which is louder and sharper in alarm.
HABITAT/BEHAVIOUR Typically found in saline lagoons, pools, saltpans and estuaries as well as tidal mudflats and occasionally freshwater lakes. Gregarious. Feeds mainly on aquatic invertebrates which are caught in shallow water, often using a sideways sweeping of the bill.
RANGE/STATUS Occurs over large areas of Africa, Eurasia and Australasia. Not globally threatened. Monotypic. A vagrant to Madagascar which has only been recorded twice.
WHERE TO SEE A rare vagrant that is unlikely to be seen. Most likely to occur in suitable habitat on the west coast.
SIMILAR SPECIES The pied plumage and slender, strongly upturned bill make this species easy to iden-tify. In flight, may be mistaken for Crab Plover but easily distinguished by the bill shape, the black on the head and the white secondaries which contrast with the black coverts (reverse in Crab Plover).

96　Madagascar Pratincole　*Glareola ocularis*

DESCRIPTION A typical pratincole, being a short-legged wader, somewhat tern-like in shape and behav-iour. Sexes alike, plumage varies with age. **Adult:** Forehead and crown dark chocolate-brown shading to dark grey-brown on the rest of the upperparts which in good light show an olive hue. Flight feathers brown-black. Uppertail-coverts white, shallowly forked tail black with white at the base of the outer tail-feathers and on the tips of the central tail feathers. Lores blackish, face grey-brown with a conspicuous white line running from the gape to the rear of the ear-coverts. Chin, throat and breast grey-brown, upper belly and underwing-coverts rich chestnut. Rest of underparts white. Iris dark brown, bill short and heavy, black with a red base, legs and feet dark grey. **Juvenile:** Similar to adult, though upperparts with buff fringes, the line on the face is buff and they show rufous-buff streaking on the upper breast.
VOICE Frequently calls while feeding on the wing. Call is reminiscent of a tern, *wick-e-wick*.
HABITAT/BEHAVIOUR Breeds in loose colonies on rocky islets in rivers, saltmarsh and coastal rocky areas. Also found in short grasslands and lake edges. Gregarious, often roosting and foraging in flocks. Catches insect prey mostly on the wing, frequently feeding just before dusk.
RANGE/STATUS Endemic Breeder to Madagascar, it is present in Madagascar from approximately Sep-tember to late March/April. Spends the non-breeding season in East Africa. Not globally threatened. Monotypic. Occurs throughout the island except for the extreme south-west. Appears to be mainly a mi-grant in the west with most known breeding areas being situated in the east. A few colonies, including near Mahajanga, have recently been found in the west. Found from sea level to 1,500m.
WHERE TO SEE Most easily seen in the east where it is best looked for at Ambanizana and around Nosy Mangabe on the Masoala Peninsula, over the river at Ranomafana and on the Mangoro river crossing (west of Perinet-Analamazaotra and crossed if driving from Antananarivo to Moramanga en route to Perinet-Analamazaotra).
SIMILAR SPECIES The only pratincole found on Madagascar, easily recognised by its distinctive shape, dark plumage contrasting with white uppertail-coverts and prominent white face line.

5a. *Pied Avocet, adult.*

5b. *Pied Avocet, juvenile.*

96. *Madagascar Pratincole, adult.*

97 Ringed Plover *Charadrius hiaticula*

DESCRIPTION Size: 18-20cm. A small stocky plover. Plumage varies seasonally and with age. Only likely to be recorded in Madagascar in non-breeding plumage. **Adult non-breeding:** Crown and upperparts brownish-grey. Forehead and short supercilium behind the eye buffish-white and broken by a blackish frontal bar. Lores and ear-coverts dark greyish-brown. Underparts white with a variable broad blackish-brown band across the breast. White of throat continues along the back of the ear-coverts to form a complete white collar around the hindneck. In flight shows a prominent white wing-bar, white sides to the rump and a white tip to the tail. Iris dark brown, bill short, black with a dull orange base, legs and feet orange. **Adult breeding:** Similar to non-breeding plumage, though frontal band, ear-coverts and breast-band black, the latter forming a complete band around the hindneck, supercilium white and bill base more extensively bright orange. **Juvenile:** Similar to non-breeding, though shows dark subterminal marks and pale fringes on the upperpart feathers and the bare parts are duller.
VOICE Typical call is a distinctive, inflected, mellow whistle, *tuuleee*.
HABITAT/BEHAVIOUR In the non-breeding season has a preference for coastal areas, particularly intertidal mudflats, beaches and lakes near the coast. Usually found in small groups. Feeds on various invertebrates.
RANGE/STATUS Breeds in north-east Canada, Greenland, northern Europe and northern Asia and winters in Europe, Africa and south-west Asia. Not globally threatened. In Madagascar, represented by the race *C. h. tundrae*. A common non-breeding visitor to Madagascar, it may be found in suitable coastal areas throughout the island during the austral summer with small numbers of non-breeding birds staying during the austral winter. Observed at and near to sea level.
WHERE TO SEE Fairly common and easily found at suitable coastal sites such as the Toliara and Maroantsetra areas.
SIMILAR SPECIES Easily distinguished from all other similar plovers in Madagascar by the orange legs. In addition, the combination of dark brownish-grey upperparts, a complete white collar and dark breast-band are unique.

98 Kittlitz's Plover *Charadrius pecuarius*

DESCRIPTION Size: 12-14cm. A small plover. Plumage varies seasonally and with age. **Adult breeding:** Narrow black eye-stripe broadens behind the eye and continues down the side of the neck where it joins across the nape. A black frontal band isolates the white forehead. Bright white supercilia meet narrowly on the forecrown and join at the nape isolating the dark brown crown. Upperparts dark brown, narrowly fringed buff. Underparts white with a variable, pale cinnamon suffusion on the lower breast and belly. In flight shows contrastingly dark lesser coverts, a moderate white wing-bar and white sides to the rump and tail. Iris dark brown, bill black, legs and feet dark greenish-grey. Female may be slightly duller than male. **Adult non-breeding:** Similar to adult breeding, though duller with the black in the plumage replaced by brown. Shows a buffish supercilium and collar and shows a variable brown suffusion on the sides of the breast. **Juvenile:** Similar to non-breeding, though with broader pale fringes on the upperparts.
VOICE Fairly quiet. Typical calls include a short *trit* and a plaintive *tu-lit* given in flight.
HABITAT/BEHAVIOUR Coastal and inland wetlands including lakes, rivers, estuaries, mudflats and adjacent short grassland. Gregarious, often found in small groups and roosts communally. Feeds on various invertebrates. Nest is a shallow scrape made in dry mud or sand.
RANGE/STATUS Occurs in Egypt and sub-Saharan Africa. Not globally threatened. Represented in Madagascar by the nominate subspecies which is common to most of the species' range. A common resident in Madagascar, present in suitable habitat throughout, though most common in the east, south and west. Found from sea level to 1,400m.
WHERE TO SEE Easily seen at wetlands in the Toliara area. Also common in wetlands around Ampijoroa.
SIMILAR SPECIES Most similar to Madagascar Plover, which see for differences. Non-breeding individuals and in particular, juveniles, are similar to the larger White-fronted Plover and Lesser Sand Plover. They are best separated from both by their smaller size, longer-legged appearance, clear buff collar, contrastingly dark lesser coverts and pale fringed upperparts which give a scaly effect.

°7. *Ringed Plover, adult non-breeding.*

°8. *Kittlitz's Plover, adult breeding.*

99 Madagascar Plover *Charadrius thoracicus*

DESCRIPTION Size: 13-14cm.. A small plover. Plumage varies seasonally and with age. **Adult breeding:** Narrow black eye-stripe broadens behind the eye and continues down the side of the neck where it joins across the nape and meets the broad black breast-band. A black frontal band isolates the white forehead. Bright white supercilia meet narrowly on the forecrown and join at the nape isolating the dark brown crown. Upperparts dark brown, narrowly fringed buff. Underparts white but for the black breast-band and a pale cinnamon suffusion on the lower breast and belly. In flight shows a narrow white wing-bar and white sides to the rump and tail. Iris dark brown, bill black, legs and feet dark grey. **Adult non-breeding:** Similar to adult breeding, though duller with black in plumage tinged brown. **Juvenile:** Similar to non-breeding, though duller still with broader pale fringes to the upperparts and the breast-band is less distinctive.
VOICE Typical call is a short *pit* or *tsewit* and a *pi-pi-pi* given during distraction display.
HABITAT/BEHAVIOUR Typically inhabits short coastal grassland and the edges of brackish pools, intertidal mud, sandy beaches and mangroves. Typically prefers drier areas than Kittlitz's Plover. Usually found in pairs and occasionally in small groups. Feeds on various invertebrates. The nest is a small scrape made in dry grassland adjacent to the coast or a lake.
RANGE/STATUS Endemic to Madagascar. Globally Threatened and currently classified as **Vulnerable.** Monotypic. Scarce to rare along the west and south-west coasts from Mahajanga to Tsimanampetsotsa. Found at and near to sea level.
WHERE TO SEE Best searched for in the Toliara area where it is frequently seen at a pool adjacent to the airport and on saltpans just south of Ifaty. May also be seen on beaches south of Morondava.
SIMILAR SPECIES Most similar to Kittlitz's Plover. Adult Madagascar Plover may easily be separated from Kittlitz's by its prominent black breast-band. Juveniles are more similar but can again be identified most easily by the presence of a greyish-brown breast-band. Easily distinguished from the larger Ringed Plover by smaller size, scaly upperparts, longer, dark grey, as opposed to orange, legs and head pattern.

100 Three-banded Plover *Charadrius tricollaris*

DESCRIPTION Size: 17-18cm. A small, long-winged plover. Plumage varies with age. **Adult:** White upper forehead joins the bright white supercilia which join across the nape isolating the dark brown crown. Upperparts uniform dark brown. Tail long, extending beyond the wing tips at rest. Lores, lower forehead, face, chin and throat smoky-grey bordered below by a narrow black breast-band. Rest of the underparts white with a second, broader, black breast-band, separated from the upper band by a white band. The upper black band and the white band extend on to the side of the hindneck forming an incomplete collar. Has a characteristic jerky flight when a very narrow white wing-bar, a white trailing edge to the secondaries and white sides to the rump and tail are visible. Iris pale brown surrounded by a prominent red orbital-ring, bill bright red tipped blackish, legs and feet reddish-brown. **Juvenile:** Similar to the adult, though duller with less distinct head pattern, forehead and breast-bands browner and shows pale fringes to the upperparts.
VOICE Fairly quiet. On taking flight or in alarm gives a shrill inflected call *tuuieet.*
HABITAT/BEHAVIOUR Favours the muddy edges of rice paddies, freshwater lakes and rivers, though also found around coastal lagoons and occasionally mudflats and mangrove areas. Usually encountered in pairs or small groups. Feeds on various invertebrates which are usually gleaned from the water's edge. The nest is a shallow scrape made in dry mud or sand close to water.
RANGE/STATUS Occurs in eastern and southern Africa. Not globally threatened. Represented in Madagascar by the endemic subspecies *C. t. bifrontatus* which differs from the nominate in being slightly larger in bill and tarsus, with a dark grey rather than pale brown face, a smaller white area below the bill (chin and upper throat only), a bicolored forehead, with dark grey lower half and white upper half, and less white in the wing, especially on the tips of the median and greater coverts and inner secondaries.It occurs throughout, though is most common in suitable habitats in the west and north. Found from sea level to 1800m.
WHERE TO SEE Frequently seen at the lake and in wetlands around Ampijoroa. Also regularly seen on pools around Toliara and in the river and surrounding wet paddies at Vohiparara in Ranomafana National Park.
SIMILAR SPECIES The red-based bill, conspicuous head pattern and two dark breast-bands are highly distinctive and this species should not be confused with any other in Madagascar.

99a. *Madagascar Plover, adult breeding.*

99b. *Madagascar Plover, adult breeding.*

100. *Three-banded Plover, adult.*

101 White-fronted Plover *Charadrius marginatus*

DESCRIPTION Size: 18cm. A small plover. Sexes differ and plumage varies seasonally and with age. **Adult male breeding:** Conspicuous white forehead bordered by a black frontal band which stops short of the eye. White supercilium joins with the white forehead and is bordered below by a narrow black eye-stripe which broadens slightly behind the eye. Crown and upperparts a pale sandy grey, sometimes richer cinnamon on the crown. Underparts white with a variable rich cinnamon-orange suffusion on the sides of the breast. In flight shows a prominent white wing-bar and white sides to the rump and tail. Iris dark brown, bill black, legs and feet grey usually tinged green. **Adult male non-breeding:** Black on head has brown mixed in and the suffusion on the breast is duller. **Adult female:** May be slightly duller than male in breeding plumage and in non-breeding plumage closely resembles the male non-breeding. **Juvenile:** Similar to non-breeding, though lacks the dark frontal band and suffusion at the sides of the breast and shows broad buff fringes to the upperparts.
VOICE Typical calls are a soft *pwit* or *woo-et*.
HABITAT/BEHAVIOUR Prefers sandy shores along coasts, large rivers and lakes. Also occasionally on rocky shores and mudflats. Gregarious, often found in pairs or small groups and occasionally in larger gatherings. Feeds on various invertebrates. The nest is a shallow scrape made in sand.
RANGE/STATUS Occurs in sub-Saharan Africa. Not globally threatened. In Madagascar, represented by the race *C.m. tenellus* which is common to eastern Africa. A common resident in Madagascar present in suitable habitat on all coasts, though rarer inland. Typically observed at or near sea level but has been recorded up to 1,500m.
WHERE TO SEE Best looked for in coastal areas such as saltpans and beaches in the Toliara area.
SIMILAR SPECIES The overall pale coloration and conspicuous white forehead are distinctive. Confusion may arise with juvenile Kittlitz's Plover and Lesser Sand Plover, which see for differences.

102 Lesser Sand Plover *Charadrius mongolus*

DESCRIPTION Size: 18-21cm. A small to medium-sized plover. Plumage varies seasonally and with age. Only likely to be recorded in Madagascar in non-breeding plumage. **Adult non-breeding:** Crown, lores, ear-coverts and upperparts greyish-brown. Forehead and supercilium buffish-white. Underparts white with extensive greyish-brown patches on the sides of the breast which occasionally meet in the centre. In flight shows an even, narrow, though obvious white wing-bar, white sides to the rump and narrow white sides and tip to the tail. Iris dark brown. Bill stout, black, about the same length or less than the distance from the base of the bill to the rear of the eye. Legs and feet dark grey. **Adult breeding:** Differs from non-breeding in much brighter coloration including black forehead and ear-coverts, extensive chestnut on the crown and nape and broad chestnut breast-band sometimes bordered by black above. **Juvenile:** Similar to non-breeding, though pale buff fringes to the upperparts give a scaly effect.
VOICE Typical call is hard *chitick*.
HABITAT/BEHAVIOUR In the non-breeding season has a preference for coastal areas, particularly intertidal mudflats and sandflats, and estuaries. Usually found singly or in small groups. Feeds on various invertebrates.
RANGE/STATUS Breeds in central and north-east Asia and winters along the coasts of East Africa through southern Asia to Australia. Not globally threatened. In Madagascar, probably represented by the race *C.m. pamirensis* which also winters on the coast of East Africa. A scarce to rare and recently discovered non-breeding visitor to Madagascar, it may occasionally be found in small numbers in suitable habitats on the west coast. Observed at and near to sea level.
WHERE TO SEE Best searched for on the intertidal mudflats at Toliara and other west coast estuaries and mudflats.
SIMILAR SPECIES Most likely to be confused with the very similar Greater Sand Plover. Best distinguished from Greater by its smaller size, shorter (especially above the knee) and darker legs which do not project beyond the tail in flight, proportionately shorter bill (the bill of Greater appears long and heavy) and differences in call. There is, however, overlap in most measurements and lone individuals can be extremely difficult to identify. The differences in size and structure become far more apparent if the two species are seen together when Lesser Sand Plover often appears rounder headed and more neatly proportioned. May also be confused with non-breeding Ringed Plover. However, this species invariably shows white on the hindneck and orange legs. White-fronted Plover is similar but is smaller, paler, shows reduced markings at the sides of the breast and more extensive white on the forehead.

5. *Grey Plover, adult transitional plumage.*

6. *Madagascar Snipe, adult in flight.*

107 Black-tailed Godwit *Limosa limosa*

DESCRIPTION Size: 36-44cm. Large, long-legged and long-billed wader. Plumage varies seasonally and with age. Bill averages longer in females. In Madagascar only in non-breeding plumage. **Adult non-breeding:** Grey-brown crown nape and upperparts. Upperparts appear uniform but at close range slightly darker shaft-streaks and paler fringes. Dark grey lores isolate the whitish supercilium. Chin and throat whitish merging into grey-brown breast. Rest of underparts white. In flight white underwings, broad white wing-bar and white patch on rump and uppertail-coverts contrast with rest of the wings and broad, black, terminal tail band. Iris dark brown, bill long and straight, basal half pink, distal half blackish. Long legs and feet blackish. **Adult breeding:** Darker, more contrastingly patterned black and rufous upperparts, rufous on face, hindneck and upper breast and black barring on the lower breast and belly. Males brighter than females. **Juvenile:** Like non-breeding, though there is a warm cinnamon-buff suffusion to breast and upperparts dark brown with bright buff fringing, spotting and notching giving a scaly effect.
VOICE Quiet on non-breeding grounds; may give a short *kek* or a *wicka-wicka-wicka* in flight.
HABITAT/BEHAVIOUR In non-breeding season occurs in coastal lagoons, intertidal mudflats and sandflats, estuaries, inland lakes and wet grasslands. Typically gregarious, though lone individuals most often seen in Madagascar. Feeds on a variety of invertebrates which are caught by probing the long bill into soft substrates.
RANGE/STATUS Breeds from Iceland across Europe to north-east Asia; winters in Europe, Africa, Asia and Australia. Not globally threatened. In Madagascar, represented by the nominate subspecies. A rare non-breeding visitor to Madagascar. Observed at and near to sea level.
WHERE TO SEE A rare visitor. Most likely to be seen in wetlands on the west coast.
SIMILAR SPECIES Wing and tail pattern renders it unmistakable in flight in all plumages.

108 Bar-tailed Godwit *Limosa lapponica*

DESCRIPTION Size: 37-41cm. A large, long-billed wader. Plumage varies seasonally and with age. Bill averages longer in females. Only likely to be recorded in Madagascar in non-breeding plumage. **Adult non-breeding:** Crown, hindneck and upperparts brownish-grey with prominent black shaft-streaks and whitish fringes especially to the coverts giving a distinctly mottled effect. Dark grey lores, conspicuous whitish supercilium, rest of the face and upper breast pale brownish-grey finely streaked with black. Rest of the underparts white with some fine black streaking, especially on the flanks. In flight shows uniform wings, a barred tail and a conspicuous white patch extending from the uppertail-coverts in a 'V' up the back. Iris dark brown, bill averages shorter than Black-tailed Godwit and is slightly upturned with the basal half pink and the distal half blackish. Legs and feet blackish, shorter than Black-tailed Godwit. **Adult breeding:** Differs from non-breeding by the darker more contrastingly patterned black and rufous upperparts and extensive rufous of varying intensity on the face, hindneck and underparts with black streaking on the breast sides. Males are brighter than females, which may recall non-breeding birds. **Juvenile:** Similar to non-breeding, though upperparts dark brown with bright buff spotting and notching giving a streaked appearance. Supercilium and underparts suffused with buff.
VOICE Usually silent, though a harsh *krruck* is occasionally given.
HABITAT/BEHAVIOUR In non-breeding season occurs on intertidal mudflats and sandflats, mangroves and estuaries. Typically gregarious, occurring in small groups. Feeds on a variety of invertebrates which are caught by probing the long bill into soft substrates.
RANGE/STATUS Breeds across northern Europe east to north-east Asia and western Alaska. Winters on the coasts of Europe, Africa, the Middle East, Asia and Australasia. Not globally threatened. In Madagascar, represented by the nominate subspecies. Occasionally small numbers of non-breeding birds are present during the austral winter. Observed at and near to sea level.
WHERE TO SEE Fairly common at suitable coastal sites such as the Toliara and Maroantsetra areas.
SIMILAR SPECIES On the ground, confusion may arise with the similar Black-tailed Godwit, which see for differences. Upperpart patterning and markings in flight may recall Eurasian Curlew and Whimbrel. However, the straight (slightly upturned) as opposed to decurved bill and overall paler plumage should easily distinguish this species.

107a. *Black-tailed Godwit, adult non-breeding.*

107b. *Black-tailed Godwit, juvenile.*

108a. *Bar-tailed Godwit, adult non-breeding.*

108b. *Bar-tailed Godwit, adult breeding.*

109 Whimbrel *Numenius phaeopus*

DESCRIPTION Size: 40-46cm. A large, dumpy, long-legged wader with a distinctly down-curved bill. Plumage varies slightly with age. **Adult:** Distinctive head pattern. A narrow pale central crown-stripe is enclosed by dark greyish-brown lateral crown-stripes. These contrast with prominent supercilia which are off-white finely streaked darker. Latter contrast with conspicuous dark eye-stripes. Hindneck grey-brown, finely streaked darker, rest of upperparts dark brown, the feathers notched and fringed with off white. Lower face, throat and breast pale grey-buff with fine darker streaking. Rest of underparts white suffused with buff, finely streaked darker and with some dark barring on the flanks. In flight, the dark upperparts contrast with the conspicuous white rump patch which extends from the uppertail-coverts in a 'V' up the back. Iris dark brown, bill fairly long and distinctly kinked downwards, blackish, though paler at the base. Legs and feet bluish-grey. **Juvenile:** Similar to non-breeding, though upperparts generally darker with clearer and neater notching and fringing.
VOICE Distinctive call, often given in flight, is a rapid series of rippling whistles which fall slightly: *wi-wi-wi-wi-wi-wi-wi-wi*. Also sometimes gives a call resembling a hoarse curlew, *cur-lew*, often when taking flight.
HABITAT/BEHAVIOUR In non-breeding season occurs in a variety of wetland habitats including intertidal mudflats and sandflats, rocky coasts, mangroves, estuaries, lake and river shores and adjacent grassland. Typically gregarious, occurring in small groups. Feeds on a variety of invertebrates.
RANGE/STATUS Breeds across northern America, northern Europe and northern Asia. Winters on the coasts of the Americas, south-west Europe, Africa, the Middle East, Asia and Australasia. Not globally threatened. In Madagascar, represented by the **Nominate** subspecies. A common non-breeding visitor to Madagascar where it may be seen on all suitable coasts during the austral summer. Small numbers of non-breeding birds are present during the austral winter. Found from sea level to 750m.
WHERE TO SEE One of the commonest and most frequently seen waders, easily found at suitable coastal sites such as the Toliara and Maroantsetra areas.
SIMILAR SPECIES On the ground, confusion may arise with the similar Eurasian Curlew which is larger, has a longer, more evenly curved bill, has paler upperparts with more extensive buff fringing and lacks the distinctive head pattern of Whimbrel. In flight, best separated by its smaller size, shorter bill, distinctive call and darker upperwing and underwing which contrast more with the white rump and back. May also be confused in flight with Bar-tailed Godwit, which see for differences.

110 Eurasian Curlew *Numenius arquata*

DESCRIPTION Size: 50-60cm. A very large, long-legged wader with a conspicuously long decurved bill. Plumage varies slightly seasonally and with age. Bill averages longer in females. Only likely to be recorded in Madagascar in non-breeding plumage. **Adult non-breeding:** Head, neck and breast buff-brown, finely streaked darker. Rest of the underparts white with darker streaking and barring, especially on the flanks. Face lacks distinct markings, giving a 'plain faced' appearance, other than a slight pale eye-ring. Upperparts dark brown, notched and fringed extensively with buff, most prominently on the wing-coverts which appear paler than the rest of the upperparts. In flight, the brown upperparts contrast with the conspicuous white tail which is barred with black and the white rump patch which extends from the uppertail-coverts in a 'V' up the back. Iris dark brown, bill long and evenly decurved, blackish, though paler at the base. Legs and feet bluish-grey. **Adult breeding:** Similar to non-breeding, though plumage appears generally warmer and more buff. **Juvenile:** Similar to adult breeding, though bill shorter.
VOICE Distinctive call is a far-carrying *cour-lew cour-lew*. Also sometimes gives the song on the wintering grounds, a sequence of bubbling phrases which accelerate and rise in pitch.
HABITAT/BEHAVIOUR In the non-breeding season prefers coastal habitats such as intertidal mudflats and sandflats, mangroves and estuaries. Typically gregarious, occurring in small groups. Feeds on a variety of invertebrates.
RANGE/STATUS Breeds across northern Europe and northern Asia. Winters on the coasts of southern Europe, Africa, the Middle East, and southern Asia to the Philippines and Greater Sundas. Not globally threatened. In Madagascar, represented by the subspecies *N. a. orientalis*. A scarce non-breeding visitor to the west coast of Madagascar during the austral summer. Observed at and near to sea level.
WHERE TO SEE Scarce, most likely to be seen in small numbers on the mudflats at Toliara and Mahajanga.
SIMILAR SPECIES Most likely to be confused with Whimbrel, which see for differences. In flight, may also be confused with Bar-tailed Godwit, which see for differences.

9. *Whimbrel, adult.*

10. *Eurasian Curlew, adult.*

111 Marsh Sandpiper *Tringa stagnatilis*

DESCRIPTION Size: 22-26cm. Medium-sized wader with long legs and long and fine bill. Plumage varies seasonally and with age. Only likely to be recorded in Madagascar in non-breeding plumage. **Adult non-breeding:** Forehead and supercilium white bordered by obscure dark eye-stripe. Rest of face and underparts white with some grey suffusion on breast. Crown and hindneck grey-brown streaked darker. Mantle, scapulars and tertials grey narrowly fringed with white and paler than darker grey wing-coverts. In flight, uniform grey-brown upperparts contrast strongly with conspicuous, elongated white patch which extends from the uppertail-coverts in a 'V' across rump and up back. The tail is largely white with indistinct barring on central tail feathers. Iris dark brown, bill longish, usually appearing straight and fine, blackish, though paler at the base. Long legs and feet grey-green to yellow-green. **Adult breeding:** Differs from non-breeding by more streaking on the head giving a less well-defined face pattern, dark streaking on the breast and brown upperparts with irregular black notching, barring and feather centres. **Juvenile:** Similar to non-breeding, though has a distinct dark cap and mask through the eye and darker upperparts with neat, dark subterminal bars and buff fringes and notches.
VOICE Typical call is a high-pitched *teu* sometimes repeated in a series which is higher than Greenshank.
HABITAT/BEHAVIOUR In non-breeding season prefers inland wetlands and brackish pools. Usually seen singly in Madagascar. Feeds chiefly on a variety of invertebrates and occasionally small fish and amphibians.
RANGE/STATUS Breeds across north-eastern Europe and northern Asia. Winters from Mediterranean and sub-Saharan Africa east to southern Asia and Australia. Not globally threatened. Monotypic. A scarce non-breeding visitor to the west coast of Madagascar during the austral summer. Observed at and near to sea level.
WHERE TO SEE Scarce, most likely to be seen at freshwater lakes on the west coast.
SIMILAR SPECIES Most likely to be confused with the very similar Common Greenshank from which it differs in its smaller size, proportionately longer, thinner legs, much finer, straighter bill, which only shows pale at the extreme base, and more delicate head and neck. Caution is required when viewing distant birds as the bill of Common Greenshank may appear fine at long range.

112 Common Greenshank *Tringa nebularia*

DESCRIPTION Size: 30-34cm. Medium-large long-legged wader. Plumage varies seasonally and with age. Only likely to be recorded in Madagascar in non-breeding plumage. **Adult non-breeding:** Forehead and indistinct supercilium and eye-ring white, crown and hindneck white with dense, fine grey streaking, rest of the face white with sparse grey streaks. Upperparts grey, narrowly fringed with white and some fine black notching. Underparts white with some grey streaking on the breast sides. In flight, the uniform grey-brown upperparts contrast strongly with the conspicuous, elongated white patch which extends from the uppertail-coverts in a 'V' across the rump and up the back. The tail pale grey with fine brown barring. Iris dark brown, bill longish, stout-based and slightly upturned, extensively greyish-green at the base becoming black distally. Long legs and feet grey-green to yellow-green. **Adult breeding:** Differs from non-breeding by more streaking on the head, dark streaking on the breast more extensive and grey-brown upperparts with irregular black notching barring and feather centres, especially on the scapulars. **Juvenile:** Similar to non-breeding, though has a darker crown, more streaking on the upper breast and darker upperparts with neat, dark subterminal bars and buff fringes and notches.
VOICE Typical call is a distinctive, ringing whistle of two to four notes: *tuu-tuu-tuu.*
HABITAT/BEHAVIOUR In the non-breeding season occurs in a variety of wetland habitats including coastal lagoons, intertidal mudflats and sandflats, estuaries, inland lakes and rice paddies. Gregarious, usually seen in small groups. Feeds chiefly on invertebrates and occasionally small fish and amphibians.
RANGE/STATUS Breeds across northern Europe and northern Asia. Not globally threatened. Monotypic. A common non-breeding visitor to Madagascar where it may be seen on all coasts and suitable habitat during the austral summer. Small numbers of non-breeding birds are present during the austral winter. Found from sea level to 1,400m.
WHERE TO SEE One of the commonest and most frequently seen waders, easily found at suitable coastal sites such as the Toliara and Maroantsetra areas, and inland freshwater marshes.
SIMILAR SPECIES A large wader with long greenish legs and a long, quite powerful, slightly upturned bill which may appear finer at long range. Most likely to be confused with the very similar, though smaller Marsh Sandpiper, which see for differences.

11a. Marsh Sandpiper, adult non-breeding.

111b. Marsh Sandpiper, juvenile.

12. Common Greenshank, adult non-breeding.

113 Green Sandpiper *Tringa ochropus*

DESCRIPTION Size: 21-24cm. A medium-sized wader with a characteristic dumpy horizontal posture. Plumage varies seasonally and with age. Only likely to be recorded in Madagascar in non-breeding plumage. **Adult non-breeding:** A short white fore-supercilium joins the prominent white eye-ring. Crown and hindneck dark brown, indistinctly streaked paler, rest of the upperparts dark olive-brown with small off-white spots and notches. Throat, face and breast grey-brown with darker streaking, rest of the underparts white. In flight, the uniform dark brown upperparts and black underwings contrast strongly with the conspicuous, square white patch on the uppertail-coverts and rump and the white tail which is barred darker towards the tip. Iris dark brown, bill shortish, straight, greyish-green at the base becoming black distally. Legs and feet grey-green. **Adult breeding:** Differs from non-breeding by darker head and breast, better-defined head pattern and more prominent spotting on the upperparts. **Juvenile:** Similar to non-breeding, though has a more obvious supercilium, a darker loral line and buffer spotting on the browner upperparts.
VOICE Call is a distinctive, high-pitched whistle with a varying number of syllables: *tee-weeeet -weeet-weeet.*
HABITAT/BEHAVIOUR In the non-breeding season occurs in freshwater habitats such as muddy pools, ditches, rice paddies and lake shores. Shy and often solitary. Feeds chiefly on a variety of invertebrates. Habitually bobs its rear end up and down while feeding.
RANGE/STATUS Breeds across northern Europe and northern Asia. Winters in Europe, Africa, the Middle East and southern Asia south to the Greater Sundas. Not globally threatened. Monotypic. A vagrant to Madagascar.
WHERE TO SEE A rare vagrant and therefore no regular sites.
SIMILAR SPECIES Most likely to be confused with Common or Wood Sandpiper. Best told from Common Sandpiper by larger size, darker upperparts which contrast more with the pale belly, spotted as opposed to plain upperparts, and dark extending evenly across the breast. In flight easily distinguished by contrasting black and white plumage and clear white rump. Separated from Wood Sandpiper by plainer, darker upperparts (distinctly spangled in Wood), shorter supercilium, more dumpy profile and sluggish nature and shorter, darker legs. In flight, further differs by blackish as opposed to pale underwings and very different flight calls.

114 Wood Sandpiper *Tringa glareola*

DESCRIPTION Size: 19-21cm. A medium-sized wader with a short straight bill and long pale legs. Plumage varies seasonally and with age. Only likely to be recorded in Madagascar in non-breeding plumage. **Adult non-breeding:** Prominent white supercilium and eye-ring bordered below by a dark eye-stripe which is most prominent in front of the eye. Crown and hindneck brown, streaked paler, rest of the upperparts dark brown with buff spots and notches. Throat white, face and breast off-white, finely streaked darker, rest of the underparts white. In flight, the uniform brown upperparts contrast strongly with the conspicuous, square white patch on the uppertail-coverts and rump and the white tail which is finely barred darker. The underwings are pale. Iris dark brown, bill shortish, straight, deep based, greyish-green basally, black distally. Longish legs and feet dull yellow. **Adult breeding:** Differs from non- breeding by more heavily streaked head and underparts, barred flanks and stronger patterned upperparts. **Juvenile:** Similar to non-breeding, though upperparts warmer brown with more distinct buff spotting and fringing and may show a buff wash on the breast.
VOICE Call is a distinctive, clear whistled *chiff-iff* or *chiff-chiff-iff*, sometimes transcribed as *wit-wit-wit.*
HABITAT/BEHAVIOUR In the non-breeding season occurs in freshwater habitats such as rice paddies and lake shores as well as coastal lagoons and saltpans. Generally avoids the coast. Usually seen singly or in small groups in Madagascar. Feeds chiefly on a variety of invertebrates and occasionally small fish and amphibians.
RANGE/STATUS Breeds across northern Europe and northern Asia. Winters in Africa, the Middle East, southern Asia and Australia. Not globally threatened. Monotypic. A scarce visitor to the west coast of Madagascar during the austral summer. Usually observed near to sea level.
WHERE TO SEE Uncommon, most likely to be seen in freshwater habitats on the west coast.
SIMILAR SPECIES Most likely to be confused with Green or Marsh Sandpipers, which see for differences.

3. Green Sandpiper, adult non-breeding.

4. Wood Sandpiper, adult non-breeding.

115 Terek Sandpiper *Xenus cinereus*

DESCRIPTION Size: 22-25cm. A short-legged, medium-sized wader with a distinctly upturned bill. Plumage varies slightly seasonally and with age. Only likely to be recorded in Madagascar in non-breeding plumage. **Adult non-breeding:** Forehead, indistinct supercilium and eye-ring white, loral line grey, rest of the face white with indistinct fine grey streaks. Crown and hindneck grey-brown with fine darker streaking, rest of the upperparts grey-brown appearing uniform, though at close range the indistinct dark shaft-streaks and narrow pale feather-fringes may be visible. Underparts snowy-white except for grey-brown breast-patches at the sides of the upper breast. In flight, the dark primaries and leading edge contrast with the grey-brown mid-wing panel and the conspicuous white trailing edge to the secondaries. Has a distinctive jerky wingbeat similar to Common Sandpiper. Iris brown, bill longish, distinctly upturned, blackish with a small yellowish-orange basal area. Short legs and feet dull yellow-orange to bright orange. **Adult breeding:** Differs from non-breeding by more obvious dark shaft-streaks on the upperparts, dark feather- centre to the upper scapulars forming a dark line and fine streaking on the breast. **Juvenile:** Similar to adult breeding though has dark sub-terminal bars and pale fringes to the wing-coverts.
VOICE Typical call is a sharp, fluty, rolling *twit-wit* or *twit-wit-wit*.
HABITAT/BEHAVIOUR In the non-breeding season prefers coastal habitats such as intertidal mudflats and sandflats, mangroves and estuaries. Usually found singly or in small groups. Feeds energetically on a variety of invertebrates. Has a characteristic habit of bobbing its head and rear-end up and down. When feeding, dashes about very actively.
RANGE/STATUS Breeds across north-eastern Europe and northern Asia. Winters in Africa, the Middle East, southern Asia and Australasia. Not globally threatened. Monotypic. A fairly common non-breeding visitor to Madagascar where it may be seen on all coasts during the austral summer though is most common on the west coast. Observed at and near to sea level.
WHERE TO SEE Small numbers may be found at suitable coastal sites such as the Toliara and Maroantsetra areas.
SIMILAR SPECIES Unlikely to be confused with any other species. From Common Sandpiper by larger size and long, upturned bill.

116 Common Sandpiper *Actitis hypoleucos*

DESCRIPTION Size: 19-21cm. A small sandpiper. Plumage varies slightly seasonally and with age. Only likely to be recorded in Madagascar in non-breeding plumage. **Adult non-breeding:** Indistinct whitish supercilium extends behind the eye and joins with the white eye-ring. Crown, hindneck and upperparts uniform dark brown with some indistinct paler fringes to the wing-coverts. Ear-coverts and face washed grey-brown, throat white, breast white with conspicuous, isolated grey-brown 'thumb-prints' on either side of the upper breast. Rest of the underparts white. In flight, has highly distinctive flickering wingbeats and shows a broad white wing-bar and white sides to the tail. Iris dark brown, bill shortish, straight, brownish with an ill-defined paler base. Short legs and feet vary in colour from greyish-olive to dull yellow. **Adult breeding:** Differs from non-breeding by narrow dark streaking on the breast and dark shaft-streaks and narrow dark bars on the upperparts. **Juvenile:** Similar to non-breeding though upperparts show narrow buff fringes and the tertials show dark and buff notches and the wing-coverts are barred brown and buff.
VOICE Call is a distinctive series of descending clear piping whistles, *swee-wee-wee*.
HABITAT/BEHAVIOUR In the non-breeding season occurs in most freshwater and brackish wetland habitats, including rice paddies and river banks, though tends to avoid large intertidal mudflats. Usually seen singly or in small groups. Feeds chiefly on a variety of invertebrates. Has a characteristic habit of bobbing its head and rear-end up and down while feeding.
RANGE/STATUS Breeds across Europe and northern Asia. Winters in Europe, Africa, the Middle East, southern Asia and Australia. Not globally threatened. Monotypic. A common non-breeding visitor to Madagascar where it may be seen in all suitable habitats during the austral summer. Found from sea level to 2,200m.
WHERE TO SEE Common and widespread in the austral summer. May be seen at any wetland such as around Toliara, Ampijoroa and Maroantsetra.
SIMILAR SPECIES A distinctive short-legged wader with a horizontal posture and a very distinctive flight action. May be confused with Green Sandpiper at a distance, which see for differences.

115. Terek Sandpiper. 115a. Adult non-breeding. 115b (inset) adult in transitional plumage.

116. Common Sandpiper, adult non-breeding.

117 Ruddy Turnstone *Arenaria interpres*

DESCRIPTION Size: 21-25cm. A short-legged, short-billed, medium-sized wader. Plumage varies seasonally and with age. Only likely in Madagascar in non-breeding plumage. **Adult non-breeding:** Crown dark brown, indistinct pale supercilium behind the eye, forehead and throat whitish, rest of face streaked brown and white. Upperparts dark brown with dull greyish fringes and white fringes to lower scapulars. Centre of breast blackish with dark spur extending up to rear of ear-coverts and second dark spur forming breast-band and enclosing paler area which is streaked with brown. Rest of underparts snowy-white. In flight, generally dark upperparts contrast strongly with white wing-bars, white patches on back and scapulars and white rump, uppertail-coverts and tail-sides. Iris dark brown, blackish bill short and stout, short legs and feet bright orange. **Adult breeding:** Differs from non-breeding by more extensive black on underparts, piebald black and white head and extensive chestnut in the upperparts. **Juvenile:** Similar to non-breeding though differs in browner upperparts with neat, pale buff fringes and duller legs.
VOICE Typical call is a clear, rapid, rolling *chukachuk*, sometimes extended into a longer trill.
HABITAT/BEHAVIOUR In non-breeding season prefers coastal habitats, especially rocky areas, though also found on intertidal mudflats and sandflats, mangrove areas and estuaries. Rarely on freshwater near the coast. Gregarious, usually found in small flocks. Feeds on invertebrates, small fish and occasionally carrion. When feeding turns objects over in search of prey as its name suggests.
RANGE/STATUS Breeds across northern North America, northern Europe and northern Asia and winters on the coasts of the Americas, Africa, the Middle East, southern Asia and Australasia. Not globally threatened. Represented in Madagascar by the nominate subspecies which is found throughout its Old-World range. A common non-breeding visitor to Madagascar, where it may be seen on all coasts during the austral summer, though is commonest in the west. Small numbers of non-breeding birds are present during the austral winter. Observed at and near to sea level.
WHERE TO SEE Common; found at suitable coastal sites such as the Toliara and Maroantsetra areas.
SIMILAR SPECIES The distinctive pied plumage renders it unlikely to be confused with any other species.

118 Sanderling *Calidris alba*

DESCRIPTION Size: 20-21cm. A short-legged, short-billed, small pale wader. Plumage varies seasonally and with age. Only likely to be recorded in Madagascar in non-breeding plumage. **Adult non-breeding:** Strikingly pale plumage. White forehead and supercilium, pale soft-grey ear-coverts, crown, hindneck and upperparts, the latter showing narrow dark shaft-treaks and narrow pale fringes to the larger feathers. Contrasting blackish lesser coverts are often hidden when not flying. Underparts white except for light grey streaking on the sides of the breast. In flight, the generally pale plumage contrasts strikingly with the dark lesser coverts and flight feathers and the broad white wing-bar. Also shows pale, whitish sides to the rump and tail. Iris dark brown, bill short and black, deep-based and very slightly decurved. Short black legs and feet. **Adult breeding:** Differs from non-breeding by rich rufous tones to the face, neck and breast and upperparts coarsely marked with rufous and black fringed with white in fresh plumage. **Juvenile:** Similar to non-breeding though differs in darker crown and black upperparts marked with golden-buff and white giving a neat spangled effect.
VOICE Typical call is a quiet *twip twip* with feeding flocks making soft twittering calls.
HABITAT/BEHAVIOUR In non-breeding season inhabits sandy coastal shores. Gregarious, usually found in small flocks. Feeds on invertebrates and occasionally small fish. Feeds on the tide-line of sandy beaches and running at great speed in a clockwork-like manner to avoid each incoming wave and then following the retreating wave.
RANGE/STATUS Breeds in Alaska, Arctic Canada and Greenland east to northern Asia and winters on the coasts of the Americas, Europe, Africa, the Middle East, southern Asia and Australasia. Not globally threatened. Monotypic. A common non-breeding visitor to Madagascar where it may be seen on all coasts during the austral summer and occasionally non-breeding birds are present during the austral winter. Observed at and near to sea level.
WHERE TO SEE Common and may be found at suitable coastal sites such as the Toliara and Maroantsetra areas.
SIMILAR SPECIES The pale grey non-breeding plumage is unmistakable.

7. Ruddy Turnstone, adult non-breeding.

8a. Sanderling, adult non-breeding.   *118b (inset) Sanderling, adult breeding.*

119 Little Stint *Calidris minuta*

DESCRIPTION Size: 12-14cm. A very small, short-billed sandpiper. Plumage varies seasonally and with age. Only likely to be recorded in Madagascar in non-breeding plumage. **Adult non-breeding:** Whitish forehead and supercilium, ear-coverts white finely streaked darker and there is an indistinct dark loral line. Crown and hindneck grey-brown finely streaked with black. Rest of the upperparts grey-brown with darker feather centres. Underparts white except for a light grey wash across the breast which is finely streaked with brown. In flight, shows a narrow but clear white wing-bar and dark rump, uppertail-coverts and tail with white sides to the rump and grey sides to the tail. Iris dark brown, bill short and black, very slightly decurved and fine at the tip. Legs and feet black. **Adult breeding:** Differs from non-breeding by rich rufous tones to the face and sides of the breast and blackish upperparts with broad rufous fringes. **Juvenile:** Similar to adult breeding though differs in showing a darker crown, more distinct supercilium and broad pale lines on the mantle and scapulars forming two prominent Vs.
VOICE Typically gives a short *chit*.
HABITAT/BEHAVIOUR In the non-breeding season inhabits coastal habitats such as estuaries and intertidal mudflats and sandflats, coastal lagoons and the margins of adjacent freshwater lakes. Usually found singly or in small groups in Madagascar. Feeds very actively picking at the surface and taking a variety of small invertebrates and some plant matter.
RANGE/STATUS Breeds in northern Europe and northern Asia and winters in southern Europe, Africa and the Middle East, east to the Indian subcontinent. Not globally threatened. Monotypic. A scarce non-breeding visitor to lakes and coastal areas in the west of Madagascar. Observed at and near to sea level.
WHERE TO SEE Scarce. Best looked for in coastal wetlands on the west coast such as those near to Toliara and Mahajanga and possibly Lake Amboromalandy west of Ampijoroa.
SIMILAR SPECIES Unlikely to be confused with any other species in Madagascar except perhaps Sanderling, which see for differences.

120 Curlew Sandpiper *Calidris ferruginea*

DESCRIPTION Size: 18-23cm. A small to medium-sized sandpiper with a long decurved bill. Plumage varies seasonally and with age. Only likely to be recorded in Madagascar in non-breeding plumage. **Adult non-breeding:** Crown and hindneck grey-brown finely streaked with black. A prominent white supercilium contrasts with a darkish loral line and the ear-coverts are grey-brown finely streaked darker. Rest of the upperparts uniform grey-brown with indistinct dark shafts and narrow pale fringes to the feathers. Underparts white except for a light grey wash on the sides of the breast which is finely streaked with brown. In flight, shows a narrow though clear white wing-bar and a white patch across the uppertail-coverts showing as a white rump. Iris dark brown, bill long and evenly decurved, blackish though sometimes paler at the base. Long legs and feet dark grey or black. **Adult breeding:** Very different from non-breeding with extensive rich chestnut on the head and underparts, white at the base of the bill and upperparts which are coarsely marked with rufous and black and narrowly fringed with white. **Juvenile:** Similar to non-breeding though differs in showing a peachy wash on the breast and dark sub-terminal marks and pale buff fringes to the upperpart feathers producing a neat scaly effect.
VOICE Typically gives quiet, deep rippling *chirrup*.
HABITAT/BEHAVIOUR In the non-breeding season occurs in a variety of wetland habitats including coastal lagoons, intertidal mudflats and sandflats, estuaries and muddy fringes of inland lakes. Gregarious, often found in sizeable flocks. Feeds on a variety of invertebrates and occasionally seeds.
RANGE/STATUS Breeds in Arctic Siberia and winters in Africa, the Middle East, southern Asia and Australasia. Not globally threatened. Monotypic. A common non-breeding visitor to Madagascar where it may be seen on all suitable coasts during the austral summer. Small numbers of non-breeding birds are present during the austral winter. Found from sea level to 1,400m.
WHERE TO SEE One of the commonest and most frequently seen waders, easily found at suitable coastal sites such as the Toliara and Maroantsetra areas.
SIMILAR SPECIES The small to medium size, long legs, long decurved bill, white rump patch and strong supercilium are characteristic.

119. Little Stint, adult non-breeding.

120a. Curlew Sandpiper, adult non-breeding.

120b. Curlew Sandpiper, juvenile.

121 Ruff *Philomachus pugnax*

DESCRIPTION Size: Males 26-32cm, Females 20-25cm. A medium-large wader with a short, slightly decurved bill and longish legs. Plumage varies seasonally and with sex and age. Only likely to be recorded in Madagascar in non-breeding plumage. **Adult non-breeding:** Sexes similar though the larger male may retain traces of breeding plumage and may have brighter bare parts. Whitish forehead and chin, crown and hindneck grey-brown finely streaked darker. Bland whitish face with fine streaking and little or no trace of a supercilium. Rest of the upperparts grey-brown with darker feather centres. Underparts white except for variable light grey mottling on the breast sides. In flight, fairly uniform with only a narrow and indistinct whitish wing-bar and white patches at the sides of the uppertail-coverts. Iris dark brown, bill shortish, slightly decurved, blackish though sometimes orange or pink at the base in males. Longish legs and feet olive, olive-yellow or even orange in males. **Adult male breeding:** Unmistakable with heavily patterned upperparts and an extensive ruff which varies from white to all shades of brown to black and a bright pink-orange bill. Moulting males often have white heads. **Adult female breeding:** Similar to non-breeding but upperparts warmer with blacker feather centres and the breast is browner. **Juvenile:** Similar to breeding female though shows variable buff on the underparts and dark upperparts, with neat pale fringes giving a scaly effect.
VOICE Usually silent.
HABITAT/BEHAVIOUR In the non-breeding season favours freshwater lakes and marshes, wet grassland, rice paddies, coastal lagoons and estuaries. Feeds on a variety of invertebrates and occasionally seeds.
RANGE/STATUS Breeds across northern Europe and northern Asia and winters in Europe, Africa and the Middle East, east to the Indian subcontinent. Not globally threatened. Monotypic. A vagrant to Madagascar where it has been seen in the west. Observed at or near to sea level.
WHERE TO SEE Rare and unlikely to be seen except with extreme luck on the west coast.
SIMILAR SPECIES Larger and longer legged than Green, Wood and Curlew Sandpipers and lacks the white 'rump' of those species.

122 Brown Skua *Catharacta antarctica*

DESCRIPTION Size: 52-64cm. Wingspan: 126-160cm. A large, stocky, gull-like seabird. Sexes alike, plumage varies slightly with age. **Adult:** Head and upperparts warm brown, slightly darker on the crown and lightly spangled with buff shaft-streaks and fringes. Underparts brown, typically slightly paler than the upperparts and with limited paler buff mottling. Iris brown, bill stout and strong, blackish, legs and feet dark grey. In flight, there is an extensive white patch across the base of the primaries which is conspicuous on both the upper and underwing. **Juvenile:** Similar to the adult though typically darker and more uniform with less buff markings.
VOICE Usually silent at sea.
HABITAT/BEHAVIOUR In the non-breeding season it is pelagic. A predator, feeding in a variety of ways including direct predation on smaller seabirds and scavenging around fishing boats.
RANGE/STATUS Breeds on coasts of the Antarctic peninsula, many sub-Antarctic and Southern Ocean Islands, dispersing in winter into southern oceans as far north as 30^0 south. Not globally threatened. Represented in Madagascar by the subspecies *lonnbergi* which is widespread in the Antarctic peninsula and sub-Antarctic islands. An uncommon visitor to the south and east coasts of Madagascar.
WHERE TO SEE Most likely to be seen from southern and eastern headlands during the austral winter.
SIMILAR SPECIES Unlikely to be confused with any other species in Madagascar. Easily separated from the other two skuas occurring in Madagascar by its much larger size, stockier proportions and more prominent, extensive white blaze across the primaries. Young Kelp Gulls may appear superficially similar but show paler underparts and lack the white primary patch. The similar South Polar Skua (*C. maccormicki*) which could potentially occur on passage around Madagascar is difficult to separate from this species, though is slightly smaller, appears more uniform, lacking the buff markings shown by adult Subantarctic Skua, is typically a colder grey-brown colour, usually shows pale at the base of the bill and a pale nuchal collar and often shows a contrast between the dark underwings and paler underparts. However, juvenile Subantarctic Skuas may share many of these characters.

125a. Kelp Gull, adult.

125b. Kelp Gull, immature.

126a. Grey-headed Gull, adult breeding.

126b (inset). Grey-headed Gull, immature.

127 Gull-billed Tern *Sterna nilotica*

DESCRIPTION Size: 33-43cm. Wingspan 85-103cm. A medium-large, stout-billed tern. Sexes alike, plumage varies with season and age. Most likely to be seen in immature/non-breeding plumages. **Adult non-breeding:** Head white except for a black patch behind the eye and streaking on hind crown. Upperparts pale grey, tail white and shallowly forked, underparts white. Upperwings pale grey with darker tips to the outer primaries. Underwings whitish with dark tips to the primaries. Iris dark brown, bill short, stout and black, legs and feet black. **Adult breeding:** Similar to adult non-breeding except the head is white with a neat black cap. **Immature:** Similar to adult non-breeding though shows a brown wash on the crown and brown fringes on the mantle and wing-coverts.
VOICE Typical flight call is a throaty, nasal *ku-veck*.
HABITAT/BEHAVIOUR Winters on estuaries, lakes and salt-pans. Feeds mainly on insects, small fish and aquatic invertebrates. Feeds mainly by hawking rather than surface-dipping or plunge-diving.
RANGE/STATUS Occurs in Africa, Europe, Asia, Australasia and the Americas. Not globally threatened. Represented in Madagascar by the nominate subspecies which winters partly in Africa. A vagrant to Madagascar with just two records.
WHERE TO SEE A rare vagrant and therefore no regular sites.
SIMILAR SPECIES A large, pale tern with broad wings, stocky proportions and a short shallowly forked tail. The short, stout black bill is unique among terns. Most likely to be confused with Sandwich Tern from which it is best separated by its short all-dark bill. However, juvenile Sandwich Tern may lack the yellow bill tip and is best separated from Gull-billed by the proportionately longer, slimmer bill, longer wings, paler plumage and more graceful, less gull-like flight. Winter-plumaged birds resemble Black-naped Tern in the overall pale plumage and dark mask but may be separated by their larger size, stockier shape and diagnostic bill shape.

128 Caspian Tern *Sterna caspia*

DESCRIPTION Size: 48-56cm. Wingspan 127-140cm. A very large tern. Sexes alike, plumage varies slightly with season and age. **Adult breeding:** Head white with a black cap which forms a slight crest on the nape. Upperparts pale grey, underparts white. Upperwings pale grey, underwings white with prominent blackish wing-tips. Iris dark brown, bill massive, red, usually with a black sub-terminal band and a yellow tip. Legs and feet black. **Adult non-breeding:** Similar to adult breeding except the black cap is streaked with white. **Immature:** Similar to adult non-breeding though shows brown fringes on the mantle and wing-coverts giving a scaly appearance and the bill is duller orange-red.
VOICE Usual call is an unmistakable loud, deep rasping *kar-kra kar-kra*.
HABITAT/BEHAVIOUR Inhabits coastal areas and large areas of fresh or brackish water. Feeds largely on medium-sized fish which are usually caught by plunge-diving. Will occasionally predate eggs and nestlings. Nests singly or in small colonies on open sandy or shingle areas near to water. The nest is a simple scrape.
RANGE/STATUS Occurs in Africa, Europe, Asia, Australasia and North and central America. Not globally threatened. Represented in Madagascar by the nominate subspecies which is scarce to locally common on all coasts, most scarce on the east coast and most frequent on the west (where it breeds on some of the larger lakes and islands), north and south coasts. Found from sea level to 1,500m.
WHERE TO SEE Uncommon and not frequently encountered at the regular birding sites. Most likely to be seen on the west coast where the Toliara and Mahajanga areas sometimes hold this species.
SIMILAR SPECIES The very large size and massive red bill render this species unmistakable.

7a. Gull-billed Tern, adult non-breeding.

127b. Gull-billed Tern, adult breeding in flight.

8. Caspian Tern, adult non-breeding.

129 Greater Crested Tern *Sterna bergii*

DESCRIPTION Size: 43-53cm. Wingspan 100-130cm. A large tern. Sexes alike, plumage varies with season and age. **Adult breeding:** Head white with a black cap which forms a prominent shaggy crest on the nape. The black cap is separated from the bill by a narrow white patch on the forehead. Upperparts grey, rump paler, tail white and forked. Underparts white. Upperwings pale grey with some dark grey in the outer primaries, underwings white with dusky markings on the outer primaries. Iris dark brown, bill yellow, long, slightly drooping and heavy. Legs and feet black. **Adult non-breeding:** Similar to adult breeding except forehead and forecrown extensively white, rest of black cap streaked with white and the upperparts are less uniform in appearance. **Immature:** Similar to adult non-breeding though head browner, upperparts initially brown with pale grey fringes becoming grey on the back and mantle and then the wing-coverts with advancing maturity. In flight shows a dark carpal bar, dark primaries and a dark bar along the trailing edge of the secondaries.
VOICE Usual call is a harsh *kree-eck.*
HABITAT/BEHAVIOUR Inhabits coastal areas including estuaries and rocky islets. Gregarious, feeds on fish and occasionally other marine prey which are usually caught by plunge-diving. Nests colonially on offshore islands and sandy islets. The nest is a simple scrape.
RANGE/STATUS Occurs in Africa, the Middle East, southern Asia and Australasia. Not globally threatened. Represented in Madagascar by the subspecies *S. b. enigma* which also nests off Mozambique, and the nominate subspecies which may occur as a non-breeding visitor. It is commonly found on all coasts and breeds on sandy islets in the north-west and east. Observed at and near to sea level.
WHERE TO SEE Fairly easily seen at coastal localities including Toliara, Mahajanga and Maroantsetra.
SIMILAR SPECIES Easily separated from all similar species in all plumages by the large yellow bill which shows no hint of red or orange.

130 Lesser Crested Tern *Sterna bengalensis*

DESCRIPTION Size: 35-43cm. Wingspan 88-105cm. A medium-large tern. Sexes alike, plumage varies with season and age. **Adult breeding:** Head white with a complete black cap which forms a prominent shaggy crest on the nape. Upperparts grey, rump paler, tail white and forked. Underparts white. Upperwings pale grey with some dark grey in the outer primaries, underwings white with dusky markings on the tips of the outer primaries. Iris dark brown, bill long and orange, legs and feet black. **Adult non-breeding:** Similar to adult breeding except head extensively white, with some black remaining behind the eye and on the nape. **Immature:** Similar to adult non-breeding though shows a duller bill, some brown in the upperparts and in flight shows dark primaries and a dark bar along the trailing edge of the secondaries.
VOICE Usual call is a hoarse, high-pitched *kreck* or *kree-eck.*
HABITAT/BEHAVIOUR Inhabits coastal areas including estuaries and rocky islets. More pelagic than Greater Crested Tern. Gregarious, feeds mainly on fish and shrimps which are usually caught by plunge-diving. Nests colonially on offshore islands and sandy islets, though no proof of nesting in Madagascar. The nest is a simple scrape.
RANGE/STATUS Occurs in Africa, the Middle East, Asia and Australia. Not globally threatened. In Madagascar, represented by the nominate subspecies which is common to much of the western Indian Ocean coasts and in Madagascar is commonly found on all coasts. Observed at and near to sea level.
WHERE TO SEE Fairly easily seen at coastal localities including Toliara, Mahajanga and Maroantsetra.
SIMILAR SPECIES Best separated from all similar species by the prominent orange bill. Immatures are best separated from immature Greater Crested Tern by smaller size, overall paler upperparts and usually at least a hint of orange in the bill.

129a. Greater Crested Tern, adult non-breeding.

129b. Greater Crested Tern, adult non-breeding in flight.

130. Lesser Crested Tern, adult non-breeding.

131 Sandwich Tern *Sterna sandvicensis*

DESCRIPTION Size: 36-46cm. Wingspan 86-105cm. A medium-large tern. Sexes alike, plumage varies with season and age. **Adult breeding:** Head white with a complete black cap which forms a prominent shaggy crest on the nape. Upperparts pale grey, rump white, tail white and forked. Underparts white sometimes flushed with pink in breeding plumage. Upperwings pale grey with dark grey in the outer four primaries forming a darker wedge. Underwings white with dusky markings on the tips of the outer primaries. Iris dark brown, bill long and black with a conspicuous yellow tip. Legs and feet black. **Adult non-breeding:** Similar to adult breeding except head extensively white, with black remaining behind the eye and on the nape. **Immature:** Similar to adult non-breeding, though shows a shorter bill often lacking the yellow tip. Juveniles show brown scaling on the mantle and wing-coverts which abrades with age.
VOICE Usual call is a characteristic, penetrating, high-pitched *kee-wick.*
HABITAT/BEHAVIOUR Strictly coastal. Feeds mainly on fish and shrimps which are usually caught by plunge-diving.
RANGE/STATUS Occurs in the Americas, Europe, Africa and the Middle East, east to southern India. Not globally threatened. In Madagascar, represented by the nominate subspecies which is found in the Old-World part of the range. In Madagascar, it is a vagrant, with just one record from Fort Dauphin. Observed at sea level.
WHERE TO SEE A rare vagrant and therefore no regular sites.
SIMILAR SPECIES Best separated from all similar species by the long, yellow-tipped black bill and overall pale plumage. Immatures are best separated from other dark-billed terns by their larger size and paler plumage. Most likely to be confused with Gull-billed Tern, which see for differences.

132 Black-naped Tern *Sterna sumatrana*

DESCRIPTION Size: 31-35cm. Wingspan 61-65cm. A small to medium-sized tern. Sexes alike, plumage varies slightly with season and with age. **Adult breeding:** Head white except for a characteristic narrow black band which runs from eye to eye and isolates the white crown. From a side view the black band appears to sweep sharply down the back of the neck. There is a small black mark in front of the eye but this does not continue to the bill. Upperparts pale grey, rump white, tail white and deeply forked, the elongated outer tail-feathers forming streamers. Underparts white sometimes flushed pink in breeding plumage. Upperwings pale grey with a dark grey web to the outer primary which shows as a dark line. Underwings white. Iris dark brown, bill long, slender and black, occasionally with an inconspicuous pale tip. Legs and feet black. **Adult non-breeding:** Similar to adult breeding though nuchal band reduced. **Immature:** In juvenile plumage the bill is dusky yellow and the crown and upperparts are extensively marked with brown. Soon moult to first-winter plumage when they resemble the adult but for some dark mottling on the crown, some dark scales on the mantle and coverts, a dark carpal bar and shorter tail.
VOICE Usual call is a high-pitched, sharp *kick* or *kick-kick.*
HABITAT/BEHAVIOUR Strictly coastal, favouring rocky coral and sandy offshore islands. Feeds mainly on small fish which are caught by shallow plunge-diving and surface dipping.
RANGE/STATUS Occurs on islands in the tropical Indian and Pacific Oceans. Not globally threatened. In Madagascar, represented by the subspecies *S. s. mathewsi*, which breeds on islands in the western Indian Ocean including Aldabra. It is a rare vagrant, with just two records from the north. Observed at sea level.
WHERE TO SEE A rare vagrant and therefore no regular sites.
SIMILAR SPECIES Best separated from all similar species by the very pale plumage and distinctive head pattern which is evident in all plumages.

*1. Sandwich Tern, adult non-breeding.

*2. Black-naped Tern. 132a. Adult breeding. 132b (inset) adult breeding in flight.

133 Roseate Tern *Sterna dougallii*

DESCRIPTION Size: 33-43cm. Wingspan 72-80cm. A small to medium-sized tern. Sexes alike, plumage varies with season and age. **Adult breeding:** Head white with a complete, neat black cap. Upperparts pale grey, rump white, tail white and deeply forked with the outer tail-feathers extending well beyond the wing-tips when at rest. Underparts white, flushed pink in breeding plumage. Upperwings pale grey with some dark grey in the outer two or three primaries forming a darker wedge. Underwings largely white. Iris dark brown, bill long and fine, basally red with a variable amount of black at the tip. Legs and feet bright red. **Adult non-breeding:** Similar to adult breeding except forehead, crown and lores white, outer tail-feathers shorter, bill all-black and the dark wedge in the outer primaries is more conspicuous. **Immature:** Similar to adult non-breeding though shows a more or less complete dark cap, a shorter tail and some dark scaling on the mantle and wing-coverts. Lacks dark tips to the underside of the primaries.
VOICE Typical call is a wader-like *chu-wick*. Also gives a harsh rasping *zraak*.
HABITAT/BEHAVIOUR Strictly coastal, favouring rocky coral and sandy offshore islands. Gregarious, feeds almost exclusively on small fish usually caught by plunge-diving or surface-dipping. Nests colonially on sandy offshore islands where the nest is a simple scrape.
RANGE/STATUS Occurs in the Americas, Europe, Africa, the Middle East, Asia and Australia. Not globally threatened though North American and European populations are declining rapidly and are considered to be endangered. Represented in Madagascar by the subspecies *S. d. arideensis* which is common to the western Indian Ocean islands and in Madagascar is found on all coasts, where it is most common in areas with offshore islands. Some colonies near to the mainland have been deserted due to human predation of eggs. Observed at and near to sea level.
WHERE TO SEE May be seen on the east coast including on the boat journey from Maroantsetra to Ambanizana, and around Nosy Bé and Mahajanga on the west coast.
SIMILAR SPECIES Most likely to be confused with Common Tern. In all plumages, may be separated by the paler overall plumage, shorter wings and shallower stiffer wingbeats. In addition, in breeding plumage easily separated by the very long tail-streamers and very pale plumage. In non-breeding plumage shows more extensive white on the crown, a white rump and tail and less black in the wings, particularly the very white looking underwings. Immatures best separated by the extensive dark cap and extensive scaling on the mantle and wing-coverts, recalling a small juvenile Sandwich Tern.

134 Common Tern *Sterna hirundo*

DESCRIPTION Size: 32-39cm. Wingspan 72-83cm. A small to medium-sized tern. Sexes alike, plumage varies with season and age. Most likely to be seen in immature/non-breeding plumages. **Adult breeding:** Head white with a complete, neat black cap. Upperparts mid-grey, rump white, tail white and deeply forked with the outer tail-feathers falling short of the wing-tips when perched. Underparts white. Upperwings grey with dark grey tips to the outer primaries. Underwings white with dark tips to the primaries. Iris dark brown, bill red with a black tip. Legs and feet red. **Adult non-breeding:** Similar to adult breeding except forehead, and fore-crown white, outer tail-feathers shorter, rump and tail washed with grey and the bill is all-black. In flight shows extensive dark grey in the outer primaries, a dark carpal bar and a dark bar along the trailing edge. The underwing shows conspicuous dark grey tips to the primaries. **Immature:** In juvenile plumage shows a brown wash on the head and upperparts. First winter plumage is similar to adult non-breeding.
VOICE Typical calls are a drawn out *kee-aaarr* and a sharp *kik kik*.
HABITAT/BEHAVIOUR Inhabits coastal areas and large areas of fresh or brackish water, though observations in Madagascar have been restricted to coastal areas. Gregarious, feeds mainly on small fish which are caught by shallow plunge-diving and surface-dipping.
RANGE/STATUS Breeds across North America, Europe and much of central and northern Asia. Winters in coastal areas south of the Tropic of Cancer. Not globally threatened. Represented in Madagascar by the nominate subspecies which breeds in North America and Europe and winters south of its breeding range. A frequent non-breeding visitor, often in large flocks, mainly to the north and west coasts during the austral summer. Observed at and near to sea level.
WHERE TO SEE Often present at the Onilahy River mouth at St. Augustin south of Toliara, at Toliara harbour and along the north-west coast near Nosy Bé.
SIMILAR SPECIES Most likely to be confused with Roseate Tern, which see for differences.

7. *Saunders' Tern, adult non-breeding.*

8. *Whiskered Tern. 138a (inset left) adult breeding. 138b (inset right) adult non-breeding. 137c. (centre) adult non-breeding.*

139 Black Tern *Chlidonias niger*

DESCRIPTION Size: 23-28cm. Wingspan 57-65cm. A small tern. Sexes alike, plumage varies seasonally and with age. Most likely to be seen in immature/non-breeding plumages. **Adult non-breeding:** Forehead white, crown, nape, ear-coverts and patch in front of the eye black, rest of the head white. Upperparts including rump and tail grey. Underparts white except for a characteristic dark grey patch on the side of the breast. Upperwings grey with darker tips to the flight feathers. Underwings grey. Iris black, bill black, legs and feet blackish tinged red. **Adult breeding:** Body entirely blackish but for the white vent. Wings and tail silvery grey contrasting with the dark body. **Immature:** Similar to non-breeding though less uniform with dark feather centres on the back and wing-coverts and extensive dark in the outer primaries and along the trailing edge.
VOICE Usually silent outside the breeding season.
HABITAT/BEHAVIOUR Winters mainly at sea though also on coasts and estuaries. Feeds by aerial hawking, dipping and occasionally plunge-diving. Feeds mainly on fish although when breeding, aquatic insects form a much greater part of the diet.
RANGE/STATUS Breeds in Europe, Asia and North America, winters around the coasts of Africa, and Central and South America. Not globally threatened. Represented in Madagascar by the nominate subspecies which is found throughout the Old World part of the range and has been recorded just once as a vagrant in Madagascar.
WHERE TO SEE A rare vagrant and therefore no regular sites.
SIMILAR SPECIES Unmistakable in breeding plumage. In non-breeding/immature plumage most likely to be confused with Whiskered Tern (which see) and White-winged Tern. Best separated from White-winged Tern in non-breeding plumages by the characteristic dark mark at the side of the breast which is present in all non-breeding plumages of Black Tern and is always absent in White-winged Tern. In addition Black Tern is generally darker, has a longer bill, a darker crown and a grey as opposed to white rump.

140 White-winged Tern *Chlidonias leucopterus*

DESCRIPTION Size: 23-27cm. Wingspan 58-67cm. A small tern. Sexes alike, plumage varies with age. Most likely to be seen in immature/non-breeding plumages. **Adult non-breeding:** Head white except for a blackish patch behind the eye, black hindcrown and nape. Upperparts pale grey with white uppertail-coverts and rump. Upperwings pale grey with darker flight feathers. Underparts white, underwings whitish with variable grey tips to the coverts. Tail white or pale grey. Moulting birds often show remnants of black underwing-coverts which is diagnostic of this species. Iris dark brown, bill blackish, legs and feet dull red. **Adult breeding:** Blackish body and underwing-coverts contrast sharply with silvery wings and white tail and rump. Bill, legs and feet dark red. **Immature:** First winter as adult non-breeding but upperparts and upperwings less uniform with dark markings in the primary coverts, lesser coverts and along the trailing edge of the secondaries. Juveniles are similar to first-winter birds though show a conspicuous dark brown 'saddle' which contrasts sharply with the pale grey wings.
VOICE Usually silent outside the breeding season.
HABITAT/BEHAVIOUR Freshwater or brackish wetlands and surrounding grassland. Feeds mainly on terrestrial insects and their larvae, aquatic insects and fish. Feeds aerially and by surface-dipping but does not plunge-dive.
RANGE/STATUS Breeds in Europe and Asia, winters in Africa, southern Asia and Australasia. Not globally threatened. Monotypic. A scarce non-breeding visitor to Madagascar where it has been recorded on a number of occasions during the austral summer and spring at Lake Alaotra and in tern flocks at Toliara and near Mahajanga. Found from sea level to 750m.
WHERE TO SEE A rare visitor most likely to be seen at Lake Alaotra, in the Toliara area or at Lake Amboromalandy.
SIMILAR SPECIES Most likely to be confused with Whiskered or Black Terns, which see for differences.

39. *Black Tern, adult breeding in flight.*

40. *White-winged Tern, adult non-breeding.*

141 Brown Noddy *Anous stolidus*

DESCRIPTION Size: 38-45cm. Wingspan 75-86cm. A medium-sized, dark, largely pelagic tern. Sexes alike, plumage varies slightly with age. **Adult:** Forehead pale grey, grading to darker grey on the crown. Black lores contrast with the incomplete white orbital-ring. Rest of the plumage dark brown, slightly darker on the flight feathers. Iris dark brown, bill black, legs and feet black. **Immature:** Similar to the adult though shows a less well-defined head pattern with the pale grey forehead initially not apparent.
VOICE Typical call is a raucous *kraa*.
HABITAT/BEHAVIOUR Highly pelagic, favouring offshore islands in tropical and subtropical seas. Gregarious, often foraging in large flocks. Feeds almost exclusively on small fish and squid which are usually caught by surface-dipping. Nests colonially on offshore islands especially rocky islets though occasionally on cliffs, sandy islets and in trees.
RANGE/STATUS Found on many tropical and subtropical islands throughout the major oceans, dispersing to oceanic habitat after breeding. Not globally threatened. Represented in Madagascar by the subspecies *A. s. pileatus* which is common to the islands of the Indian Ocean. It is found on all coasts but is generally scarce away from nesting colonies which include islets near to Toamasina, Antsiranana, Nosy Bé and Morondava. Some colonies suffer from human predation. Observed at sea level.
WHERE TO SEE Seldom seen from land due to its pelagic habits. Most likely to be seen near to the breeding colonies.
SIMILAR SPECIES Characteristic deeply notched tail, dark plumage and rapid flight. Most likely to be confused with Lesser Noddy from which it is best distinguished by its larger size, broader wings, heavier jizz, slower wingbeats, black (as opposed to pale) lores and stouter bill. May also be confused with immature Sooty or Bridled Terns, which see for differences.

142 Lesser Noddy *Anous tenuirostris*

DESCRIPTION Size: 30-34cm. Wingspan 58-63cm. A small to medium-sized, dark, largely pelagic tern. Sexes alike, plumage varies slightly with age. **Adult:** Forehead very pale grey, grading to pale grey on the crown which merges into the grey nape. Rest of the head, including the lores, grey but for a small dark mark in front of the eye and an incomplete white orbital-ring. Rest of the plumage dark grey-brown, slightly darker on the flight feathers. Iris dark brown, bill slender and black, legs and feet black. **Immature:** Similar to adult though may show a whiter cap.
VOICE Call is a short, rattling *churr*.
HABITAT/BEHAVIOUR Highly pelagic, favouring oceanic islands in tropical oceans. Gregarious, often foraging in flocks, sometimes mixed with Brown Noddy. Feeds on small fish and invertebrates which are usually caught by surface-dipping. Nests colonially on offshore islands in trees.
RANGE/STATUS Found on tropical and subtropical islands in the Indian Ocean. Not globally threatened. Represented in Madagascar by the nominate subspecies which is common to the islands of the west Indian Ocean. It is a scarce though regular visitor to the west coast though no breeding colonies are known, the nearest being on Mauritius and the Seychelles. Observed at sea level.
WHERE TO SEE Seldom seen from land due to its pelagic habits. Most likely to be seen near to the north-west coast during stormy weather.
SIMILAR SPECIES Most likely to be confused with Brown Noddy, which see for differences. May also be confused with immature Sooty or Bridled Terns, which see for differences.

1. Brown Noddy, adult.

2. Lesser Noddy, adult.

143 White Tern *Gygis alba*

DESCRIPTION Size: 25-30cm. Wingspan 76-80cm. A medium-sized, largely pelagic, all-white tern. Sexes alike, plumage varies slightly with age. **Adult:** Entire plumage white but for a black ring around the eye and dusky shafts to the flight feathers. Iris dark brown, bill unique, black with a grey-blue base, distinctly up-turned and tapering to a point. Legs and feet blue-grey. **Immature:** Similar to adult though variable pale brown mottling on the mantle, back and wing-coverts.
VOICE Usually silent.
HABITAT/BEHAVIOUR Pelagic outside the breeding season. Occurs on oceanic islands in tropical oceans. Gregarious, feeds on small fish and invertebrates.
RANGE/STATUS Pantropical, breeding on many small islands throughout the tropical oceans. Not globally threatened. Represented in Madagascar by the subspecies *G. a. candida*, which is common to the islands of the Indian and south and central Pacific Oceans. It is a rare visitor to the north-west and north-east coast, the nearest breeding colonies being on the Seychelles. Observed at sea level.
WHERE TO SEE A scarce visitor and therefore no regular sites.
SIMILAR SPECIES Unmistakable. In flight the wings appear broad and rounded and the head and eye large.

144 Madagascar Sandgrouse *Pterocles personatus*

DESCRIPTION Size: 35cm. A stocky, gregarious, pigeon-like bird. Sexes differ. **Adult male:** Black forehead, chin and lores, face greyish-brown with a bold yellow orbital-ring, forehead and sides of the neck rufous-brown, tinged ochre. Upperparts brown with darker grey-brown centres to the scapulars, blackish barring on the rump and uppertail-coverts and a white tail-tip. Wing-coverts paler creamy-brown with two to three narrow blackish wing-bars. The pale coverts contrast sharply in flight with the blackish flight feathers and underwings. Underparts brown with narrow blackish barring on the belly. Iris dark brown, bill blue-grey with a black tip, legs and feet grey. **Adult female:** Similar to male but lacks the black mask, shows a dark mark around the eye and is overall more cryptically patterned with narrow dark bars over the entire upperparts. **Immature:** Similar to the female though duller.
VOICE The call, which is uttered especially in flight, is a distinctive, guttural, rapid *gutagutagat* and is often the first indication of the species' presence.
HABITAT/BEHAVIOUR Inhabits open areas such as sparsely vegetated lake and river shores, savanna and open rocky areas. Gregarious, often feeding and drinking in groups. Typically seen flying in flocks in the early morning and less so in the evening when moving to and from drinking and feeding areas. Feeds largely on seeds. Nest is a sparsely lined scrape situated on open ground.
RANGE/STATUS Endemic to Madagascar. Not globally threatened. Monotypic. Found in suitable habitat in the north, west and south, commonest in the south and south-west. Found from sea level to 1,200m.
WHERE TO SEE The islands in the mouth of the Onilahy River at St. Augustin, south of Toliara, seem to be a reliable area to find this species. Other sites where the species is seen regularly include Lake Ranobe north of Toliara/Ifaty, Berenty and the lake at Ampijoroa Forest Station, and the nearby Lake Amboromalandy.
SIMILAR SPECIES A large, robust sandgrouse and the only representative of the family in Madagascar. Unlikely to be confused with any other species even in flight at a distance when the stocky silhouette and rapid, powerful flight are distinctive.

3. *White Tern, adults.*

4a. *Madagascar Sandgrouse, adult male.*

144b. *Madagascar Sandgrouse, adults.*

145 Rock Dove/Feral Pigeon *Columba livia*

DESCRIPTION Size: 30-33cm. A medium-sized compact pigeon. Sexes and all plumages alike. Plumage highly variable due to selective breeding by humans but typically the plumage is grey, darker on the head and breast where there is a variable glossy green and pink suffusion. Typically shows two black wing-bars and a white rump. Iris orange, bill dark grey, legs and feet reddish. Birds vary from all-white to dark grey or reddish-brown and any combination of these colours.
VOICE Typical pigeon cooing notes.
HABITAT/BEHAVIOUR In Madagascar this species is largely confined to towns and villages and their environs. Gregarious, typically seen in flocks. Feeds largely on seeds.
RANGE/STATUS Introduced to Madagascar as it has been to much of the world. Not globally threatened. Found in populated areas at all altitudes throughout.
WHERE TO SEE Common in built-up areas.
SIMILAR SPECIES Usually encountered in flocks in towns and is unlikely to be confused with the indigenous pigeon species.

146 Madagascar Turtle Dove *Streptopelia picturata*

DESCRIPTION Size: 28cm. A small to medium-sized pigeon. Sexes alike, plumage varies slightly with age. **Adult:** Head and throat a soft dove-grey, nape grey, tinged vinaceous pink with darker mottling and spotting on the side of the neck. Upperparts vinaceous brown, browner on the wing-coverts and greyer-brown on the rump. Flight feathers and tail darker brown, the latter with extensive white tips to the outer tail-feathers. Underparts pinkish-brown, paler on the belly and whitish on the undertail-coverts. Iris red surrounded by a narrow reddish orbital ring. Bill dull red with a pale grey tip, legs and feet reddish. **Immature:** Similar to adult though duller and greyer and with some rufous fringing on the wings.
VOICE Song is a frequently repeated, disyllabic *hay-oo*, with the emphasis on the higher second syllable.
HABITAT/BEHAVIOUR Inhabits natural forest, degraded woodland, plantations and scrubby and sparsely wooded areas. Fairly shy, usually found singly or in small loose groups. Feeds on the forest floor, in clearings and on trails and roads taking fallen fruit, seeds and to a lesser extent small invertebrates. Perches in dense foliage when disturbed and when singing. Nest is a loose structure of twigs situated in the fork of a tree or in the understorey.
RANGE/STATUS Regional Endemic, occurring in Madagascar, Aldabra, the Seychelles and the Comoros and introduced to Mauritius and Réunion. Not globally threatened. Represented in Madagascar by the endemic nominate subspecies which is common in suitable habitats throughout, though is largely absent from the savanna parts of the high-plateau. Found from sea level to 2,000m.
WHERE TO SEE Common and widespread, though unobtrusive. Easily seen at sites such as Berenty, Perinet-Analamazaotra, Ranomafana and in the Toliara area.
SIMILAR SPECIES Often flushed from the ground when the white tail tip is apparent. The terrestrial habits and overall pinkish-brown coloration are distinctive and it is unlikely to be confused with any other species in Madagascar.

5. Rock Dove (Feral Pigeon).

6. Madagascar Turtle Dove, adult.

147 Namaqua Dove *Oena capensis*

DESCRIPTION Size: 28-29cm. A small, long-tailed terrestrial pigeon. Sexes differ and plumage varies slightly with age. **Adult male:** Forehead, lores, throat and centre of breast black. Rest of head and nape grey. Upperparts grey-brown with two dark bars separated by a whitish band on the lower back. Iridescent purple spots in the wing-coverts, flight feathers darker with rufous in the primaries, only visible in flight, and rufous underwings. Tail long and blackish. Underparts pale grey, whiter on the belly and flanks. Undertail-coverts black. Iris dark brown, bill orange with a pinkish-red base, legs and feet reddish. **Adult female:** Similar to the male though the forehead, lores, throat and breast are grey rather than black. Bill dark grey. **Immature:** Similar to female though shorter tailed and shows black and buff barring on the throat and upperparts.
VOICE Song is a distinctive, mournful disyllabic cooing, with the second syllable being longer and more mellow, *hoo-ooo*. Higher-pitched than Madagascar Turtle Dove and often given from an open perch.
HABITAT/BEHAVIOUR Inhabits open, sparsely wooded dry habitats. Usually found singly or in small groups. Feeds on seeds which are picked from the ground. Often perches in the open when resting or singing. Nest is a loose structure of twigs situated in the fork of a tree or bush.
RANGE/STATUS Occurs in the Middle East and sub-Saharan Africa. Not globally threatened. Represented in Madagascar by the endemic subspecies *O. c. aliena* which differs from the nominate in being slightly darker and greyer. It is very common in suitable habitats in the north, west and south, less common in open areas of the east. Found from sea level to 1,500m.
WHERE TO SEE Common and widespread in the west and south-west and easily seen around Toliara and Ampijoroa.
SIMILAR SPECIES Unlikely to be mistaken for any other species.

148 Madagascar Green Pigeon *Treron australis*

DESCRIPTION Size: 30-32cm. A stocky, medium-sized pigeon. Sexes alike, plumage varies slightly with age. Two subspecies. **Adult nominate:** Head and breast yellowish-green. Upperparts dull olive-green, yellower on the mantle. Wings grey-green with broad creamy-yellow tips to the greater coverts forming a prominent wing-bar, yellow fringes to the black flight feathers and a maroon patch on the shoulder (lesser coverts). Tail short, olive-grey with a paler grey tip. Rest of the underparts greyish with dark olive streaking on the belly and pale rufous streaked with pale grey undertail-coverts. Iris blue, bill short, pale grey with a pinkish-red base, legs and feet yellowish-orange. **Adult *T. a. xenia*:** Slightly paler and greyer. **Immature:** Similar to adult though duller.
VOICE Song is typical for a *Treron*, consisting of a series of soft, melodic, mournful whistles, *tweeeoooo tweeull woo teeewooo*.
HABITAT/BEHAVIOUR Inhabits a variety of woodland habitats including evergreen humid forest, secondary forest, parkland, dry deciduous forest and spiny forest. Gregarious, usually found in small groups. Frugivorous, taking fruit from trees and occasionally bushes. Often difficult to detect in dense canopy foliage. Nest is a loose structure of twigs built on the fork of a tree.
RANGE/STATUS Regional Endemic, occurring in Madagascar and the Comoros. Not globally threatened though is hunted for food. Represented in Madagascar by two endemic subspecies, the nominate and *T. a. xenia*. The species occurs throughout in suitable habitat though is absent from the high plateau. The nominate subspecies is found in the north, west and east with *T. a. xenia* in the south-west and south. Found from sea level to 1,000m.
WHERE TO SEE Fairly common and widespread. Easiest to see in the arid west, around Ampijoroa Forest station and at sites around Toliara.
SIMILAR SPECIES Easily identified by its green coloration and yellow wing-bar. In flight, shows a longer, more pointed tail than Madagascar Blue Pigeon and the pale wing-bar is usually conspicuous on the narrower wings.

7a. *Namaqua Dove, adult male. 147b (inset) Namaqua Dove, adult female.*

8. *Madagascar Green Pigeon, adult.*

149 Madagascar Blue Pigeon *Alectroenas madagascariensis*

DESCRIPTION Size: 28cm. A stocky, medium-sized, short-tailed pigeon. Sexes alike, plumage varies slightly with age. **Adult:** Most of plumage dark blue. Large area of bare red skin around the eye. Throat, upper breast, nape and upper mantle appear silvery-blue in good light. Flight feathers grey. Undertail-coverts and short tail deep reddish-chestnut. Iris dull yellow, bill short, greyish green with a paler tip, legs and feet reddish. **Immature:** Similar to adult though duller, lacking the silvery appearance to the breast, nape and upper mantle shown by the adult and shows a reduced area of bare red skin around the eye.
VOICE Seldom heard. Gives a soft cooing call, particularly when attending the nest.
HABITAT/BEHAVIOUR Inhabits evergreen humid forest and adjacent secondary forest and parkland. Gregarious, usually found in small groups. Frugivorous, taking food from trees and occasionally bushes. Often perches in the open on dead branches. Nest is a loose structure of twigs built on the fork of a tree.
RANGE/STATUS Endemic to Madagascar. Not globally threatened. Monotypic. Occurs commonly in suitable habitat in the north-west, north and east, though as with the previous species it is hunted for food. Found from sea level to 2,000m.
WHERE TO SEE Common and fairly easy to see at Perinet-Analamazaotra, Ranomafana and in the forests of the Masoala Peninsula.
SIMILAR SPECIES Easily identified by its blue coloration and reddish tail.

150 Greater Vasa Parrot *Coracopsis vasa*

DESCRIPTION Size: 50cm. A large, all-dark parrot. Sexes alike, plumage varies slightly with age. Two subspecies. **Adult nominate:** Plumage entirely blackish-brown, slightly paler on the wing-coverts and undertail-coverts and darker on the tips of the flight feathers. Usually shows an area of prominent, pale, yellow-pink bare skin around the eye and some birds even show largely bald yellow-orange heads. Iris dark brown. Bill massive, usually pale yellowish-brown with a darker grey cere which is cut off squarely from the pale bill forming a straight line between the pale upper mandible and the darker cere. Legs and feet pinkish-brown. **Adult *C. v. drouhardi*:** Generally slightly smaller and paler. **Immature:** Similar to adult though duller, bill appears smaller and darker and the bare skin around the eye may be absent.
VOICE Loud, raucous and parrot-like. Typical calls include a loud, screeching *gweep-chuee* or *gweep-chuee-chull* sometimes followed by a loud *kuuk-kak-kak-kak-kak.* This may be the territorial song. Other calls include a shrill *weeaa* and deep, throaty scolding calls, *kraaaah kraaaah*, which are slightly inflected.
HABITAT/BEHAVIOUR Inhabits all native forest types, secondary forest, trees surrounding villages, open country and parkland, though scarce far from primary forest. Gregarious, usually found in small groups. Feeds on fruit and seeds which are taken from trees and bushes or when foraging on the ground. Roosts communally and may be active on bright nights. Nests in a tree hollow.
RANGE/STATUS Regional Endemic, occurring in Madagascar and the Comoros. Not globally threatened though frequently caught for food and kept as pets. Represented in Madagascar by two endemic subspecies, *drouhardi* in the drier west and south and the nominate subspecies in the east. Occurs commonly in suitable habitat throughout. Found from sea level to 1,500m.
WHERE TO SEE Relatively common though generally scarcer than Lesser Vasa Parrot. Most easily seen in the west where it is usually easy to find around Ampijoroa Forest Station, at Zombitse Forest and around Toliara.
SIMILAR SPECIES Cannot be confused with any species other than Lesser Vasa Parrot from which it must be separated with care. Greater Vasa Parrot is substantially larger (though this may be hard to judge), appears larger headed with a more massive and typically paler bill. The division between the pale upper mandible and the darker cere is straight and there is typically a large area of pale bare skin around the eye and in extreme cases a bald yellowish-orange head. By contrast, Lesser Vasa Parrot appears smaller headed with a smaller, often darker bill, the dark cere protrudes as a rounded point on to the upper mandible and the dark bare skin around the eye is not conspicuous. In addition, typical calls of the two species are quite different. Immature Greater Vasa Parrot has a darkish bill and reduced bare skin around the eye and thus appears more similar to Lesser Vasa Parrot. These birds are best separated by size, voice and the pattern of the cere, though they are often accompanied by adults which are easier to identify.

149a. Madagascar Blue Pigeon, adult.

149b. Madagascar Blue Pigeon, adults.

150. Greater Vasa Parrot. 150a (centre) adult. 150b (inset left) adult head. 150c (inset right) adult in flight.

151 Lesser Vasa Parrot *Coracopsis nigra*

DESCRIPTION Size: 35cm. A medium-sized, all-dark parrot. Sexes alike, plumage varies slightly with age. Two subspecies. **Adult nominate:** Plumage entirely blackish-brown, slightly darker on the tips of the flight feathers and with a slight greenish gloss to the upperparts in the breeding season. Usually shows an inconspicuous, small area of greyish bare skin around the eye. Iris dark brown. Bill smaller than the previous species, pinkish-grey to dusky brown with a darker grey cere which protrudes as a dark rounded point on to the upper mandible. Legs and feet brownish. **Adult *C. n. libs*:** Generally slightly smaller and paler. **Immature:** Similar to adult though browner and the bare skin around the eye is absent or reduced.

VOICE Call and song quieter and less raucous than Greater Vasa Parrot. Most frequently heard call, which is probably the territorial song, is a series of melodic whistles which are atypical for a parrot - *teer-tee-tee-too-tee*, and other similar variations. Within each phrase, the notes typically descend in pitch with the last note higher-pitched giving the phrase an almost quizzical quality. Also a frequently repeated *teer-tee-too teer-tee-too*, often ending in two or three subdued notes. Other calls include a quiet *chack-chack tewee* and a sharp *chwick-cheer*.

HABITAT/BEHAVIOUR Inhabits all native forest types, secondary forest and occasionally mangroves. Gregarious, usually found in small groups. Feeds on fruit, flowers and seeds which are taken from trees and bushes or when foraging on the ground. Roosts communally and may be active on bright nights. Nests in a tree hollow.

RANGE/STATUS Regional Endemic, occurring in Madagascar, the Comoros and the Seychelles. Not globally threatened though frequently caught for food and kept as pets. Represented in Madagascar by two endemic subspecies, *C. n. libs* in the drier west and south and the nominate subspecies in the east. Occurs commonly in suitable habitat throughout. Found from sea level to 2,000m.

WHERE TO SEE Relatively common and easy to see at most sites including Perinet-Analamazaotra, Ranomafana and Ampijoroa.

SIMILAR SPECIES Can only be confused with the larger Greater Vasa Parrot, which see for differences.

152 Grey-headed Lovebird *Agapornis canus*

DESCRIPTION Size: 14-16cm. A small, plump, bright green parrot. Sexes differ and plumage varies slightly with age. Two subspecies. **Adult male nominate:** Pale grey head and breast. Upperparts green with darker, blackish fringes to the flight feathers, black underwing-coverts, blackish tip to the tail and a brighter green rump. Underparts bright yellowish green. Iris dark brown. Bill small, pale grey, legs and feet pale grey. **Adult female nominate:** Similar to male though differs in being slightly duller with dull green head and breast and green underwing-coverts. *A. c. ablactanea* from the south is similar to the nominate, though is slightly darker and the underparts are less yellowish. **Immature:** Similar to female though duller with a dirty yellowish bill with some dark at the base.

VOICE Vocal, with flocks constantly uttering characteristic sparrow-like chirping calls, *chree chree*, especially in flight.

HABITAT/BEHAVIOUR Favours dry open habitats including spiny desert, forest clearings, sparsely wooded areas and savanna. Gregarious, usually found in small groups. Forages on the ground, feeding on small seeds, often perching in the open when disturbed or when resting. Nests in a tree hollow.

RANGE/STATUS Endemic to Madagascar though introduced to other Indian Ocean islands including the Comoros and the Seychelles. Not globally threatened. Found throughout Madagascar where it is common in the west and south, scarce in the east and rare on the high plateau. Two subspecies, the nominate subspecies occurs throughout the range except in the south where it is replaced by the subspecies *A. c. ablactanea*. Found from sea level to 1,500m.

WHERE TO SEE Relatively common and easy to see at sites in the south and west including Ampijoroa Forest Station, Zombitse Forest, Berenty and sites around Toliara.

SIMILAR SPECIES Cannot be mistaken for any other species.

55. *Giant Coua, adult.*

56. *Coquerel's Coua, adult.*

157 Running Coua *Coua cursor*

DESCRIPTION Size: 40cm. A medium-sized, slim, long-legged, terrestrial coua. Sexes alike, plumage varies with age. **Adult:** Crown, nape and upperparts bronze, tail slightly darker bronze with all but central tail feathers tipped white. Brightly coloured ovoid patch of bare facial skin surrounds eye and is outlined boldly in black. Bare skin is bicoloured, deep ultramarine blue around and in front of the eye and bright pink behind the eye. Throat and upper breast pale rufous-orange, deep peachy-orange sides to the neck, pinkish-grey breast grading to pale buff on belly and whitish undertail-coverts. Iris dark red, bill, legs and feet black. **Immature:** Differs from adult in duller plumage, duller blue facial skin and pale spots on the wing-coverts. Bill is initially pale.
VOICE Frequently repeated, hurried series of six to seven gruff whistles, first three to four are similar high-pitched notes followed by one to three shorter, quieter, gruffer notes - *gweerr-gweerr-gweerr gulk-gulk-gulk.* A variation is a single whistle followed by a series of descending gruffer notes: *weeer gulk-gulk-gul-gu.*
HABITAT/BEHAVIOUR Inhabits spiny desert, thorn scrub and dry forests, especially areas with limited undergrowth or grassy vegetation. Secretive, usually found alone or in pairs. Forages on the ground where its diet consists largely of insects. Usually runs swiftly to escape danger. Builds a bowl-shaped nest of twigs, usually in a dense bush.
RANGE/STATUS Endemic to Madagascar. Not globally threatened though trapped and hunted for food. Monotypic. Common in south-west and south. Found from sea level to 200m.
WHERE TO SEE Usually easy to find in the spiny desert around Ifaty and in the coral rag scrub south and east of Toliara. Also present in arid habitats near Berenty in the vicinity of Lake Anony.
SIMILAR SPECIES The facial skin coloration and underpart patterning is highly distinctive. Occurs more or less sympatrically with Coquerel's Coua (which see for differences) though the two are separated by habitat. Readily separated from both subspecies of Red-capped Coua by the overall brighter coloration, the bright pink skin behind the eye and the bright peachy-orange sides to the neck.

158 Red-breasted Coua *Coua serriana*

DESCRIPTION Size: 42cm. A medium-sized, stocky, terrestrial coua. Sexes alike, plumage varies with age. **Adult:** Crown, nape and upperparts dark bronze. Flight feathers darker and tail blackish with, in good light, a blue gloss. A brightly coloured ovoid patch of bare facial skin surrounds the eye and is in turn outlined in black, the lower border of which merges with the blackish chin and throat. The bare skin is bicoloured, being sky-blue above the eye and darker, ultramarine blue in front of, behind and below the eye. Breast deep reddish-chestnut, rest of the underparts dark brown, becoming blackish on the lower belly and undertail-coverts. Iris dark red, bill black, legs and feet dark grey. **Immature:** Differs from the adult in duller plumage including dull chestnut breast, duller blue facial skin and pale buff spots on the upperparts with blackish subterminal markings. Bill is initially pale.
VOICE Typical call is a characteristic high-pitched descending whistle which is frequently repeated and usually ends in a soft growl, *cheeoow-ugh*, though from a distance sounds like a clear whistle, *keyew*. Also gives a deeper, resonant, frequently repeated *hoor - ha-ha* with the first syllable being the longest and the last two syllables drooping slightly in pitch. Other calls include a repeated disyllabic *chee-guall*, the second syllable having a somewhat growling quality and when alarmed a harsh, resonant growl *eeowll*.
HABITAT/BEHAVIOUR Restricted to evergreen humid forest. Secretive and highly terrestrial, usually found alone or in pairs. Forages on the ground where its diet consists largely of insects and small fruits. Frequently observed sunbathing in sun-lit areas of the forest floor. Usually runs swiftly to escape danger. Builds a bowl-shaped nest of twigs, usually in a low fern or palm.
RANGE/STATUS Endemic to Madagascar. Not globally threatened though is trapped and hunted for food. Monotypic. Fairly common in the north-east and east. Found from sea level to 1,000m.
WHERE TO SEE Common, though somewhat secretive, in forest on the Masoala Peninsula where it may be readily seen in the vicinity of Ambanizana. Also present at Perinet-Analamazaotra, near to southern edge of its range. Although it is not uncommon and easy to hear, difficult to observe.
SIMILAR SPECIES Easily recognised by distinctive dark plumage and the characteristic deep reddish-chestnut breast. Overlaps with Red-fronted Coua and is easily distinguished from it by the overall darker plumage, the distinctive reddish-chestnut breast and the dull bronze (as opposed to bright rufous in Red-fronted Coua) crown. Vocalisations of the two species are also significantly different.

7. Running Coua, adult.

8a. Red-breasted Coua, adult.   158b. Red-breasted Coua, adult.

159 Red-fronted Coua *Coua reynaudii*

DESCRIPTION Size: 40cm. A medium-sized, slim, largely terrestrial coua. Sexes alike, plumage varies with age. **Adult:** Bright rufous crown. Upperparts olive-brown with a green gloss, wings and tail darker with, in good light, a green or blue gloss. A brightly coloured, narrow ovoid patch of bare facial skin surrounds the eye and is in turn outlined narrowly in black. The bare skin is bicoloured, being ultramarine blue around and in front of the eye and bright sky-blue behind the eye. Underparts smoky-grey becoming darker on the belly and undertail-coverts. Iris dark brown, bill, legs and feet black. **Immature:** Differs from the adult in duller plumage including dull rufous crown, dull rufous underparts, dull facial skin and pale buff feather-edgings on the upperparts.

VOICE Typical calls include a repeated, hollow, squawking *gwuarr* and an explosive, sharp *jick* or *chweck*. Also a long, guttural rattle which increases gradually in volume.

HABITAT/BEHAVIOUR Restricted to evergreen humid forest and well-developed secondary forest. Secretive and largely terrestrial, usually found alone or in pairs. Forages on the ground and on lower branches and creepers. Diet consists largely of insects and small fruits but will also take small frogs. Usually runs swiftly to escape danger but if flushed will fly a short distance first. Builds a bowl-shaped nest of twigs and dry stalks, usually in a low fern or palm.

RANGE/STATUS Endemic to Madagascar. Not globally threatened though is trapped and hunted for food. Monotypic. Fairly common in the north-west and the eastern evergreen humid forest belt. Observed in suitable habitat at all altitudes, though commoner above 800m.

WHERE TO SEE Common, though somewhat secretive, in forest on the Masoala Peninsula where it may be readily seen in the vicinity of Ambanizana, at Perinet-Analamazaotra and at Ranomafana.

SIMILAR SPECIES Easily recognised by the distinctive bright rufous crown. Overlaps with Red-breasted Coua, which see for differences. Also narrowly overlaps with Coquerel's Coua in the north-west from which it is easily separated by the rufous crown, darker, greener upperparts and grey underparts (lacking the rufous-orange tones of Coquerel's Coua).

160 Red-capped Coua *Coua ruficeps*

DESCRIPTION Size: 40cm. A medium-sized terrestrial coua. Sexes alike, plumage varies with age. Two subspecies. **Adult nominate:** crown bright rufous, nape, back and wings brown with a green gloss. Uppertail-coverts and tail maroon-brown, the latter darkening distally and with all but the central tail feathers tipped white. A bright, deep ultramarine-blue coloured patch of bare facial skin surrounds the eye and is in turn outlined in black, narrowly above the eye, broadly behind and below. Underparts pale sandy-rufous except for the breast which is deep pinkish-grey. Iris dark reddish brown, base of bill blue-grey, culmen and tip black. Legs and feet black. **Adult *C. r. olivaceiceps*:** Similar to the nominate though is overall duller with a brown crown and slightly paler underparts. **Immature:** Differs from the adult in overall duller plumage, showing pale spots on the tips of the upperwing-coverts. Bill is initially pale pink on the base.

VOICE Typical call is a rapid, ringing *quer-quer-quer-quee-quee* which rises up the scale and is quite unlike other coua species.

HABITAT/BEHAVIOUR Inhabits dry deciduous forest, spiny desert, thorn scrub and degraded open wooded country. Secretive, usually found alone or in pairs. Forages on the ground where its diet consists largely of insects. Usually runs swiftly to escape danger though may fly short distances. Will perch in trees when calling and when warming in the early morning sun. Builds a bowl-shaped nest of twigs in a tree.

RANGE/STATUS Endemic to Madagascar. Not globally threatened though is commonly trapped and hunted for food. Common in suitable habitat in the west, south-west and south. The nominate subspecies occupies the northern part of the range from Mahajanga south to Morondava with *C. r. olivaceiceps* taking over in the south-west and south. Found from sea level to 900m.

WHERE TO SEE The nominate subspecies is very common in dry deciduous forest at Ampijoroa while *C. r. olivaceiceps* is common in the spiny desert around Ifaty and in the coral rag scrub south and east of Toliara. It also occurs in arid habitats near Berenty.

SIMILAR SPECIES The long legs, long neck and small head, long tail and slim body give it a distinctly rakish silhouette. Overlaps and may possibly be confused with the similarly-sized Running and Coquerel's Couas, which see for differences.

159. Red-fronted Coua, adult.

160a. Red-capped Coua, adult nominate.

160b. Red-capped Coua,
adult C. r. olivaceiceps

161 Crested Coua *Coua cristata*

DESCRIPTION Size: 40-44cm. A medium-sized, largely arboreal coua. Sexes alike, plumage varies with age. Four subspecies. **Adult nominate:** Head and neck dove grey with a prominent crest which is usually fluffy in appearance. Upperparts greyish with a green gloss. Wings and tail slightly darker and glossier, the latter bluish glossed with violet and with broad white tips to all but the central tail feathers. A brightly coloured ovoid patch of bare facial skin surrounds eye and is in turn narrowly outlined in black. Bare skin is bicoloured, lilac in front of and around eye and bright turquoise behind the eye. Chin and throat dove grey, pinkish-grey grading into peachy-orange on the lower breast. Rest of underparts white. Iris dark brown, bill, legs and feet black. *C. c. dumonti*: Differs in its larger size, paler plumage, more extensive white tips to the tail feathers and pale rufous undertail-coverts. *C. c. pyropyga*: Similar to *C. c. dumonti* though is larger and paler and shows bright rufous undertail-coverts. *C. c. maxima*: Larger and darker than all the other subspecies. **Immature:** Generally duller plumage, bare skin around the eye absent or reduced and pale buff spots on the greater coverts.
VOICE Series of loud, clear well-separated calls often given at dusk- *guay - guay - guay - guay - gwuck*. Also a loud *guilp*, a chicken-like clucking *wuk-wuk-wuk* in alarm and low cooing similar to Madagascar Hoopoe.
HABITAT/BEHAVIOUR Occurs in all native forest types though rare in primary eastern evergreen humid forest and second growth. Secretive, usually found alone or in pairs. Forages in the foliage moving from one tree to the next with a long glide. Will also take food from the ground. Diet consists largely of insects, though also eats fruit and small reptiles. Nest is a bowl-shaped structure of twigs built in a tree.
RANGE/STATUS Endemic to Madagascar. Not globally threatened. Scarce in the east and south, common in the north, north-west and west and very common in the south-west. The nominate subspecies occurs in the east, north and west south to Mahajanga, *C. c. dumonti* in the west between Mahajanga and Morondava, *C. c. pyropyga* in the south-west and south, south of Morondava and *C. c. maxima* is known from just one specimen collected near Fort Dauphin in the south-east. Found from sea level to 1,000m.
WHERE TO SEE Easiest to see in south and west. Common at Ampijoroa and Berenty.
SIMILAR SPECIES Can only be confused with the superficially similar Verreaux's Coua which occurs sympatrically in the south-west and south. Verreaux's Coua is smaller, shows a more pointed, dark-tipped crest, lacks the black surround to the bare facial skin, shows blue rather than lilac skin in front of the eye and shows largely white underparts, lacking the brightly coloured breast and undertail-coverts of the sympatric *C. c. pyropyga* form of Crested Coua. The calls of the two species are also significantly different.

162 Verreaux's Coua *Coua verreauxi*

DESCRIPTION Size: 38cm. A small, slim, largely arboreal coua. Sexes alike, plumage varies with age. **Adult:** Head grey, tinged green with a prominent spikey crest which darkens towards the tip and is sometimes held vertically upright or even pointing forwards. Upperparts grey tinged green, wings slightly darker, glossed green. Uppertail-coverts glossed purple, tail darker glossed with blue and purple, darkening towards the tip and with broad white tips to all but the central tail feathers. A small patch of bare facial skin surrounds the eye, and unlike all other couas, is not outlined in black. The bare skin is bicoloured, deep ultramarine blue around and in front of the eye and bright sky blue behind the eye. Underparts off-white, sullied with grey on the throat and breast and sometimes showing a small buff patch on the sides of the breast. Iris dark brown, bill, legs and feet black. **Immature:** Differs from adult in generally duller plumage, and reduced and duller bare skin around the eye.
VOICE Calls include a loud descending series of squawking notes, frequently given at dusk- *crick-crick-crick-corick-corick*. Higher-pitched and more rasping than the corresponding call of Crested Coua and may be followed by a series of descending growls, *gwuorr-gwuorr gorr-gorr-gor-gor*, which may also be given separately.
HABITAT/BEHAVIOUR Restricted to subarid thorn scrub. Habits as for Crested Coua. Diet consists largely of insects, though also eats fruit. Nesting habits undescribed.
RANGE/STATUS Endemic to Madagascar. Currently considered **Near Threatened** globally. Monotypic. Locally common in suitable habitat within its restricted range along the coastal strip in the south-west and south from just south of Toliara to just east of Cap Ste. Marie. Found from sea level to 200m.
WHERE TO SEE Best looked for in the coral rag scrub near Toliara. The areas around La Mangrove Hotel on the St. Augustin road south of Toliara is a good place to try. Also occurs around Cap Ste. Marie at the southern tip of Madagascar.
SIMILAR SPECIES Can only be confused with Crested Coua, which see for differences.

1a. Crested Coua, adult nominate.

161b. Crested Coua, adult C. c. pyropyga.

162a (inset) Verreaux's Coua, adult. 162b. Verreaux's Coua, adult.

163 Blue Coua *Coua caerulea*

DESCRIPTION Size: 50cm. A large, arboreal, all-blue coua. Sexes alike, plumage varies with age. **Adult:** Entire plumage bright, dark blue, the wings and tail glossed with violet. A brightly coloured ovoid patch of bare facial skin surrounds the eye and is in turn outlined narrowly in black. The bare skin is bicoloured, deep ultramarine blue around and in front of the eye and bright sky blue behind the eye. Iris dark brown, bill, legs and feet black. **Immature:** Differs from the adult in generally duller plumage, bare skin around the eye absent or reduced, gloss to wings and tail lacking and some brown in the plumage.
VOICE Typical call, which is frequently heard, is a short, loud, explosive trill which lasts for less than a second and drops slightly in tone - *drrrr   drrrr*. Also occasionally gives a loud series of evenly spaced, descending call notes, *guack - guack - guack - guack - gwuck*, which is often answered by a neighbour.
HABITAT/BEHAVIOUR Occurs in evergreen humid forest and adjacent second growth and locally in the north-west in drier forest. Arboreal, usually found alone or in small groups. Moves clumsily through the canopy, travelling along the larger branches gleaning its prey from the foliage. Diet consists of insects, small reptiles and fruit. Flight is weak and when moving from tree to tree or crossing an open area, flies from high up and glides heavily across, usually losing height. Builds a bowl-shaped nest of twigs which is usually situated in dense foliage.
RANGE/STATUS Endemic to Madagascar. Not globally threatened. Common throughout the remaining eastern evergreen humid forest and also occurs locally in forest in the north and north-west. Found from sea level to 2,000m.
WHERE TO SEE Common and easy to see in eastern evergreen humid forests such as Perinet-Analamazaotra and Ranomafana.
SIMILAR SPECIES Unmistakable.

164 Madagascar Coucal *Centropus toulou*

DESCRIPTION Size: 42-47cm. A typical coucal. Sexes alike, plumage varies seasonally and with age. **Adult breeding:** Entire plumage glossy black with the exception of the wings and back which are deep chestnut. Iris red, bill, legs and feet black. **Adult non-breeding:** Similar to adult breeding though duller with entire head, mantle, back, throat and breast finely streaked rufous-buff and black and bill paler, pinkish-brown. **Immature:** Similar to adult non-breeding though spotted rather than streaked on the head and body, the mantle and wing-coverts are barred dark brown rather than chestnut and the underside of the tail is barred.
VOICE Vocal, especially in the early morning and evening. Most commonly heard call is a series of typically five to ten deep hoots which decrease in volume - *toop toop toop toop tup*. Also gives a harsh scolding hiss.
HABITAT/BEHAVIOUR Occurs in a wide variety of habitats including forest, scrub, mangroves, rice-paddies and any other habitats which provide dense cover, especially abundant in reedbeds. Usually found alone or in pairs and generally remains under cover except in the early morning when it frequently suns itself in the open. Moves through dense foliage and on the ground when foraging. Diet is varied and includes insects, small reptiles and amphibians and eggs and chicks which are taken from nests. Often mobbed by small passerines presumably because it is recognised as a nest predator. Seldom flies and when it does the flight is weak with vigorous flaps followed by periods of gliding. The nest is a large domed structure built from grass and situated low down in dense foliage.
RANGE/STATUS Regional Endemic, occurring in Madagascar and Aldabra. Not globally threatened. Represented in Madagascar by the endemic nominate subspecies which is common in suitable habitat throughout. Found from sea level to 1,800m.
WHERE TO SEE Common and widespread, present at most birding sites.
SIMILAR SPECIES The only coucal occurring in Madagascar. The large size, long tail and black and chestnut plumage render it unmistakable.

3. *Blue Coua, adult.*

4. *Madagascar Coucal, adult breeding.*

165 Madagascar Red Owl *Tyto soumagnei*

DESCRIPTION Size: 30cm. A medium-sized owl. Sexes alike, plumage variation with age unknown. **Adult:** Heart-shaped facial disk is outlined in chestnut-orange. Face greyish-buff with darker brown around the eyes and extending towards the bill as dark 'teardrops'. Crown, nape and entire upperparts chestnut-orange with fine black spotting, most dense on the crown. The inner webs of the flight feathers are marked with four to five widely spaced narrow black bars. Underparts buffy-orange with fine black spots. Iris blackish, bill pale grey, legs greyish-buff, feathered, feet pale pinkish-grey with darker claws. **Immature:** Unknown, though immature *Tyto* species typically show retained down initially but fairly soon appear similar to the adult.

VOICE The call is typical for the genus and is often given when leaving the roost. It is a loud hissing screech which drops in pitch halfway through the call - *cheeerrrooorrr*.

HABITAT/BEHAVIOUR Nocturnal. Occurs in and adjacent to evergreen humid forest. Roosts during the day usually on a concealed perch and hunts by night. Recent observations have shown that open habitats adjacent to forest including rice paddies are used for hunting. Usually solitary. Diet includes small mammals. The nests is located in a natural tree cavity.

RANGE/STATUS Endemic to Madagascar. Globally Threatened and currently classified as **Endangered**. Monotypic. Very little known, with records being confined to the east and north-east. The species may have been overlooked and future work may reveal it to be less rare than feared. Found from sea level to 1,200m.

WHERE TO SEE Very rare. Best searched for in and around forests on the Masoala Peninsula including Ambanizana. There have also been recent records from forest near Perinet-Analamazaotra including at Mantadia.

SIMILAR SPECIES Easily recognised as a *Tyto* by the stocky shape and heart-shaped facial disk. Could only be confused with the larger Barn Owl from which it is readily separated by the overall orange coloration and in particular the buffy-orange, as opposed to white, underparts. Barn Owl often appears very pale, almost white.

166 Barn Owl *Tyto alba*

DESCRIPTION Size: 32-36cm. A medium-large owl. Sexes alike, plumage varies slightly with age. **Adult:** Heart-shaped facial disk is outlined in dark brown. Face whitish with darker brown around the eyes and extending towards the bill as dark 'teardrops'. Crown, nape and entire upperparts grey with buff barring and fine black and white spotting. Tail and flight feathers show darker barring. Underwing white with dark barring on the flight feathers. Buff wash across the breast, the rest of the underparts white with fine black spots. Iris blackish, bill off-white, legs white, feathered, feet yellowish with darker claws. **Immature:** Similar to adult, initially shows retained down but fairly soon appears similar to the adult.

VOICE The typical call is a loud, rasping hiss.

HABITAT/BEHAVIOUR Nocturnal. Occurs in a variety of open and sparsely wooded habitats. Roosts during the day in a concealed area such as a tree hollow or cave and emerges at or just before dusk to hunt. Hunts over open areas from dusk onwards, seldom during the day. Usually solitary. Diet includes small mammals and occasionally insects and small birds. The nests is located in a natural tree cavity, cave or rocky cavity or in a disused building.

RANGE/STATUS Distributed widely in the Americas, Europe, Africa, Asia and Australia. Not globally threatened. Represented in Madagascar by the subspecies *T. a. affinis* which is common to sub-Saharan Africa though some authors treat the birds on Madagascar and the Comoros as a separate subspecies, *T. a. hypermetra*. Widespread and possibly increasing in suitable habitat throughout the island. This species is persecuted by villagers as it is, along with all species of owl, perceived as a bird of ill-omen. Found from sea level to 1,500m.

WHERE TO SEE Could be seen anywhere and most likely to be seen if driving at night. Common in the vicinity of Antananarivo.

SIMILAR SPECIES Easily recognised as a *Tyto* by the stocky shape and heart-shaped facial disk. Could only be confused with the smaller Red Owl, which see for differences.

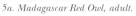

5a. Madagascar Red Owl, adult.

165b. Madagascar Red Owl, adult.

6. Barn Owl, adult.

167 Madagascar Scops Owl *Otus rutilus*

DESCRIPTION Size: 22-24cm. A small owl. Sexes and all plumages similar though coloration of plumage varies between individuals. Face grey to rufous-brown with a darker line extending from the forehead to the bill with paler marks either side which extend over the eyes and form pale eyebrows. Has ear-like tufts on the head which may be conspicuous, especially when roosting, but at times are held flat and are not visible. Crown, nape and entire upperparts vary from grey to rufous with fine paler and darker speckling and barring. A row of large pale spots on the scapulars form a conspicuous paler line. The flight feathers show dark and whitish bars. Underparts are similarly coloured to the upperparts, though are paler, having conspicuous blackish striations with inconspicuous, fine cross-barring and often a whitish centre to the breast. Iris yellow, bill blackish, legs feathered, feet pinkish with darker claws. Birds from the humid parts of the range tend to show more rufous plumage tones while those from the drier west tend to be greyer.

VOICE In the evergreen humid forests of the east, the call is a distinctive series of five to fifteen clear, soft hoots, lasting for 1.5 to 5 seconds in total. Notes increase slightly in volume and tail off slightly with the final one or two notes. In the west, the call is a shorter series of three to seven notes, delivered more slowly (call duration is 2 to 3 seconds). Each note is less pure, tremulous and has an overall barking quality to it, sounding more forceful than the birds from the east.

HABITAT/BEHAVIOUR Nocturnal. Occurs in woodland habitats including all native forest, second growth and even trees around villages. Usually solitary or in pairs. Roosts during the day, concealed in dense foliage. Feeds mainly on insects taken at night. The nest is usually located in a tree cavity.

RANGE/STATUS Regional Endemic, occurring in Madagascar and the Comoros. Not globally threatened. Represented in Madagascar by the nominate subspecies which is endemic and is common in suitable habitat throughout except in the high plateau where it is rare. There are clearly two 'forms' occurring in Madagascar which can easily be separated by voice. Further work is required to determine the taxonomic relationship between these forms, particularly where they meet, but they are likely to represent separate species. They may possibly prove to be good species in their own right. In addition, at least one form on the Comoros may prove to be a good species based on morphology and calls. Found from sea level to 2,000m.

WHERE TO SEE Widespread and relatively easy to see at Perinet-Analamazaotra ('eastern form') and at Ampijoroa and Berenty ('western form'). At the latter site the guides can often find roosting individuals.

SIMILAR SPECIES The smallest owl in Madagascar, easily recognised by its small size, yellow eyes, cryptic plumage, distinctive vocalisations and, when visible, the characteristic ear-tufts.

168 White-browed Owl *Ninox superciliaris*

DESCRIPTION Size: 30cm. A medium-sized owl. Sexes and all plumages alike. Face buffy-grey with conspicuous white eyebrows which meet over the bill. Forehead brown with fine white spotting, upperparts brown with white spotting in the scapulars and coverts and white barring in the flight feathers. Underparts show a white line under the bill, which may be obscured if the bird is hunched-up, and a brown band on the upper breast. Rest of underparts white with conspicuous brown barring across the breast which may be broken in the centre of the breast. Iris dark brown, bill yellowish surrounded by numerous dark rictal bristles, legs and feet yellowish-brown with dark grey claws.

VOICE Has a variety of calls. Typically announces its presence by a long series of notes which begin quietly and accelerate and increase in volume - *ar-ook ook-ook-ook-angk-angk-angk* - with the *angk* note being repeated about 15 times. Usually follows this with hooting calls - *ho-oool* - with the emphasis being on the second syllable which is louder and higher pitched. Sometimes gives the hooting call only and occasionally calls during the day.

HABITAT/BEHAVIOUR Nocturnal. Occurs in evergreen humid forest-edge habitats, thorn scrub, dry deciduous forest, gallery forest and second growth. Usually solitary or in pairs. Roosts during the day, usually concealed in dense foliage. Feeds on insects taken at night. Nest usually situated in a tree cavity.

RANGE/STATUS Endemic to Madagascar. Not globally threatened. Monotypic. Uncommon in evergreen humid forest in the north-east, common in dry forest in the west and south. Found from sea level to 800m.

WHERE TO SEE Easy to find at Berenty where the guides can usually find roosting birds. Also common at Zombitse and Kirindy.

SIMILAR SPECIES Easily recognised by its long wings and tail, conspicuous white eyebrows and barred underparts.

167a. Madagascar Scops Owl, adult 'western form'.

168a. White-browed Owl.

167b. Madagascar Scops Owl, adult 'eastern form'.

168b. White-browed Owl.

169 Madagascar Long-eared Owl *Asio madagascariensis*

DESCRIPTION Size: 40-50cm. The largest owl in Madagascar. Sexes alike, plumage varies with age. Female larger than male. **Adult:** Face brown, around the eyes and with paler marks either side of the bill which extend to just above the eyes. Has prominent ear-like tufts on the head which are usually conspicuous, especially when roosting. Crown, nape and entire upperparts brownish-black with rufous-brown mottling and barring. The wings and tail are conspicuously barred blackish and buff. Underparts are buff with conspicuous blackish striations. Iris dull orange, bill grey, legs and feet huge and feathered with massive, dark grey claws. **Immature:** When first fledged the face is black and the head and body are covered in creamy-white down which is gradually replaced by adult plumage.
VOICE Call is a long series of barking notes, *harkh* or *ankh*, not unlike a dog, which may last for 20 seconds. The calls are initially quiet but accelerate and increase in volume before slowing down and dropping in tone at the end. One series may consist of up to 50, possibly more, separate 'barking' notes though typically 8-20 notes are given in a series. Newly fledged juveniles give a distinctive, short, high-pitched rasping hiss when begging - *kwearr* - which is repeated every 5 to 15 seconds.
HABITAT/BEHAVIOUR Nocturnal. Occurs in a variety of woodland habitats including evergreen humid forest, dry deciduous forest, gallery forest and degraded and dense secondary forest. Usually solitary or in pairs. Roosts during the day, usually concealed in dense foliage. Diet consists largely of small mammals. The species may also be found at night in open areas adjacent to forest.
RANGE/STATUS Endemic to Madagascar. Not globally threatened. Monotypic. Occurs throughout in suitable habitat though is seldom observed. Found from sea level to 1,600m.
WHERE TO SEE Occurs at many sites including Perinet-Analamazaotra, Ranomafana, Kirindy and Berenty. However, it is difficult to track down and the best chance is likely to be if the local guides know of roosting birds.
SIMILAR SPECIES Unmistakable.

170 Marsh Owl *Asio capensis*

DESCRIPTION Size: 37-40cm. A large owl. Sexes alike, plumage varies with age. **Adult:** Face greyish-buff with darker brown marks around the eyes. The facial disc is outlined with an indistinct white line which in turn is edged by a darker line. Small ear-like tufts on the forecrown are sometimes visible. Upperparts greyish-brown with fine and inconspicuous pale vermiculations. Upperside of primaries show conspicuous rufous-buff barring and the tail is also conspicuously barred. Underside of the wings buff with a conspicuous dark carpal crescent and dark bars on the flight feathers. Underparts grey-brown, finely vermiculated, becoming paler on the belly and undertail-coverts. Iris dark brown, bill grey, legs feathered, feet partly feathered with grey toes and darker claws. **Immature:** When first fledged, some down is still visible but soon moults into adult type plumage, though the face tends to be darker.
VOICE Gives various croaking and hissing calls when disturbed and in flight.
HABITAT/BEHAVIOUR Nocturnal and crepuscular, often hunting just before dusk when it quarters open ground. Occurs in grassland, particularly near to water and often near to towns. Usually encountered singly or in small groups. Roosts during the day on the ground, sometimes communally. Diet includes insects, small mammals and occasionally birds. The nests is a simple hollow constructed in dense grass usually near to a wetland.
RANGE/STATUS Occurs in Africa. Not globally threatened. In Madagascar, represented by the endemic subspecies *A. c. hova* which differs from the nominate by being larger and darker, with less contrasted markings on the wings and tail. It is uncommon and patchily distributed in suitable habitat throughout. Found from sea level to 1,500m.
WHERE TO SEE Uncommon and seldom seen. Occasionally seen at dusk in grasslands between Ranohira and Ihosy and occurs in and around Antananarivo.
SIMILAR SPECIES Easily recognised by the uniform brown upperparts, small ear-tufts, faintly marked brown underparts and in flight by the long wings which are marked with rufous-buff barring in the primaries and supple, buoyant flight.

169a. Madagascar Long-eared Owl, adult.

169b. Madagascar Long-eared Owl, juvenile.

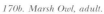

170a. Marsh Owl, adult.

170b. Marsh Owl, adult.

171 Collared Nightjar *Caprimulgus enarratus*

DESCRIPTION Size: 24cm. A large, large-headed, forest nightjar which is seldom seen away from the forest floor. Sexes alike, plumage varies with age and there is some individual variations between grey and buffy extremes. **Adult:** Dark rusty-brown band expends from the bill and broadens behind the eye to form a dark mask which is darker on the lower border. Forehead, crown and lower face grey with pale scaling on the forecrown and black spots on the crown. Narrow golden-buff hind collar joins a less conspicuous pale lower border to the face and is backed by a broad, deep rufous collar. Upperparts grey with buff and black markings, scapulars pale grey-buff with conspicuous black spots, coverts grey-brown with indistinct darker spots, tertials pale grey-buff with terminal black spots, flight feathers and tail black with rufous barring, the latter with white tips to the outer tail-feathers. Buff underparts with black spots on the breast and fine dark barring on the belly and undertail-coverts. Iris dark brown, bill dark grey surrounded by long black rictal bristles, legs and feet pinkish-grey, short and weak. **Immature:** When first fledged shows traces of down and is more cryptically patterned than the adult.
VOICE Vocalisations are unknown. It appears that the birds are silent for much of the year.
HABITAT/BEHAVIOUR Evergreen humid forest and adjacent second growth and in dry forest in some areas. Usually encountered singly or in family groups, roosting on the forest floor. Seldom observed foraging and may do so largely within the forest. Feeds on insects. The nest is made on a small palm or in a fork in a tree up to 2m above the ground from where the adult and young move to the forest floor sometime after hatching. Also reported to nest on the forest floor though this may well be erroneous.
RANGE/STATUS Endemic to Madagascar. Not globally threatened. Monotypic. Generally scarce and seldom seen though this may be in part due to its secretive behaviour. Most records are from the evergreen humid forests of the east though also present in the north and north-west. Recent records from sea level to 1,200m.
WHERE TO SEE Uncommon and seldom seen. The best chance is at Perinet-Analamazaotra where the local guides are often able to find roosting birds. May also be found at Ankarana in the north where it seems to be fairly common.
SIMILAR SPECIES The vividly marked plumage make this one of the most beautiful and distinctive nightjars. If seen well, cannot be mistaken for Madagascar Nightjar. In flight, no white is visible in the primaries.

172 Madagascar Nightjar *Caprimulgus madagascariensis*

DESCRIPTION Size: 21cm. A typical nightjar. Sexes alike though plumage varies between individuals with some birds very grey, others overall buffer. **Adult:** Brownish ear-coverts with a paler, off-white submoustachial-stripe which joins a paler buffy area behind the ear-coverts. Crown and upperparts grey with fine black streaking, pale white to buff spots on the coverts and a pale line on the scapulars formed by off-white fringes to one row. Flight feathers and tail barred with tan, with prominent white patches on the centre of the outer four primaries and at the tip of the outer four pairs of tail feathers. Underparts grey or grey-buff with fine black streaks and narrow darker cross-barring. Usually shows prominent white marks on the sides of the throat which are bordered below with black spots. Iris dark brown, bill dark grey surrounded by black rictal bristles, legs and feet grey, short and weak. **Immature:** When first fledged shows traces of down, is short-tailed and short-winged and is more cryptically patterned than the adult.
VOICE Call is a distinctive series of hollow notes which accelerate like a ping-pong ball bouncing on a table, *took tuk-tuk-tr-r-r-r*, each series lasting for 1 to 2 seconds and repeated every 2 to 5 seconds. Also a bubbling growl and peculiar *weer-wuk, weer wer-wuk* given occasionally.
HABITAT/BEHAVIOUR Occurs in most open habitats and avoids dense forest. Usually encountered singly or in family groups. Roosts on the ground during the day, foraging on the wing at night and in particular at dawn and dusk. Feeds on insects. The nest is a scrape, usually made on leaf litter.
RANGE/STATUS Regional Endemic, restricted to Madagascar and Aldabra. Not globally threatened. Represented in Madagascar by the endemic nominate subspecies which is common throughout. Found from sea level to 2,000m. Some authors treat this species as a subspecies of the Indian Nightjar *C. asiaticus* from Asia.
WHERE TO SEE Common and easy to see, especially in the dry south-west where it is very common around Toliara.
SIMILAR SPECIES A typical, cryptically coloured greyish nightjar with prominent white tail and wing patches. Could only be confused with Collared Nightjar which is larger, lacks white in the wing, is distinctively patterned and is largely restricted to forest habitats.

*71a. Collared Nightjar, adult with
  juvenile mostly hidden behind.*

171b. Collared Nightjar, adult with two chicks.

72a. Madagascar Nightjar, adult.

172b. Madagascar Nightjar, adult.

173 Madagascar Spinetail *Zoonavena grandidieri*

DESCRIPTION Size: 12cm. A small swift. Sexes and all plumages alike. Head black-brown, throat paler greyish-brown with brown streaks. Upperparts and tail black-brown, rump whitish with noticeable brown shaft-streaks. Underparts grey-brown with darker brown on the breast, forming an indistinct breast-band, and darker undertail-coverts. Upperwing and underwing black-brown, the underwing clearly darker than the underbody. Rectrix spines longest at centre of tail (extending up to 3mm on males and 1.5mm on females), but very difficult to see in the field. Iris dark brown, bill black.

VOICE Generally quiet though utters a shrill, brief *zree* call when feeding which is sometimes given as a series and when displaying utters three or four notes which rise in pitch followed by a dropping trill given as the bird 'stalls' with its wings held in an inverted 'V'.

HABITAT/BEHAVIOUR Almost always over forest or adjacent secondary forest, savanna and open country. Usually seen in pairs or small groups feeding on insects just above stands of trees. The flight is characteristic, gliding with the wings held below the horizontal. Builds nest of twigs and other vegetation in hollow trees.

RANGE/STATUS Regional Endemic occurring in Madagascar and the Comoros. Not globally threatened. Represented in Madagascar by the endemic nominate subspecies which is distributed throughout the island except on the high plateau. Frequent in the east, scarcer in the west and south. Found from sea level to 2,000m.

WHERE TO SEE Widespread. Regularly seen at Perinet-Analamazaotra and Zombitse Forest and also along the forest edge at Ambanizana on the Masoala Peninsula.

SIMILAR SPECIES Readily identified by its somewhat fluttering flight, square or only shallowly forked tail and pale whitish rump. Most likely to be confused with Little Swift which is stockier, has a stronger and more direct flight, shows a pale forehead and a larger, cleaner white rump.

174 African Palm Swift *Cypsiurus parvus*

DESCRIPTION Size: 16cm. A small, all-brown swift with an extremely long tail which is characteristically held closed. Sexes alike, plumage varies slightly with age. **Adult:** Head brown-grey, throat greyish with indistinct brown streaking. Upperparts, upperwings and tail uniformly brown. Underparts and underwings pale grey brown except for darker brown underwing-coverts. The tail is deeply forked though it is usually held tightly closed and appears as a thin spike. Iris dark brown, bill black. **Immature:** Similar to adult though narrow pale fringes give a scaly effect.

VOICE Vocal, especially near roosting and nesting sites. Call is a shrill, chattering *si-si-si-si-si-sri-sri*.

HABITAT/BEHAVIOUR Closely associated with the presence of tall palms, especially near water, through a wide range of habitats. Fairly gregarious, feeds on insects. Nests in palm trees and sometimes on bridges.

RANGE/STATUS Occurs in sub-Saharan Africa, south-west Arabia and the Comoros. Not globally threatened. Represented in Madagascar by the endemic subspecies *C. p. gracilis* which is smaller and darker than the nominate, with a more heavily streaked throat. The tail of the juvenile is also more strongly forked. It is common in coastal areas except in the south. Some authors suggest that this subspecies may merit elevation to specific status. Found from sea level to 1,100m.

WHERE TO SEE Common and widespread wherever suitable palm trees occur, especially in coastal lowlands.

SIMILAR SPECIES Most likely to be mistaken for the Madagascar Spinetail, from which it is distinguished by the long, deeply forked tail, which usually appears pointed.

3. *Madagascar Spinetail, adult in flight.*

4a *(inset) African Palm Swift, adult in flight. 174b. African Palm Swift, juvenile.*

175 Alpine Swift *Apus melba*

DESCRIPTION Size: 20-22cm. A very large swift. Sexes alike, plumage varies slightly with age. **Adult:** Head brown with a dark eye patch and a broad white throat. At a distance and in poor light the throat may appear dark. Upperparts and tail brown. Breast and belly white separated from the throat by a brown breast-band. Flanks, vent and undertail-coverts brown. Upperwing and underwing brown. At close range, the plumage has a scaly effect formed by narrow pale fringes to the plumage. Iris dark brown, bill black. **Immature:** Similar to fresh adult with the plumage being extensively fringed white, especially on the wing-coverts.
VOICE A loud, shrill, accelerating trill which slows towards the end. Especially vocal when close to a roost or breeding colony.
HABITAT/BEHAVIOUR An aerial feeder which may be found foraging for insects over any habitat where prey is plentiful. Gregarious, often feeds at great heights. Throughout most of its range, nests on ledges or in holes on cliff faces.
RANGE/STATUS Occurs in southern Europe, the Middle East, western Asia and northern and sub-Saharan Africa. Not globally threatened. Represented in Madagascar by the endemic subspecies *A. m. willsi* which is smaller and darker than the nominate, with the darkest plumage of any race, and a broad breast-band. Occurs throughout Madagascar with populations ranging widely in response to changes in food availability. Found from sea level to 2,000m.
WHERE TO SEE May be encountered anywhere, most likely to be seen in mountainous areas or feeding at low levels during adverse weather conditions.
SIMILAR SPECIES Easily separated from all other swifts in Madagascar by its large size and clear white throat and belly separated by a broad brown breast-band.

176 African Black Swift *Apus barbatus*

DESCRIPTION Size: 16cm. A medium-large swift with a shallowly forked tail. Sexes alike. **Adult:** Head black with a well-defined white throat. Rest of the plumage blackish, darkest on the mantle. There is a distinct contrast on both the upperwing and underwing between the very dark body, lesser-coverts and primaries and the paler inner wing. At close range, the plumage has a scaly effect formed by narrow pale fringes to the feathers. Iris dark brown, bill black. **Immature:** Similar to fresh adult with the plumage being extensively fringed greyish. The throat patch is normally more extensive.
VOICE A high-pitched, shrill scream.
HABITAT/BEHAVIOUR A gregarious aerial feeder which may form large flocks, sometimes with other swift species. Forages for insects over any habitat where prey is plentiful. Usually nests in crevices on cliff faces.
RANGE/STATUS Occurs patchily in sub-Saharan Africa and the Comoros. Not globally threatened. Represented in Madagascar by the endemic subspecies *A. b. balstoni* which is smaller and somewhat darker than the nominate, especially on the lesser coverts, which are more similar to the mantle in colour. It occurs throughout Madagascar with populations ranging widely in response to changes in food availability. There is circumstantial evidence to suggest that birds from Madagascar may migrate to Africa, though this is as yet unproven. Found from sea level to 2,000m. Some authors regard the Madagascar subspecies as a good species, Madagascar Black Swift *Apus balstoni*.
WHERE TO SEE Common and widespread. Seen regularly around the cliffs near the mouth of the Onilahy River near St. Augustin south of Toliara and in roadside cliffs in the Isalo Massif. Also regularly over Antananarivo.
SIMILAR SPECIES The all-dark plumage except for the white throat and paler inner wing is distinctive. Larger and darker than either Madagascar Spinetail or African Palm Swift.

75. *Alpine Swift, adult in flight*

76. *African Black Swift, adult in flight.*

177 Little Swift *Apus affinis*

DESCRIPTION Size: 12cm. A small stocky swift with broad wings and a square tail. Sexes alike. **Adult:** Well-defined white throat patch. Greyish forehead, lores and supercilium contrast with the blackish eye-patch. Rest of plumage blackish-brown except for a prominent and well-defined, broad white rump band which extends on to the rear flanks. The plumage is darkest on the mantle, breast and underwing-coverts and the mantle appears glossy in good light. Iris dark brown, bill black. **Immature:** Similar to fresh adult with the plumage being fringed greyish but lacks the glossy saddle.
VOICE Typical call is a rippling, high-pitched trill.
HABITAT/BEHAVIOUR A gregarious aerial feeder which may form flocks, sometimes with other swift species. Forages for insects over any habitat where prey is plentiful.
RANGE/STATUS Occurs commonly in sub-Saharan Africa and patchily from North Africa east to the Middle East and the Indian sub-continent. Not globally threatened. Presumably represented in Madagascar by the subspecies *A. a. theresae* which occurs in adjacent southern Africa. In Madagascar there have been regular sightings of this species over the capital Antananarivo since 1987 and it may be a recent colonist. There have also been records in the north over Amber Mountain. Most records have been in the period September-November. Found around 1,300m.
WHERE TO SEE Best searched for by checking swift flocks over Antananarivo.
SIMILAR SPECIES Easily recognised by the all-dark plumage with prominent white throat and rump patches.

178 Madagascar Malachite Kingfisher *Alcedo vintsioides*

DESCRIPTION Size: 13-15cm. A small, bright blue and orange kingfisher. Sexes alike, plumage varies slightly with age. **Adult:** Forehead and crown greenish-blue with black barring. The long feathers on the crown can be erected to form a crest. Lores and face bright rufous-orange with a conspicuous white throat and white patch on the side of the neck. Upperparts bright blue, brighter and paler on the lower back, rump and tail and darkest on the flight feathers. Underparts washed with rufous-orange, palest in the centre of the breast and belly. Iris dark brown, bill long and dagger-like, black with a variable dull reddish base. Legs and feet bright red. **Immature:** Similar to adult though duller. In particular, the wing-coverts are dull blackish-blue with brighter blue spangling and the underparts are browner, less orange.
VOICE Typical call is a thin, high-pitched *tlip* or *tsee*.
HABITAT/BEHAVIOUR Found in any habitat adjacent to fresh, brackish or saltwater habitats including mangroves, rivers lakes and pools. Generally seen alone or in pairs. Tame, often perching on a conspicuous perch by water from which it locates its prey. Feeds on a variety of insects, small fish and amphibians. The nest is excavated in a bank, usually adjacent to water and consists of a tunnel leading to a nesting chamber.
RANGE/STATUS Regional Endemic, occurring in Madagascar and the Comoros. Not globally threatened. Represented in Madagascar by the nominate subspecies which is endemic and is common in suitable habitat throughout except in the south where it is rare. Found from sea level to around 1,800m. It is sometimes considered conspecific with the mainland African species Malachite Kingfisher *A. cristata*, from which it differs by being rather duller orange underneath, slightly darker duller blue on the back, having green in the crest and having a bill that is largely dark.
WHERE TO SEE Common and widespread and easily found at most sites with suitable aquatic habitats such as Lake Alarobia in Antananarivo.
SIMILAR SPECIES Unmistakable.

177a. Little Swift, adult in flight.

177b. Little Swift, adult in flight.

178a. Madagascar Malachite Kingfisher, adult.

178b. Madagascar Malachite Kingfisher, adult.

179 Madagascar Pygmy Kingfisher *Ceyx madagascariensis*

DESCRIPTION Size: 12-14cm. A small, bright, rufous and white forest kingfisher. Sexes alike, plumage varies slightly with age. **Adult:** Head and upperparts bright rufous with a violet gloss which is most obvious on the crown, ear-coverts, back and rump. There is an inconspicuous buff patch on the lores and a conspicuous white stripe on the side of the neck. Flight feathers dark grey. Underparts snowy-white except for orange-rufous sides to the breast and flanks. Iris dark brown, bill long and dagger-like, bright red. Legs and feet bright red. **Immature:** Similar to adult though duller, lacking the violet gloss and initially showing a pale-tipped, blackish bill.
VOICE Typical call is a harsh, high-pitched *chweip* or *tsieck*.
HABITAT/BEHAVIOUR Found in evergreen humid forest and dry deciduous forest wherever there is a dense understorey including secondary growth. Generally secretive and usually solitary though often approachable. Locates prey from a perch in the understorey from which it dives down to snatch the prey before returning to a perch to eat it. Feeds on a variety of invertebrates and small vertebrates including frogs, lizards and chameleons. The nest is excavated in a bank often at the edge of a forest trail or road and consists of a tunnel leading to a nesting chamber.
RANGE/STATUS Endemic to Madagascar. Not globally threatened. Two subspecies are currently recognised, the nominate which is widespread in suitable habitat in the east, north and north-west and is most common in the east and *C. m. diluata* which is known from a single specimen taken near to Sakaraha in the south-west in the 1970s. Observations in the west and south are very irregular. Found from sea level to around 1,500m.
WHERE TO SEE Common though elusive in suitable habitat in the east. Best looked for at Périnet-Analamazaotra and at Ranomafana. It is frequently seen from the road at both of these sites. Also regularly seen at Ampijoroa Forest Station.
SIMILAR SPECIES Unmistakable.

180 Madagascar Bee-eater *Merops superciliosus*

DESCRIPTION Size: 27-33cm, including tail-streamers up to 7cm. A medium-large, green bee-eater. Sexes alike, plumage varies slightly with age. **Adult:** Crown and nape bronze-green. Rest of the upperparts green with a blue tinge to the tertials and black tips to the primaries and secondaries. Shows a conspicuous black mask, bordered above by a narrow creamy-yellow supercilium. Chin and a stripe across the cheek creamy yellow, throat pale rufous. Rest of underparts pale green. Tail green with pointed projections on the central tail feathers extending for up to 7cm. Iris dark red, bill long and black, legs and feet brownish. **Immature:** Similar to the adult though duller and lacks the elongated central tail-projections.
VOICE Typical call is a soft, rolling *cheleep cheleep* which is frequently uttered, especially by flying birds and is often the first sign that the species is present.
HABITAT/BEHAVIOUR Found in a variety of open habitats such as forest clearings and rice paddies. Generally gregarious often perching conspicuously. Insect prey is taken on the wing. Nests colonially, the nests are excavated in a bank such as a river bank, roadside embankment or ravine.
RANGE/STATUS Occurs in East Africa and Madagascar. Not globally threatened. Represented in Madagascar by the nominate subspecies which is common to East Africa and the Comoros. Common in suitable habitat throughout the island and present year round, though may undertake migrations to Africa. Found from sea level to 1,700m. This species is sometimes considered conspecific with Blue-tailed Bee-eater (*M. philippinus*) and even Blue-cheeked Bee-eater (*M. persicus*) but this group is more usually treated as three closely related allospecies.
WHERE TO SEE Common and widespread in open habitats.
SIMILAR SPECIES Could only be confused with the vagrant European Bee-eater from which it is easily separated by its predominantly green plumage with a rufous as opposed to yellow throat. European Bee-eater shows a very distinctive and unmistakable plumage pattern.

179a. *Madagascar Pygmy Kingfisher, adult.*　　　　179b. *Madagascar Pygmy Kingfisher, adult.*

180a. *Madagscar Bee-eater, adult.* 180b *(inset) Madagascar Bee-eater, adult.*

181 European Bee-eater *Merops apiaster*

DESCRIPTION Size: 25-28cm, including tail-streamers up to 3cm. A medium-large bee-eater. Sexes similar, plumage varies slightly with age. **Adult male:** Forehead whitish, extending as a narrow, pale blue supercilium above the black mask. Crown, nape and mantle rich chestnut, oval patch on the scapulars and rump golden-buff. Wings green, tinged blue, with chestnut secondary-coverts but for the green lesser coverts and black tips to the primaries and secondaries. Tail green with short, pointed central tail-projections. Throat bright yellow, separated from the turquoise underparts by a black bar. Iris dark red, bill long and black, legs and feet brownish. **Adult female:** Similar to the male though scapulars tinged green, and the chestnut coverts have green fringes. **Immature:** Similar to the adult though duller, and lacks the elongated central tail-projections.
VOICE Typical call is a soft, rolling, liquid *prruip* which is frequently uttered, especially by flying birds and is often the first sign that the species is present.
HABITAT/BEHAVIOUR Found in a variety of open habitats such as forest clearings and rice paddies. Generally gregarious often perching conspicuously. Insect prey is taken on the wing.
RANGE/STATUS Occurs in Europe, and northern and southern Africa. European populations migrate to southern Africa to winter though there is also a resident population in southern Africa. Not globally threatened. In Madagascar it is a rare vagrant with just one record from Ifaty, north of Toliara in November 1995. Observed once at sea level.
WHERE TO SEE A rare vagrant with just one record and consequently no regular sites.
SIMILAR SPECIES Could only be confused with Madagascar Bee-eater from which it is easily separated by its very distinctive plumage pattern.

182 Broad-billed Roller *Eurystomus glaucurus*

DESCRIPTION Size: 29-32cm. A medium-sized roller. Sexes alike, plumage varies slightly with age. **Adult:** Head and upperparts dark rufous with a lilac wash on the face. Primaries, secondaries, greater secondary-coverts and primary-coverts deep blue. Uppertail-coverts and tail paler azure blue, the latter darker distally. Underparts lilac except for the blue lower belly and undertail-coverts. Iris brown, bill short and stubby, bright yellow. Legs and feet greyish-green. **Immature:** Similar to adult though duller and paler, appearing washed-out.
VOICE Very vocal, giving a variety of harsh, discordant, guttural calls. Typical calls include a harsh *griaow grak grak grak grak grak*, a long rattling *kik-k-k-k-k-k-r-r-r-r* and in flight a loud *grik-grik-grik*.
HABITAT/BEHAVIOUR Prefers forest edge, open forest and sparsely wooded areas. Usually found alone or in small groups. Often perches conspicuously, remaining motionless for long periods. Typically hunts from a perch, swooping down to take prey, though also often feeds on the wing at dusk. Feeds largely on invertebrates, though will take small vertebrates such as lizards. Nests in a tree cavity.
RANGE/STATUS Occurs in sub-Saharan Africa. Not globally threatened. In Madagascar it is represented by the nominate subspecies which is an endemic breeder, breeding in Madagascar and migrating to eastern Africa during the Austral winter (May-September). Common throughout Madagascar except on the high plateau where it is rare. Found from sea level to 1,500m.
WHERE TO SEE Common and widespread between October and April. Easily seen at most birding locations.
SIMILAR SPECIES The only roller occurring in Madagascar. It is easily recognised by a combination of the overall rufous and lilac plumage, the bright yellow bill and blue wings.

181a. European Bee-eater, adult non-breeding.

181b. European Bee-eater, adult breeding in flight.

182a. Broad-billed Roller, adult.

182b. Broad-billed Roller, adult.

183 Short-legged Ground-roller *Brachypteracias leptosomus*

DESCRIPTION Size: 38cm. A large, thickset, roller-like species which appears large headed with a puffed-out throat. Sexes alike, plumage varies slightly with age. **Adult:** Crown, nape and upperparts brown with, in good light, a purple gloss to the crown and nape and a bronze-green gloss to the rest of the upperparts. Tail bronze-brown, darker distally with white tips to all but the central tail feathers. The wings show prominent white crescent-shaped markings on the coverts which are outlined in black. The noticeably large eye is bordered above by a conspicuous white supercilium. Rest of face brown with prominent white spotting. Throat brown with white spotting and streaking, the feathers of the throat often held puffed-out. A prominent white breast-band extends on to the side of the neck and separates the throat from the rest of the underparts which are white with brown barring, heaviest on the upper breast and flanks. Iris brown, bill stout, blackish, legs and feet yellowish-brown. **Immature:** Similar to adult though duller with a less conspicuous breast-band and a plainer, brown head.
VOICE Song is a very long series of hollow, resonant notes *hoop* repeated monotonously with intervals between each note being approximately one second, though the notes are sometimes repeated more rapidly. Often sings from a perch 5-15m above the ground. Contact call is a quiet *kroo-kroo*.
HABITAT/BEHAVIOUR Inhabits eastern evergreen humid forest, particularly undisturbed humid areas. Secretive and difficult to locate if not calling. Usually found singly or occasionally in pairs. Spends long periods perched motionless often 3-5m off the ground. Drops down to the ground to take prey which largely consists of invertebrates such as snails and small vertebrates.
RANGE/STATUS Endemic to Madagascar. Globally Threatened and currently classified as **Vulnerable** due to habitat destruction and degradation. Monotypic. It is a scarce and secretive resident in evergreen humid forests in the east between Iharanä in the north and Andohahela in the south. Found from sea level to 1,100m, rarely higher.
WHERE TO SEE Difficult to find outside the breeding season. Best searched for in forest around Ambanizana on the Masoala Peninsula, at Vohiparara in Ranomafana National Park and at Mantadia.
SIMILAR SPECIES Easily separated from the other ground-rollers by its more arboreal habits.

184 Scaly Ground-roller *Brachypteracias squamigera*

DESCRIPTION Size: 27-31cm. A medium-sized, long-legged, terrestrial Ground-roller. Sexes alike, plumage varies with age. **Adult:** Distinctive head pattern with a prominent black central crown-stripe, black eye-stripe behind the eye and a prominent black line from below the eye which extends diagonally across the ear-coverts. Rest of the head pale buff with prominent black feather centres which gives a scaly effect. Broad rufous hind collar, rest of the upperparts green with prominent white crescent-shaped markings on the scapulars and coverts which are outlined in black. Primaries and secondaries darker with a white patch at the base of the primaries. Tail rufous, basally bronze-green with a subterminal black bar and bright blue tips to all but the central feathers. Underparts white with prominent black feather centres to each feather giving a scaly effect though this is less pronounced on the belly and undertail-coverts which are largely off-white. Iris brown surrounded by bare pink skin which extends as a patch behind the eye. Bill heavy and blackish, legs and feet pink. **Immature:** Similar to the adult though shows more extensive rufous on the upperparts, duller buffy underparts and a less well-defined head pattern.
VOICE Song is a series of soft, hollow, hoots - *hoo-oo* - which are inflected upwards slightly (though this is not noticeable from a distance) and repeated every 5 to 10 seconds. The notes are somewhat higher pitched than Short-legged Ground-roller. Also gives a dry churring call, possibly in alarm.
HABITAT/BEHAVIOUR Inhabits lowland eastern evergreen humid forest, particularly undisturbed areas with dark undergrowth and good leaf litter. Secretive and difficult to locate if not calling. Usually found singly or occasionally in pairs. Runs along the forest floor and will also perch on low horizontal branches, particularly when calling. Diet consists of invertebrates and small vertebrates. The nest cavity is situated at the end of a tunnel 0.5-1m long which is excavated in loose soil on an embankment.
RANGE/STATUS Endemic to Madagascar. Globally Threatened and currently classified as **Vulnerable** due to habitat destruction and degradation. Monotypic. It is a scarce and secretive resident in evergreen humid forests the length of the eastern escarpment. Found from sea level to 1,000m.
WHERE TO SEE Best searched for in forest around Ambanizana on the Masoala Peninsula or at Mantadia.
SIMILAR SPECIES Easily separated from the other ground-rollers by its distinctive green and rufous plumage with prominent scaly markings and the long, pink legs.

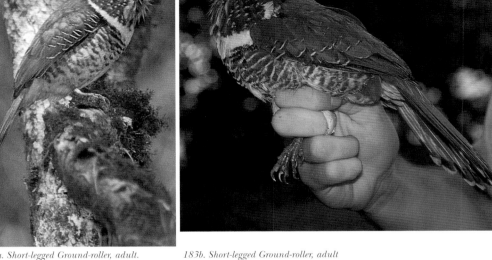

183a. Short-legged Ground-roller, adult.

183b. Short-legged Ground-roller, adult

184a. Scaly Ground-roller, adult.

184b. Scaly Ground-roller, adult.

185 Pitta-like Ground-roller *Atelornis pittoides*

DESCRIPTION Size: 27cm. A medium-sized, long-legged, terrestrial Ground-roller. Sexes alike, plumage varies with age. **Adult:** Distinctive head pattern with a broad black eye-stripe which merges with the blue ear-coverts and extends as a band around the breast, though sometimes broken in the centre of the breast. A white supercilium above and behind the eye is bordered above by black which in turn is flecked with white. Crown blue with sparse white flecking. Rest of upperparts green except for darker brownish primaries which show a white basal patch, pale blue outer tail-feathers and an orange-rufous hind collar. This extends on to the breast sides, along the flanks and forms a second band across the breast, bordering the blue breast-band. Throat, belly and undertail-coverts white. Iris brown, bill heavy and blackish, legs and feet pink. **Immature:** Differs from adult in generally duller plumage and some dark smudging on the throat.
VOICE Song is a series of soft, quiet, muffled hoots, *gwoop* or *whop*, each note rather shorter than that of Scaly Ground-roller. Calls are typically repeated every 4 to 10 seconds. Also gives a sharp scolding alarm call which consists of a combination of dry tacking notes and a loud scolding hiss, *tac tac tashhhhhhrr*.
HABITAT/BEHAVIOUR Inhabits eastern evergreen humid forest, particularly undisturbed areas with dark undergrowth, a good leaf litter and plentiful dead wood. Also occurs in degraded forest and even in plantations adjacent to primary forest. Secretive and difficult to locate if not calling. Usually found singly or occasionally in pairs. Habits similar to Scaly Ground-roller.
RANGE/STATUS Endemic to Madagascar. Currently considered **Near Threatened** due to habitat loss and degradation. Monotypic. It is a locally common though secretive resident in evergreen humid forests in the north and in the eastern evergreen humid forest belt and is the most common and widespread ground-roller. Found from sea level to 2,000m though most common from 800 to 1,600m.
WHERE TO SEE Difficult to find outside the breeding season. In the breeding season birds may be located by call and are usually easy to find at Ranomafana. May also be seen at Mantadia and at Amber Mountain in the north where it is the only ground-roller.
SIMILAR SPECIES Easily separated from the other ground-rollers by its distinctive plumage, the blue, black and white head-markings rendering it unmistakable.

186 Rufous-headed Ground-roller *Atelornis crossleyi*

DESCRIPTION Size: 25cm. A small, long-legged, terrestrial Ground-roller. Sexes alike, plumage varies with age. **Adult:** Head entirely rufous. Upperparts green except for an iridescent pale-blue patch on the lesser coverts which may be concealed when at rest and darker brownish primaries which show a white basal patch. Underparts rufous, becoming green on the lower belly and undertail-coverts and with a prominent, black, 'cut-throat' marking which is broadest in the centre of the throat and is finely streaked with white. Iris brown, bill blackish and finer than other ground-rollers. Legs and feet dark brown. **Immature:** Differs from the adult in generally duller plumage and a poorly defined black throat-patch.
VOICE Song is a series of clear hoots, *woop* or *whop*, which are typically repeated every 3 to 6 seconds. Each note sounds slightly inflected, almost disyllabic and the call is higher-pitched than those of the the three other eastern evergreen humid forest Ground-rollers.
HABITAT/BEHAVIOUR Inhabits eastern evergreen humid forest, particularly areas with dark tangled undergrowth, dense thickets and fallen timber especially in the dense understorey of mossy montane forest. Secretive though not especially shy and difficult to locate if not calling. Usually found singly or occasionally in pairs. Runs along the forest floor, foraging on the ground. Diet consists of insects.
RANGE/STATUS Endemic to Madagascar. **Globally Threatened** and currently classified as **Vulnerable** due to habitat destruction and degradation. Monotypic. It is a scarce resident in evergreen humid forests in the east though its apparent scarcity may be due in part at least to its retiring nature and skulking habits, making it easy to overlook. All recent well-documented records come from above 900m, suggesting the species prefers montane habitats and it is most frequent above 1,200m where it is usually the only ground-roller and is common in places.
WHERE TO SEE Difficult to find outside the breeding season. In the breeding season may be located by call at Ranomafana, especially at Vohiparara, at Perinet-Analamazaotra and at the nearby Maromizaha forest. Also present at some other eastern evergreen humid forest sites such as Marojejy.
SIMILAR SPECIES Easily separated from the other ground-rollers by its small size and largely green and rufous plumage.

185a. *Pitta-like Ground-roller, adult.* 185b (inset) *Pitta-like Ground-roller, adult.*

186a. *Rufous-headed Ground-roller, adult.*   186b. *Rufous-headed Ground-roller, adult.*

187 Long-tailed Ground-roller *Uratelornis chimaera*

DESCRIPTION Size: 47cm. A long-tailed and long-legged terrestrial ground-roller. Sexes similar, plumage variation with age unknown. Chocolate-brown ear-coverts form a prominent mask which is bordered above by a pale buff supercilium and below by a broad white submoustachial-stripe. A broad chocolate-brown malar stripe continues across the breast isolating the white throat and is bordered behind by a white stripe which is a continuation of the sub-moustachial. Crown and upperparts pale buff streaked with black. Wings tinged olive with paler blotches, a prominent sky-blue patch in the wing-coverts and a white patch at the base of the primaries. Extraordinarily long buff tail is marked with numerous dark brown bars and shows sky-blue outer tail-feathers. Breast and belly pale buff. Iris brown, bill blackish, long legs and feet pale pinkish-brown.
VOICE Generally quiet and seldom heard. Typical call is a series of five to six quiet, descending *tuc* notes. Also sometimes gives a variety of muffled hoots including a series of chuckling *too-tuc too-tuc too-tuc* notes which end in a harsh scratching note and are only audible from close range. The calls are similar to Madagascar Coucal, though are typically softer and delivered more rapidly.
HABITAT/BEHAVIOUR Dry, spiny forest with much leaf litter and little herbaceous growth. Can tolerate more open, slightly degraded forest providing there are areas of shade and leaf litter. Terrestrial and usually solitary or in pairs. Forages by probing into the leaf litter. Feeds mainly on insects. Usually runs to escape danger, frequently perches on low branches, especially when calling and spends long periods motionless. Often cocks its tail, especially when alarmed. The nest cavity is situated at the end of a tunnel *c.* 1m long which is excavated in the sand.
RANGE/STATUS Endemic to Madagascar. Globally Threatened and currently classified as **Vulnerable.** Threatened by habitat loss and trapping and predation by rats. Monotypic. Uncommon and restricted to a coastal strip *c.* 70km wide and *c.* 200km long between the Mangoky and Fiherenana rivers in south-west Madagascar. None of its habitat is protected at present. Found from sea level to 100m.
WHERE TO SEE Most readily seen in the spiny forest north of Toliara in the vicinity of Ifaty. Without the assistance of local guides the species can be very difficult to locate.
SIMILAR SPECIES An extremely distinctive ground-roller which cannot be confused with any other species.

188 Cuckoo-Roller *Leptosomus discolor*

DESCRIPTION Size: 50cm. A large roller-like bird with a distinctly large head. Sexes differ and plumage varies with age. **Adult male:** Head grey with a black eye-stripe and a narrow black crown-stripe which is joined to the eyes by a black band. Upperpart green with a purple sheen except for the flight feathers which are dark blue. Underparts grey becoming pale grey on the belly and undertail-coverts. In flight the undersides of the wings are white except for blackish wing-tips. Iris brown, bill small, blackish, legs and feet pale yellowish-brown. **Adult female:** Head brown, finely and extensively barred with dark brown. Upperparts dark brownish-green with chestnut tips and fringes to most feathers which are especially prominent on the scapulars and wing-coverts. Underparts buff with prominent blackish-brown spotting. **Immature:** Similar to female though duller.
VOICE Extremely vocal, the loud far-carrying song being one of the characteristic sounds of Madagascar. Typical song, which is often given in flight by a displaying male, is a series of three or four loud whistles which drop slightly in tone and intensity - *weeell weeell weeell weell.* Also gives a woodpecker-like *woo we-we-we-wer-war* possibly when alarmed and a quiet though very distinctive whistled contact call, *wheeu.*
HABITAT/BEHAVIOUR Dry and wet forests including degraded areas, parkland and even plantations, though rarely far from primary forest. Usually seen singly, in pairs or in small groups. Spends much of the time in the canopy, often motionless, though frequently flies above the canopy, particularly when displaying when it circles, often high, calling. Feeds mainly on large insects and small vertebrates which are gleaned from the canopy. Nests in a tree cavity.
RANGE/STATUS Regional Endemic, occurring in Madagascar and the Comoros. Not globally threatened. Represented in Madagascar by the endemic nominate subspecies which is common throughout except for the south where it is restricted to gallery forests. Found from sea level to 2,000m.
WHERE TO SEE Common and widespread. Present and relatively numerous at all forests sites though perhaps easiest to see in the dry forests of the west at sites such as Zombitse and Ampijoroa.
SIMILAR SPECIES Unlikely to be confused with any other species, though in flight the broad wings and slow flight recall a raptor at first glance. However, the unique shape and markings are highly distinctive.

187a. Long-tailed Ground-roller, adult.   187b. Long-tailed Ground-roller, adult.

188. Cuckoo-Roller. 188a (left) adult male. 188b (right) female/immature. 188c (inset) adult male in flight.

189 Madagascar Hoopoe *Upupa marginata*

DESCRIPTION Size: 32cm. Sexes differ slightly and plumage varies with age. **Adult male:** Orange-rufous head with elongated black-tipped crown feathers which may be raised to form crest. Orange-rufous neck merges into duller mantle. Rest of upperparts, including wings, black with broad white (variably tinged orange) bars. Tail black with white bar across centre. Underparts buffy orange becoming paler on breast, belly and undertail-coverts which are almost white. Iris brown, bill long, decurved, brown with a pink base. Legs and feet dark grey. **Adult female:** As male though duller. **Immature:** As female though duller.

VOICE Gives two distinctive calls. The first a soft, resonant, rolling purr which lasts for about one second repeated at regular intervals. The second a harsh, scolding growl *aaaahhhrrr.*

HABITAT/BEHAVIOUR Most common in heavily wooded margins of forest. May even occur well inside primary western forest. Usually seen singly. Forages on the ground where it walks busily, probing the ground with its long bill. Feeds mainly on insects. Nests in a tree cavity.

RANGE/STATUS Endemic to Madagascar. Not globally threatened. Common in the north, west and south, scarce on the high plateau and largely absent from east. Found from sea level to 1,500m. The taxonomy of the hoopoe complex is much debated. Madagascar Hoopoe is often treated as a subspecies of Eurasian Hoopoe (*U. epops*). However, the distinctive plumage, and in particular very different vocal characteristics of Madagascar Hoopoe, suggest that it merits specific treatment.

WHERE TO SEE Easily seen in the drier habitats of the west at sites such as Ifaty and Ampijoroa.

SIMILAR SPECIES Unmistakable. In flight, the broad wings and slow, floppy, undulating flight are characteristic and recognisable from a great distance.

190 Velvet Asity *Philepitta castanea*

DESCRIPTION Size: 14-16.5cm. A small, stocky passerine found in mid-storey. Sexes differ and the plumage of the male varies seasonally. **Adult male breeding:** Plumage velvety-black but for browner flight feathers and a concealed golden-yellow shoulder patch which is only exposed during display. Large, bright lime-green caruncle extending above the eye from the forehead to the rear of the ear-coverts. Caruncle protrudes upwards to form a laterally compressed wattle above bill. Lower part of the caruncle immediately over eye is bright sky blue though usually concealed except during display. Iris brown, bill black, legs and feet olive. **Adult male non-breeding:** Caruncle much reduced and velvety-black plumage concealed by broad yellow feather fringes giving a black and yellow scaly appearance. Face and throat unmarked and black. **Adult female:** Crown, nape and upperparts entirely olive. Dark olive ear-coverts and moustachial stripe contrast with paler, scaled yellow, submoustachial stripe and indistinct supercilium. Underparts off-white to yellow-olive with olive streaking giving a scaly effect. Centre of breast often more yellow and undertail-coverts unmarked creamy yellow. Bare parts as male but shows a narrow olive orbital-ring. **Immature:** Similar to the female, the male gradually acquiring the black plumage.

VOICE Typically gives a variety of thin, high-pitched calls. Usual call is a series of thin *weee-do* notes sometimes extending into a series lasting several seconds. Also gives quiet *tsip-tsip* notes and a thin *teeee* call.

HABITAT/BEHAVIOUR Primary evergreen humid forest and secondary and degraded forests. Unobtrusive species found singly or in small groups in the understorey. Feeds on small fruits and occasionally nectar and insects. Occupies small territories in breeding season where males appear to have communal display areas. Displays include flicking wings out to reveal yellow shoulder patches. The nest is a conspicuous pear shaped structure, usually 2-5m off the ground and suspended from a branch, sometimes over water.

RANGE/STATUS Endemic to Madagascar. Not globally threatened. Monotypic. In evergreen humid forests in north-west and along the entire length of the eastern forests where it is fairly common. Found from sea level to about 1,500m.

WHERE TO SEE Fairly common in east coast forest sites such as forest on the Masoala Peninsula and the easily accessible Perinet-Analamazaotra and Ranomafana.

SIMILAR SPECIES Male unmistakable. Female very similar to the largely allopatric Schlegel's Asity. Where their ranges overlap in forests of the north-west (Sambirano) the two must be separated with care. Female Velvet is larger and has a distinctive yellow submoustachial stripe and contrasting dark moustachial stripe both of which are lacking in female Schlegel's. In addition, female Schlegel's is shorter billed, shows obvious pink orbital-ring, has yellow fringes to flight feathers and has clearer yellow belly and undertail-coverts.

189a. Madagascar Hoopoe, adult.

189b. Madagascar Hoopoe, adult.

190a. Velvet Asity, adult male breeding.

190b. Velvet Asity, adult female.

191 Schlegel's Asity *Philepitta schlegeli*

DESCRIPTION Size: 12.5-14cm. A small, stocky passerine found in mid-storey and canopy. Sexes differ and plumage of the male varies seasonally. **Adult male breeding:** Head black with a large multi-lobed wattle (caruncle) around the eye which is mostly bright lime green, but sky-blue above and below the eye. Upperparts olive with a broad yellow patch on the upper mantle, limited black scaling on the mantle and darker flight feathers. Underparts entirely yellow, sullied with olive. Iris brown, bill black with a conspicuous orange gape. Legs and feet grey. **Adult male non-breeding:** Crown, nape and upperparts entirely olive with yellower fringes to the flight feathers and variable yellow and black markings on the upper mantle. Face and ear-coverts olive with paler mottling and an indistinct supercilium. Throat and breast off-white to yellow-olive with olive streaking giving a scaly effect. Belly and undertail-coverts unmarked yellow. Bare parts as male breeding but shows a distinct orbital-ring and a reduced caruncle. **Adult female:** Similar to non-breeding male though lacks the caruncle and the black and yellow markings on the back. Bare parts as male but shows a prominent pinkish-yellow orbital-ring. **Immature:** Similar to female. Some males with fully developed caruncles but otherwise resembling female plumage may be sub-adult males.
VOICE Song is quiet and distinctive and consists of a series of approximately seven to nine weak high-pitched notes which rise in pitch and fall at the end and lasts for 1 to 2 seconds.
HABITAT/BEHAVIOUR Occurs in evergreen humid forest in the north-west and dry deciduous forests in the west. An unobtrusive species generally found singly or in small groups. Often in the canopy though may also be seen lower in the understorey. Feeds largely on small fruits and nectar. The nest is a conspicuous, ragged, globular, woven structure usually 2-5m off the ground and suspended from a branch.
RANGE/STATUS Endemic to Madagascar. Currently considered **Near Threatened** on a global scale. Monotypic. Occurs in evergreen humid forest in the north-west (Sambirano) where it is reported to be common and in dry forests in the west where it is scarce and most frequently encountered in humid valleys and near limestone outcrops. Found from sea level to 800m.
WHERE TO SEE Widespread though generally scarce.
SIMILAR SPECIES The stocky, short-tailed appearance, and distinctive plumage make this species highly distinctive. Female very similar to the largely allopatric Velvet Asity, which see for differences.

192 Common Sunbird-Asity *Neodrepanis coruscans*

DESCRIPTION Size: 9.5-10.5cm. A small, short-tailed, sunbird-like species. Sexes differ; male plumage varies seasonally. **Adult male breeding:** Head bright blue with large, rectangular sky blue wattle around and behind eye where it is distinctly rounded at the rear. Below the eye, the wattle is deep ultramarine blue. Upperparts dark metallic blue except for yellowish-fringed greater coverts and secondaries and yellow-fringed brownish primaries. Underparts dull yellow variably sullied with olive, brightest on the flanks and undertail-coverts. Distinct grey mottling on the breast. Iris brown, bill long, strongly decurved and very fine at the tip, black with a conspicuous ultramarine base to the upper part of the upper mandible and a bright pale green base to the lower mandible. Legs and feet greyish-olive. **Adult male non-breeding:** Head and upperparts olive green lacking or with a vestigial wattle, underparts paler olive grey with bright yellow flanks and undertail-coverts. Retains some blue in the uppertail-coverts and wing-coverts. Bare parts as male breeding except the bill is all black. **Adult female:** As non-breeding male but lacks blue in the upperparts. **Immature:** As female. As with other asities, some apparently female-plumaged birds with well developed wattles occur.
VOICE Rapid, strident, high-pitched *sisisisisisi*. Also gives single *si* notes and more drawn out *swee*.
HABITAT/BEHAVIOUR Occurs in the eastern evergreen humid forests. An extremely active species generally found singly or in small numbers. Often calls from the canopy though may also be seen moving through the understorey. Forages at flowers, often in parasitic *Bakerella* spp., presumably feeding on nectar and possibly insects attracted to the flowers. The nest is an untidy suspended structure, usually a few metres above the ground.
RANGE/STATUS Endemic to Madagascar. Not globally threatened. Monotypic. Occurs in evergreen humid forest along the entire length of the eastern forests where it is fairly common. Found from sea level to 1,400m, scarcer below 700m and is replaced by Yellow-bellied Sunbird-Asity in montane or mossy forest where the two species occur together.
WHERE TO SEE Fairly common in east coast forest sites, such as Perinet-Analamazaoatra and Ranomafana.
SIMILAR SPECIES Most likely to be confused with Yellow-bellied Sunbird Asity, which see.

191a. Schlegel's Asity, adult male breeding.

191b. Schlegel's Asity, adult female.

192a. Common Sunbird-Asity, adult male breeding.

192b. Common Sunbird-Asity, adult male non-breeding.

193 Yellow-bellied Sunbird-Asity *Neodrepanis hypoxantha*

DESCRIPTION Size: 9-10cm. A small, short-tailed, sunbird-like species. Sexes differ and the plumage of the male varies seasonally. **Adult male breeding:** Crown and nape bright blue with a large, conspicuous, rectangular sky-blue wattle which extends around and behind the eye and is lime green around the eye. Upperparts dark metallic blue except for duller brownish-black flight feathers. Underparts bright golden yellow. Iris brown, bill long, decurved and very fine at the tip, black with a conspicuous ultramarine base to the upper part of the upper mandible which is surrounded by pale green and a bright pale green base to the lower mandible. Legs and feet brown. **Adult male non-breeding:** Head and upperparts olive-green, lacking or with a vestigial wattle, underparts bright yellow with some indistinct olive streaking on the breast sides and flanks. Retains some blue in the uppertail-coverts and wing-coverts. Bare parts as male breeding except bill is all black. **Adult female:** As non-breeding male but lacks blue in the upperparts. **Immature:** As female though may show more olive suffusion on the breast. As with other asities, some apparently female- plumaged birds with well-developed wattles occur.
VOICE Typical call is a very high-pitched, clipped metallic *tip* which is almost insect like. The *tip* call is often given in a long series and sometimes accelerates into a rapid series *tip-tip-tip-tip-tip* and then decelerates. Juveniles give a thin *seee* call when begging.
HABITAT/BEHAVIOUR Occurs in humid montane forests. Behaviour little known but similar to Common Sunbird-Asity.
RANGE/STATUS Endemic to Madagascar. Currently considered **Endangered** on a global scale due to the deforestation of much of its original habitat. Monotypic. Occurs patchily in montane forests in the east. Observed at altitudes above 1,000m and is commoner at higher altitudes up to 2,000m. Generally occurs at higher altitudes than Common Sunbird-Asity.
WHERE TO SEE The most accessible site where the species is seen regularly is Vohiparara in Ranomafana National Park (where the species occurs alongside Common Sunbird-Asity). Best searched for by checking flowering plants, especially pink *Bakerella* spp. flowers. Most easily detected by call. May also be seen at Marojejy and Maromizaha near to Perinet-Analamazaotra.
SIMILAR SPECIES The small size, short tail, long, strongly decurved bill and distinctive plumage make this species unlike any other except the closely related Common Sunbird-Asity. Common Sunbird-Asity is larger with a longer more strongly decurved bill. Voice is a useful tool for separating the two species (see relevant sections). In breeding plumage, males are best distinguished by underpart colour which is clear bright yellow in Yellow-bellied, duller and marked with grey mottling in Common. In addition, the wattle of Yellow-bellied is larger, squarer-ended and with a green central section. Yellow-bellied also lacks the yellow greater covert and secondary fringes of Common and instead shows uniform deep blue upperparts with blackish flight feathers. Females, non-breeding males and immatures are best separated by underpart colouring, size and bill shape. In Yellow-bellied the underparts are clear bright yellow with at most some light and indistinct olive streaking on the sides of the breast and flanks. In Common the underparts are dull olive with contrasting yellow flanks and undertail-coverts. Female Souimanga Sunbird is superficially similar but is larger and much longer tailed.

194 Madagascar Bush Lark *Mirafra hova*

DESCRIPTION Size: 13cm. A typical lark. Sexes and all plumages alike. Crown buff streaked with dark brown. A prominent off-white supercilium and crescent under the eye contrast with the dark brown eye-stripe and moustachial-stripe. Ear-coverts off-white streaked darker. Upperparts brown with darker blackish-brown streaking, particularly on the mantle and scapulars. Tail brown with buff outer fringes to the outer tail-feathers. Underparts whitish with prominent blackish streaking on the throat and upper breast. Iris brown, bill fleshy-pink, short and stout, legs and feet pink.
VOICE Vocal species, the melodious song has a liquid quality and is usually given in a hovering song-flight.
HABITAT/BEHAVIOUR Occurs in open habitats including grassland, sparsely wooded areas and lake edges and is frequently seen on the road. Usually found in pairs or small groups foraging on the ground. Feeds on seeds and small insects. Nests on the ground, the nest is constructed from grass.
RANGE/STATUS Endemic to Madagascar. Not globally threatened. Common in suitable habitat throughout the island. Found from sea level to 2,500m.
WHERE TO SEE Common and easy to see. Frequently seen on the road during journeys.
SIMILAR SPECIES Only lark occurring in Madagascar and unlikely to be confused with any other species.

193a. Yellow-bellied Sunbird-Asity, adult male breeding.

193b. Yellow-bellied Sunbird-Asity, adult male non-breeding.

194a. Madagascar Bush Lark, adult.

194b. Madagascar Bush Lark, adult.

195 Mascarene Martin *Phedina borbonica*

DESCRIPTION Size: 15cm. A large stocky martin which in flight shows a slightly forked tail and broad triangular wings. Sexes alike, plumage varies slightly with age. **Adult:** Head and upperparts grey-brown with indistinct darker shaft-streaks. Wings darker blackish-brown. Underparts whitish, heavily streaked with dark brown on the chin, throat and breast and lightly streaked on the belly and undertail-coverts which are largely white. Iris dark brown, bill black, legs and feet dark grey. **Juvenile:** Similar to adult though shows white tips to the tertials.
VOICE The song is a soft twittering warble which is usually given in flight. Calls include a sharp *phreeezz* and short *chip* notes given as contact calls.
HABITAT/BEHAVIOUR Occurs in a variety of open, forested and wetland habitats. Usually found in small groups either foraging on the wing or perched, often close to water. Feeds on small insects. The nest is constructed from twigs and other vegetable matter and is situated on a ledge above water, in a little-used building, cave or similar location.
RANGE/STATUS Regional Endemic, occurring in Madagascar, Réunion and Mauritius. Not globally threatened. In Madagascar it is represented by the endemic subspecies *P. b. madagascariensis* which has a longer bill than the nominate race, and is paler, particularly on the undertail-coverts, and more clearly streaked. It is common in suitable habitat throughout the island. Although present all year, the birds in Madagascar are somewhat migratory, undertaking local and long distance migrations with birds reaching the African mainland most years. Breeding may occur on Pemba Island off the Kenya coast, though this is not proven. Found from sea level to 2,400m.
WHERE TO SEE Common and easy to see.
SIMILAR SPECIES Most likely to be confused with Brown-throated Sand Martin from which it differs in its larger size, slower flight and distinctly streaked underparts.

196 Common Sand Martin *Riparia riparia*

DESCRIPTION Size: 12cm. A small, slim martin which in flight shows a slightly forked tail. Sexes alike, plumage varies slightly with age. **Adult:** Head and upperparts brown, chin and throat white separated from the white lower breast and belly by a brown breast-band. Iris dark brown, bill black, legs and feet blackish. **Juvenile:** Similar to adult though upperparts shows narrow pale buff fringes.
VOICE The typical call is a characteristic dry rasping *tchrrip.*
HABITAT/BEHAVIOUR Occurs in a variety of open habitats, particularly around water. A scarce visitor to Madagascar, usually seen singularly. Feeds on small insects.
RANGE/STATUS Breeds right across the Northern Hemisphere in North America, Europe and Asia, wintering in South America, sub-Saharan Africa and southern Asia. Not globally threatened. In Madagascar the birds occurring are presumably of the nominate subspecies. It is a scarce visitor to Madagascar with just a handful of records during the austral summer at sites including Ihotry Lake and Maroantsetra.
WHERE TO SEE A rare visitor which is most likely to be found by checking hirundines, particularly around wetlands, during the austral summer.
SIMILAR SPECIES Differs from the similarly sized Brown-throated Sand Martin by the white throat and distinctive brown breast-band. Alpine Swift shows similar plumage but is unlikely to cause confusion due to its much larger size and long, sickle-shaped wings.

195a. Mascarene Martin, adult.

195b. Mascarene Martin, adult.

196. Common Sand Martin, adult.

197 Brown-throated Sand Martin *Riparia paludicola*

DESCRIPTION Size: 12cm. A small, slim martin which in flight shows a slightly forked tail. Sexes alike, plumage varies slightly with age. **Adult:** Head and upperparts brown, chin, throat and upper breast paler grey-brown merging into the white lower breast and belly. Iris dark brown, bill black, legs and feet blackish. **Juvenile:** Similar to adult though upperparts shows narrow pale buff fringes.
VOICE A fairly quiet species. The song is a weak, high-pitched twitter. The typical call is a repeated, weak *svee-wee* and a louder oscillating *pirirer.*
HABITAT/BEHAVIOUR Occurs in a variety of open habitats, particularly close to water. Usually found in small groups either foraging on the wing or perched, often close to water. Feeds on small insects. Nests alone or commonly in colonies. The nest is excavated in a sand or earth bank.
RANGE/STATUS Occurs in north-east and sub-Saharan Africa, India and southern Asia. Not globally threatened. In Madagascar it is represented by the endemic subspecies *R. p. cowani* which is smaller than the nominate, with less grey underparts and a pale grey-white rather than dull brown throat. It is common in suitable habitat in the north-west, east and the high plateau. Found from sea level to 2,400m, though it is scarce at altitudes below 500m.
WHERE TO SEE Widespread though somewhat localised. Common in marshes between Moramanga and Perinet-Analamazaotra and along the river and in wetlands at Ranomafana.
SIMILAR SPECIES Could be confused with Mascarene Martin or the scarce Common Sand Martin, which see for differences.

198 Barn Swallow *Hirundo rustica*

DESCRIPTION Size: 18cm. A long-tailed slender swallow which in flight shows a deeply forked tail and whitish underwings. Sexes alike, plumage varies slightly with age. **Adult:** Head and upperparts metallic blue except for the forehead and chin and throat which are rusty red. Tail shows elongated outer tail-feathers giving the tail a deeply forked appearance and there is an indistinct white sub-terminal bar in the tail formed by white inner webs to the feathers which are only visible from above when the tail is spread. Underparts whitish separated from the reddish throat by a blue breast-band. Iris dark brown, bill black, legs and feet blackish. **Juvenile:** Similar to adult though duller and lacking the elongated outer tail-feathers.
VOICE Has a varied vocabulary, though typical calls include a high-pitched twittering and a disyllabic *tsee-wit.*
HABITAT/BEHAVIOUR Occurs in a variety of open habitats, particularly around water. A scarce visitor to Madagascar, usually seen singly. Feeds on small insects.
RANGE/STATUS Breeds right across the Northern Hemisphere in North America, Europe and Asia, wintering in South America, sub-Saharan Africa and southern Asia. Not globally threatened. In Madagascar the birds occurring are presumably of the nominate subspecies. It is a scarce visitor to Madagascar with just a handful of scattered records during the austral summer, including several records in the Toliara area.
WHERE TO SEE A rare visitor which may occasionally be found in the Toliara and Ifaty areas during the austral summer.
SIMILAR SPECIES The reddish throat and dark breast-band contrasting with the white underparts and underwing-coverts is unique among Malagasy hirundines.

*7. Brown-throated Sand Martin, adult.

*8. Barn Swallow, adult.

199 Madagascar Wagtail *Motacilla flaviventris*

DESCRIPTION Size: 19cm. A large wagtail. Sexes and all plumages similar though female and immature average paler than the male. **Adult:** Grey crown and nape, the former bordered below by a prominent though narrow white supercilium. Dark grey eye-stripe and moustachial. Rest of head grey but for a white crescent under the eye and a variable whitish spot on the ear-coverts. Rest of upperparts mouse grey, more olive on the rump and uppertail-coverts. Wings and tail blackish brown with an indistinct, whitish, greater covert wing-bar, whitish tertial fringes and prominent white outer tail-feathers. White at the base of the flight feathers shows as a prominent white wing-bar in flight. Underparts white with a prominent lemon-yellow wash across the belly and flanks and a narrow black band across the upper breast which joins the moustachial-stripes enclosing some white on the neck sides. Iris brown, bill blackish, legs and feet dark grey.
VOICE Frequently heard, the usual call is a loud melodious buzzy phrase, *trrree trrree-oou*, which is frequently repeated and is sometimes followed by a melodious phrase, *tsee-eee-wee-oo tsee-wee-oo*. Calls are given from the ground, a perch or in flight.
HABITAT/BEHAVIOUR Occurs in open habitats especially those near to water and even in towns and villages. Not shy, usually found in pairs or small groups. Walks jerkily on the ground when foraging. Feeds on small invertebrates. The bowl-shaped nest is usually situated close to the ground in a variety of locations such as dense foliage, a tree fork, rock crevice or under a roof, but nearly always near to water.
RANGE/STATUS Endemic to Madagascar. Not globally threatened. Monotypic. Common in suitable habitat throughout the island except in the south where it is uncommon. Found from sea level to 2,500m.
WHERE TO SEE Common and conspicuous and easy to see at many sites.
SIMILAR SPECIES The only wagtail occurring in Madagascar and unlikely to be confused with any other species.

200 Ashy Cuckoo-shrike *Coracina cinerea*

DESCRIPTION Size: 24cm. A typical cuckoo-shrike. Sexes differ and plumage varies slightly with age. Two subspecies. **Adult male nominate:** Blackish hood encompasses the whole of the head, chin, throat and neck. Upperparts grey, darker on the flight feathers. Tail grey, darker on the outer tail-feathers which show white at the tip and on the underside. Underparts uniform pale grey. Iris dark reddish-brown, bill, legs and feet blackish. **Adult female nominate:** The blackish hood of the male is replaced with grey and the upperparts are paler than on the male. **Immature nominate:** Similar to the female though the wing-coverts are edged with buff. *C. c. pallida* is similar to the nominate though is paler, the male also differing in showing a grey hood which is separated from the pale grey underparts by a whitish area and white undertail-coverts. The female and immature differ from the nominate subspecies in overall paler plumage.
VOICE Frequently heard, the usual song is very distinctive, consisting of a series of hard notes followed by a series of fluted notes which decrease in volume and gradually tail off - *kyup kyup kyup kyup kyup teeteetee-tee-tee-tee*. Often repeated several times, the second part of the phrase sometimes being replaced by a series of *kick-oo* notes.
HABITAT/BEHAVIOUR Occurs in lowland and mid-altitude evergreen humid forest, dry forest and gallery forest. Accompanies mixed-species flocks where it is usually to be found in the canopy. Feeds on a variety of invertebrates. The shallow, bowl-shaped nest is usually placed on a horizontal branch high in a tree.
RANGE/STATUS Regional Endemic, occurring in Madagascar and the Comoros. Not globally threatened. Represented in Madagascar by two endemic subspecies: the nominate form which is common in suitable habitat in the north-west, east and on the high plateau and *C. c. pallida* which is common in suitable habitat in the west and south. Found from sea level to 1,600m.
WHERE TO SEE Fairly common and relatively easy to see at many sites including Perinet-Analamazaotra, Ranomafana, Ampijoroa and Berenty.
SIMILAR SPECIES The only cuckoo-shrike in Madagascar. May be confused with Tylas or the *Xenopirostris* vangas. Differs from the latter three species in plumage pattern and, importantly, in lacking the large laterally compressed bill. Tylas Vanga is best separated by its darker plumage which shows olive tones to the upperparts and usually a buff or orange wash to the underparts.

199a. Madagascar Wagtail, adult.

199b. Madagascar Wagtail, adult.

200a. Ashy Cuckoo-shrike, adult male nominate.

200b. Ashy Cuckoo-shrike, adult male nominate.

201 Madagascar Bulbul *Hypsipetes madagascariensis*

DESCRIPTION Size: 24cm. A slender, medium-sized dark bulbul. Sexes and all plumages similar. Plumage mostly dark slate-grey, with a black cap, lores and chin. Tail and wings slightly browner. Bill orange, with a dark tip to the upper mandible. Iris dark brown, feet and legs dull horn.
VOICE Usual call is a conversational, thrush-like, three-note *tchi-churr-tchi*, given by several individuals in a group at the same time, in flight and perched. Also a characteristic single cat-like mewing call which may be difficult to locate.
HABITAT/BEHAVIOUR Found very commonly in forest and second growth, less common in savanna or around habitation. Often perches high in trees in small groups, feeding on fruit or insects, or seen flying across forest gaps. Nest is built from plant matter, usually low down.
RANGE/STATUS Regional Endemic, occurring in Madagascar, the Comoros and Aldabra. Not globally threatened. Represented on Madagascar by the endemic nominate subspecies which is abundant over the whole island, from sea level to 2,000m at least.
WHERE TO SEE Any forest or second growth.
SIMILAR SPECIES The dark grey plumage in combination with the orange bill make this species unmistakable.

202 Long-billed Greenbul *Phyllastrephus madagascariensis*

DESCRIPTION Size: 17.5-20cm. A medium-sized understorey insectivore. Sexes similar, plumage varies slightly with age, two subspecies. **Adult:** Head shows a dull dark eyestripe and narrow pale supercilium, more conspicuous in front of the eye. Upperparts dull, dark green-brown, paler and greyer in the western subspecies *P. m. inceleber*. Wings slightly darker than upperparts, with indistinct pale yellow fringes to the primaries and secondaries. Underparts dull off-white, with a yellow wash over the throat and breast, darker, olive on the belly, flanks and undertail-coverts. Iris mid-brown, bill dark grey-brown, long and tweezers-like, with a hook tip; male's bill is noticeably longer than the female's. Legs and feet brown. **Juvenile:** Similar to adult though duller and browner above, and supercilium and eyestripe less well marked and the underparts are less yellow. In addition, the bill is paler and shorter than the adult's.
VOICE The alarm is a short 'chacking' rattle. Song is a long melodious series of notes (based on irregular series of *whit* and 'chirrip' notes) usually given from *c.* 10m up, often with a few well-separated *tchip* notes before it. Contact call is a short characteristic *chep*, often repeated, and a short rattle.
HABITAT/BEHAVIOUR In primary western or eastern forest and adjacent secondary areas. Feeds in dense vegetation (dead leaf clumps, fallen trees, palm-frond bases) between 1-20m up. Feeds on insects and very small vertebrates. A regular member of mixed-species flocks.
RANGE/STATUS Endemic to Madagascar. Not globally threatened. The two subspecies are very common in mid-altitude evergreen humid forest and western forest, although restricted to primary forest and adjacent secondary habitats. Found from sea level to about 1,300m in eastern forest, rarely up to 1,500m. In western forest, from sea level to about 1,000m.
WHERE TO SEE Common at most forest sites, including Perinet-Analamazaotra, Ranomafana, Ampijoroa, Kirindy and Masoala.
SIMILAR SPECIES Most likely to be confused with Spectacled Greenbul from which it can be distinguished by the longer, more hooked bill, duller green-brown upperparts, less yellow underparts, lack of conspicuous spectacle, and deeper, 'chacking' calls.

201. Madagascar Bulbul, adult.

202a. Long-billed Greenbul, adult.

202b. Long-billed Greenbul, adult.

203 Spectacled Greenbul *Phyllastrephus zosterops*

DESCRIPTION Size: 16-17cm. A medium-sized understorey insectivore. Plumage varies slightly with age, two subspecies. **Adult nominate:** Fairly bright olive-green on head, neck and mantle, darker brownish-olive on the wings and tail. Variable olive-green below with yellow throat and upper breast (also rather variable in extent and coloration), forming a yellow throat-patch and an olive-green breast-band. Head shows a slight dark eyestripe and a wide, broken yellow spectacle and line to the bill. **Adult *P. z. fulvescens*:** The pattern is similar but the bird is much greyer and slightly paler in the Amber Mountain subspecies. Iris mid-brown, culmen dark brown, lower half of upper mandible and lower mandible pinkish-brown. **Juvenile:** Similar to adult, often with a shorter tail, indistinct spectacles and a duller throat-patch.
VOICE Quite loud but very high-pitched seeping and twittering noises, quite unlike any Long-billed Greenbul calls but very similar to the three other small Malagasy greenbuls. Usual call is a high-pitched, slightly hoarse *tsit* repeated irregularly, also a spluttering *ptrrr*. Song is an irregular descending series of similar notes.
HABITAT/BEHAVIOUR The understorey of primary eastern evergreen humid forest, characteristically feeding 0.5-5m from the ground, frequently perching on vertical stems of understorey shrubs and feeding on insects sally-gleaned from the undersides of leaves. Almost always in small groups, often with other greenbuls or in mixed-species flocks with other understorey species. The cup-shaped nest is made from moss and other vegetation and is typically situated low in a shrub.
RANGE/STATUS Endemic to Madagascar. Not globally threatened. The nominate subspecies is very common in low and mid-altitude eastern evergreen humid forest between sea level and about 1,100m, rare above this. Subspecies *P. z. fulvescens* is found in the Sambirano and at Amber Mountain.
WHERE TO SEE Common at Perinet-Analamazaotra, Ranomafana, on the Masoala Peninsula and at Amber Mountain.
SIMILAR SPECIES From Long-billed Greenbul by shorter, mostly pink bill, brighter yellow on the throat and breast, olive-green breast-band, brighter green on the back, high 'seeping' calls and habit of feeding from stems of low shrubs. From Dusky Greenbul by distinctly green back, wider band of yellow on the throat, much wider yellow spectacle, longer tail (in adult) and lack of ground-feeding habits.

204 Appert's Greenbul *Phyllastrephus apperti*

DESCRIPTION Size: 15cm. A small, mostly terrestrial insectivore. Plumage variation unknown. **Adult:** Above greenish with a brown tinge to the mantle. Cap and cheeks blue-grey, with a buffy-white or pale grey supercilium, which is broad and diffuse (though faint) behind the eye. Eyestripe (to eye) dark grey, faint behind the eye. Underparts except throat warm yellow, brightest on the flanks, centre of belly whitish. Throat white except for small black speckles at the bill junction. Wings short, slightly darker than the back, with slight pale yellow fringes to primaries and secondaries. Iris dark brown. Narrow bill pale pink, except for dark culmen; often held pointing slightly upwards. Legs rather thin, short, and pale horn.
VOICE Call is a high shivering trill, similar to Grey-crowned Greenbul.
HABITAT/BEHAVIOUR Forages in small groups in the low understorey of deciduous western forest, often walking along the ground with its wings drooped. Feeds on small invertebrates gleaned from leaves and branches and the ground.
RANGE/STATUS Endemic to Madagascar. Globally Threatened and currently classified as **Vulnerable.** Monotypic. Very rare and localised. Known only from Zombitse and Vohibasia forest in south-western Madagascar, but seems to be scarce over much of this area, except in the south-eastern corner of Zombitse. Observed at altitudes of around 600 to 800m.
WHERE TO SEE The only site is Zombitse and Vohibasia forests, near Sakaraha, recently gazetted as a National Park. Appert's Greenbul is most easily found near the main road to the east of the village of Andranomaitso, 15km east of Sakaraha.
SIMILAR SPECIES Similar to Grey-crowned Greenbul, but stockier, much less arboreal, with a better defined pale supercilium and brighter peachy-yellow underparts. The two species' ranges are not known to overlap.

203a. Spectacled Greenbul, adult nominate.

203b. Spectacled Greenbul, adult nominate.

204. Appert's Greenbul, adult.

205 Grey-crowned Greenbul *Phyllastrephus cinereiceps*

DESCRIPTION Size: 14cm. A small to medium-sized understorey insectivore. Sexes alike, plumage varies slightly with age. **Adult:** Cap and cheeks blue-grey, nape and back olive-green, wings and tail slightly darker with dull, pale yellow fringes to the primaries and secondaries. Throat white, rest of the underparts are pale yellow though darker, more olive on the flanks and undertail-coverts. Head lacks a dark eyestripe, instead showing paler grey lores. Iris mid-brown, rather short and slim bill dark horn on the upper mandible, pale pink on the lower mandible. Legs and feet mid-grey. **Juvenile:** Acquires the grey crown and cheeks and the white throat gradually, having an olive-green crown and whitish-yellow throat in the early stages, when they are identifiable as juveniles by their orange gape-lines and short tails.
VOICE As with the other small greenbuls, single or multiple high-pitched *tsip* calls and spluttering trills. The song, delivered from a shrub-layer perch, is a series of spluttering and seeping calls.
HABITAT/BEHAVIOUR Usually feeds in the understorey of montane evergreen humid forest, often in mixed flocks with Spectacled Greenbul (in their narrow range of altitudinal overlap) and Wedge-tailed Jery. Forages in small shrubs, on the ground and characteristically on mossy tree-trunks, hopping up like a nuthatch. The bowl-shaped nest is built in a fork of a small horizontal branch, 1-2m off the ground.
RANGE/STATUS Endemic to Madagascar. Globally Threatened and currently classified as **Vulnerable**. Monotypic. A montane greenbul, rarely found below 800-1,000m, and most common in moist montane forest between 1,000 and 1,700m, along the length of the eastern evergreen humid forest.
WHERE TO SEE Fairly common at Ranomafana, (e.g. Vohiparara) and also at Mantadia and Maromizaha.
SIMILAR SPECIES A small and slim greenbul, distinguished from Spectacled Greenbul by its shorter thinner bill, grey head with no conspicuous yellow eye-ring or dark eyestripe, and white throat. Often feeds by clinging to vertical mossy stems. Usually present at higher altitudes than Spectacled Greenbul. For distinction from Appert's Greenbul, see that species.

206 Dusky Greenbul *Phyllastrephus tenebrosus*

DESCRIPTION Size: 14-15cm. A small, mostly terrestrial insectivore. No known plumage variation. Crown, nape, mantle, wings and tail dark dull olive-brown (appearing slightly more greenish when well-lit). Shows a narrow whitish-yellow eye-ring, broken in front of and behind the eye. Throat with an oval strip of bright yellow, breast, flanks and belly similar colour to upperparts. Centre of belly and vent paler brown-yellow. Iris mid-brown, bill fairly short, dull pale pinkish-orange except for dark culmen. Legs pale fleshy pink. Shape rather rotund, with strong fairly long legs, a full belly and a rather short tail.
VOICE Like the other small greenbuls, a series of quiet, high-pitched hissing and twittering calls. Single contact call a quiet *tseip*, similar to Madagascar Yellowbrow but quieter. Groups call with a series of notes of a rhythm rather like that of Common Sunbird-Asity, but deeper and more inflected.
HABITAT/BEHAVIOUR Mostly terrestrial or in low shrubs, in the understorey of lowland or mid-altitude evergreen humid forest. Hops rapidly along the ground like a Madagascar Yellowbrow, but flies more, between perches and across paths or obstructions. Not restricted to dense understorey. Sometimes in company with other ground or low understorey species.
RANGE/STATUS Endemic to Madagascar. Globally Threatened and currently classified as **Endangered**. Monotypic. Seems to be extremely scarce, in low or mid-altitude evergreen humid forest. Recorded recently at sites between Marojejy and Ranomafana, but probably present in all large evergreen humid forest blocks between sea level and 1,000m.
WHERE TO SEE Recent records from Perinet-Analamazaotra, Ranomafana and the Masoala Peninsula. However, it appears to be extremely scarce at these sites and is seldom observed.
SIMILAR SPECIES Similar to Spectacled Greenbul, but much more terrestrial, with longer, more robust legs, fuller belly and a shorter tail. Upperparts and underparts are darker (though this is often difficult to judge in dull forest understorey), the breast is almost the same colour as the upperparts (dull olive-green on Spectacled Greenbul) and the yellow on the throat is narrower and more contrasted with the darker breast and head. The spectacle is distinctly narrower, and the bill slightly thicker. Juvenile Spectacled Greenbul is brighter green above, with wider spectacles, more yellow on the throat and with weaker legs and a longer tail. They feed very rarely on the ground. Short-tailed juvenile Spectacled Greenbuls would almost always be accompanied by adults and be food-begging. Juvenile White-throated Oxylabes are terrestrial, with rather dark olive-tinged rufous upper- and underparts and a buffy-white throat, but they have longer tails, lack the narrow eye-ring and have dark, rather long bills, usually with an obvious yellow gape.

05. *Grey-crowned Greenbul, adult.*

06. *Dusky Greenbul.*

207 Red-tailed Vanga *Calicalicus madagascariensis*

DESCRIPTION Size: 14cm. A small tit-like vanga. Plumage varies with sex and age. **Adult male:** Crown, nape, mantle, scapulars, greater-coverts and tertials grey, lesser and median-coverts, rump and uppertail-coverts brick-red. The tail is also brick-red, except for inner webs of the central feather which are grey-brown. Primaries and primary-coverts blackish, fringed greyish. There is a wide black patch around the eye, extending to the base of the bill, and a narrow white band over the forehead. Ear-coverts white, chin and throat black, forming neat bib up to lower margin of ear-coverts. Rest of underparts whitish, often with a brick-red suffusion on flanks. Iris dark brown, bill blackish, legs and feet dark grey. **Adult female:** Crown, upper ear-coverts and nape mid-grey, contrasting with olive-brown mantle and scapulars. Wing feathers and inner webs of tail feathers darker brown; rump, uppertail-coverts and outer webs of tail feathers brick-red. Area around eye is off-white, forming a conspicuous eye-ring. Lower ear-coverts and sides of neck are buffy, throat whitish contrasting with broad buffy breast-band, grading to whitish on belly. Bare parts as for male. **Juvenile:** Similar to female though shows buff shaft streaks and tips to upperpart feathers.
VOICE In eastern evergreen humid forest and in north, males sing *per-whew* like a wolf-whistle, the syllable dropping. In west, males typically sing *pew-poo-whee* or *oo-oo-whi*, last syllable higher. Another different song heard in west (near Morondava): *plee-plee tich-che-weh*. Calls are equally variable; both sexes use wooden *tk-tk trrt* or *trrk tikatik*, repeated many times, and males have a hissing, swearing *kschrrr*.
HABITAT/BEHAVIOUR Found in eastern evergreen humid forest, western deciduous forest and sparingly in southern subdesert. Will use fairly degraded habitat. Usually found in pairs or small groups, often in mixed-species flocks. Forages for medium-sized insects gleaned from leaves or caught by short sally-gleans.
RANGE/STATUS Endemic to Madagascar. Not globally threatened. Monotypic. The commonest vanga in the eastern evergreen humid forest. In west, its distribution more patchy. Fairly common in north, around Ankarana, and occurs near Bemaraha to as Ifaty, about 30km north of Toliara. Found from sea-level to 1,800m.
WHERE TO SEE Common at Perinet-Analamazaotra, Mantadia, Ranomafana and Lombitse.
SIMILAR SPECIES Adult males only likely to be confused with Red-shouldered Vanga, from which they differ by having dark, not yellow, iris and grey greater coverts instead of brick-red. Female could be confused with female Red-shouldered Vanga, but they too have dark irides, and lack red lesser coverts of female Red-shouldered Vanga. Female could also easily be confused with Red-tailed Newtonia, which see.

208 Red-shouldered Vanga *Calicalicus rufocarpalis*

DESCRIPTION Size: 14-15cm. A small, recently described, tit-like Vanga. Larger overall than Red-tailed Vanga, with longer bill, tail and tarsi, and shorter wings giving it rather elongated appearance. Plumage varies with sex, other variation unknown. **Adult male:** Pale grey crown, nape, and mantle. Tertials, primaries and secondaries brown, lesser, median and greater wing-coverts brick-red. Tail appears pale brick-red. The ear-coverts are white, as on Red-tailed Vanga, but more white on forehead. Black bib sometimes more extensive than that of Red-tailed Vanga, extending further down breast and up over the sides of neck. Rest of underparts whitish with pale pink suffusion over breast and flanks. Iris pale lemon yellow, bill black, legs and feet mid-pinkish-grey. **Adult female:** Upperparts even olive-grey-brown with pale reddish rump and tail (reddish colour restricted to outer webs), and brick-red lesser and median-coverts. Broad pale buffy eye-ring, blends into slightly darker buffy lower ear-coverts. Throat whitish, rest of underparts washed buff, blending to whitish on belly. Bare parts as for the male.
VOICE The alarm or contact call is a peevish *karr-trkkk*, initial note like a sunbird, dropping into a low wooden rattle. This may be modified into a rolling *kwoiroikk*, again with a slight rattle on the end. A contact call may be a loud *ksisisisisususu*, a rapid, dropping, rolling cadence with a slight whistling quality. Male song is a loud *tyuh-tee* or *pu-teer*, the second note louder and more whistled. Female often gives contact call immediately after male song in duet-like fashion. At a distance, the second note is more clearly audible and sounds not unlike the song of Hook-billed Vanga *Vanga curvirostris*.
HABITAT/BEHAVIOUR Found in euphorbia scrub, so far in a very restricted area in SW. Forages low, catching small invertebrates by sally-gleaning and gleaning.
RANGE/STATUS Endemic to Madagascar. Global conservation status not yet evaluated. Known from a very small area and may be globally threatened. Monotypic. Distribution not known beyond the small area of forest between the main Antananarivo-Toliara road and St Augustin, although the species may well occur elsewhere in similar habitat. Found at altitudes around 100m.
WHERE TO SEE Best looked for on the road to St Augustin, in euphorbia scrub on hillsides.
SIMILAR SPECIES See under Red-tailed Vanga.

7a. Red-tailed Vanga, adult male.

207b. Red-tailed Vanga, adult female/immature.

8. Red-shouldered Vanga; adult female, left, adult male, right.

209 Rufous Vanga *Schetba rufa*

DESCRIPTION Size: 20cm. A medium-sized vanga. Plumage varies with sex and age. Two subspecies. **Adult male nominate:** Entire head, nape and upper breast glossy black. Mantle, scapulars, and tail bright rufous-brown, somewhat darker on the flight feathers. Rest of underparts white. Iris dark red, bill blue-grey, legs and feet blue-grey. **Adult female nominate:** Cap, to just below eye, and upper nape glossy black. Mantle, scapulars, wing feathers and tail mid-rufous-brown. Cheeks, chin, throat and upper breast variably tinged grey, in a shadow of the male pattern. The rest of the underparts are white. **Juvenile:** Resembles the female but distinguishable when young by the black of the crown being variably mixed with brown and the rufous on the wings being duller. **S. r. occidentalis:** Differs only in a slightly longer, heavier bill.
VOICE A species with an amazing variety of beautiful calls. Possible song, is a smooth whistled rippling trill down the scale. Also gies a loud and ringing *ti-ti-tong* (the *tong* much lower) may also be a song, the female singing *twit-twit-twit* in response. Call is a nasal *eesh*, probably an alarm. Also gives a *whip whip whip whip whip* which is accompanied by bill-snapping.
HABITAT/BEHAVIOUR Found in lowland eastern evergreen humid forest and western deciduous forest, in areas with open understorey and large trees. Requires primary forest. Usually found in family groups or mixed-species flocks, often low down. Feeds on medium or large invertebrates and small vertebrates gleaned from the ground or sally-gleaned from leaves or branches. The cup-shaped nest is usually placed in the fork of a tree.
RANGE/STATUS Endemic to Madagascar. Not globally threatened. Nominate subspecies found in lowland eastern evergreen humid forest from the far south to near Sambava, *S. r. occidentalis* in western forest from near the Sambirano to the Mangoky. Appears to be absent from the far north. Rather patchily distributed in evergreen humid forest, but often very common in primary western deciduous forest. Found from sea level to about 800m.
WHERE TO SEE Scarce at Ranomafana and the Masoala peninsula, very common at Kirindy, Ampijoroa and Zombitse.
SIMILAR SPECIES A very distinctive species, unlikely to be mistaken if seen well. Several calls resemble those of Helmet Vanga, but those of the Rufous Vanga are finer and more modulated.

210 Hook-billed Vanga *Vanga curvirostris*

DESCRIPTION Size: 25-29cm. A medium-large vanga. Plumage varies with age. Two subspecies. **Adult nominate:** Front half of crown white, rear half (in a band extending up from just in front of the eye) glossy black. Rest of head, nape, sides of neck and collar white. Mantle, scapulars and wing feathers black, the median and greater coverts with wide white outer fringes and tips forming a white panel in the closed wing. The primaries and secondaries have narrower white fringes. Tail basal two-thirds mid-grey, subterminal band black, tip white. The underparts are white, with a grey tinge to the flanks. Iris dark red, large bill black with a small pale spot behind the hooked tip. Legs and feet dark blue-grey. **Juvenile:** Similar to adult but the black upperparts are variably marked with brown. The base of the bill is grey in young juveniles. *V. c. cetera:* Longer bill with a wider white collar, extending to the upper mantle.
VOICE The song is a very penetrating, high-pitched, single-note whistle. Somewhat ventriloquial and very difficult to place. Often two birds may be heard counter-singing. The call of western birds is usually two or three loud bill-claps uttered while calling *karr-karr-karr* followed by an angry *tew-tew-tew-tew*. Eastern and southern birds often omit the *karr*-notes and bill-claps. Contact call is a quiet *pew*.
HABITAT/BEHAVIOUR A predatory passerine, found in dense scrub, degraded and primary forests (east, west and south) and even in plantations far from forest. Hunts in dense vegetation. Feeds on large insects and small vertebrates, including medium-sized chameleons, which it dismembers by wedging into horizontal forks and pulling off limbs. Discreet species and difficult to find when not calling. The bulky, cup-shaped nest is usually placed in the fork of a tree.
RANGE/STATUS Endemic to Madagascar. Not globally threatened. The nominate subspecies is rather thinly scattered in evergreen humid forest and degraded areas and plantations in the lowlands and is more common in the west. *V. c. cetera* is common in spiny forest from the Mangoky south and east to near Fort-Dauphin. Found from sea level to 1,500m though scarce above about 1,000m.
WHERE TO SEE Present but difficult to find at Perinet-Analamazaotra, Mantadia, Ranomafana and Masoala. Much more common and conspicuous at Ampijoroa, Kirindy, Ifaty and Berenty.
SIMILAR SPECIES The pied plumage and heavy bill render it unmistakable.

209a. Rufous Vanga, adult male.

209b. Rufous Vanga, adult female.

210a. Hook-billed Vanga, adult.

210b. Hook-billed Vanga, adult.

211 Lafresnaye's Vanga *Xenopirostris xenopirostris*

DESCRIPTION Size: 24cm. A medium-sized vanga. Plumage varies with sex and age. **Adult male:** Cap, ear-coverts and chin glossy black, isolated from the upperparts by a white collar. Mantle, scapulars, upperwing-coverts and tail mid-grey tinged brown (though can appear darker in some lights), flight feathers somewhat darker and browner. Tail uniform mid-grey-brown. Underparts other than the chin are off-white. Iris dark brown, bill remarkable, bluish-white (sometimes with a dark spot at the tip), flattened and heavy, with a slight gap between the mandibles when closed. Legs and feet, dark greyish-blue. **Adult female:** Differs from the male in showing off-white lores and forecrown, white cheeks and dull mid-grey-brown upperparts. **Juvenile:** Similar to female but upperparts browner.

VOICE The most frequent calls are a loud, whistled and highly characteristic *tseeang* or *tseeeo*, and a loud *whip*, often delivered from the top of a *Didierea* stem. Also a slow *chuck chuck chuck* rather like a Chabert's Vanga. Other calls are less distinctive but are mainly downwardly-inflected whistles.

HABITAT/BEHAVIOUR Found in primary spiny forest and coastal euphorbia scrub, and adjacent degraded areas. Feeds by searching methodically in nooks in dead and broken wood, especially under dead bark and in twigs; frequently close to the forest floor. Preys on large insects and small vertebrates. Often joins other large vangas in mixed-species groups. The cup-shaped nest is usually placed in the fork of a tree.

RANGE/STATUS Endemic to Madagascar. Not globally threatened. Monotypic. Found only in the southern subdesert biome, between just north of the Mangoky river to just east of Fort Dauphin. Found from sea level to 100m.

WHERE TO SEE Fairly common at Ifaty, near St. Augustin, Berenty, and Lake Anony.

SIMILAR SPECIES Very similar to Van Dam's Vanga. Male Lafresnaye's is paler on the mantle and wings, and all ages and sexes of Van Dam's Vanga appear to have mostly black bills. Recent reports of Van Dam's Vanga within the range of Lafresnaye's are probably incorrect as there appears to be a clear distributional difference between the species, with a six-hundred kilometre gap between the Mangoky and Ankarafantsika with no *Xenopirostris* vangas at all.

212 Pollen's Vanga *Xenopirostris polleni*

DESCRIPTION Size: 24cm. A medium-sized vanga. Plumage varies with sex and age. **Adult male:** Entire head and throat glossy black with a black spur extending on to the upper breast. Collar white, mantle, scapulars, back and rump mid-grey tinged olive, wing-coverts and flight feathers dark grey, tail mid-grey. There is a narrow, pale blue eye-ring. The rest of the underparts are whitish, occasionally flushed with pale orange, sometimes tinged greyer. Iris dark red, bill bluish-white (bluer at the base), laterally flattened and powerful. Legs and feet strong, dark grey. **Adult female:** Similar to the male except that the blackish hood lacks the extension on to the upper breast, being restricted to the chin and throat, the breast is variably tinged orange, sometimes strongly. There is usually a white band below the hood lacking orange coloration, and the upperparts have a stronger olive tinge. **Juvenile:** Similar to the adult though very young juveniles are pale orange underneath, paler than the female, with a complete but slightly less extensive hood compared to the female. They have pale pink bills and a conspicuous orange gape. Birds that may be one-year-old males have a blotchy orange breast and some black spots on the breast.

VOICE Pollen's Vanga has a wide variety of calls, including the characteristic loud *Xenopirostris tseeang* or *tseeeo* and a loud *whip*. Other calls include a quiet *chuck-chuck-chuck* when alarmed, and a range of loud off-key whistles. A contact call sounds similar to Tylas Vanga, *whit-whit-whit*.

HABITAT/BEHAVIOUR Found in or adjacent to primary eastern evergreen humid forest, from lowland to sclerophyllous, where it feeds in a similar manner to the above species. It often joins other large vangas in mixed-species groups. The large cup-shaped nest is usually placed in the fork of a tree.

RANGE/STATUS Endemic to Madagascar. **Globally Threatened** and currently classified as **Vulnerable**. Monotypic. Rather patchy in distribution; quite common between 400 and 2,000m in the far south of the evergreen humid forest belt near Andohahela and as far north as Ranomafana, but scarce or apparently absent from many other forest blocks further north such as Mantadia, Masoala, Perinet-Analamazaotra and Marojejy.

WHERE TO SEE Can be seen at Ranomafana and Manantantely Forest Station near Fort Dauphin.

SIMILAR SPECIES The massive pale blue bill and complete black hood make this species easy to identify. Males could be confused with Ashy Cuckoo-shrikes and females with Tylas Vangas, but in both cases the bill is immediately diagnostic. Often occur in mixed groups with Tylas Vangas.

1a. Lafresnaye's Vanga, adult female.

211b. Lafresnaye's Vanga, adult male.

2a. Pollen's Vanga, adult.

212b. Pollen's Vanga, adult.

213 Van Dam's Vanga *Xenopirostris damii*

DESCRIPTION Size: 23cm. A medium-sized vanga. Plumage varies with sex and age. **Adult male:** Forehead, crown, and ear-coverts glossy black, isolated from the rest of the upperparts by a white collar. Mantle, scapulars, back, rump and tail dark charcoal-grey (may appear darker in some lights), wing-coverts and flight feathers blackish. Underparts entirely whitish. Iris dark red, bill thick, laterally flattened and dark charcoal-grey. Legs and feet dark grey. **Adult female:** Similar to male but the glossy black cap is less extensive, lacking completely on the lores and forehead where the feathers are buffy or whitish. The back is paler and browner and the breast and belly may be tinged with buff, contrasting with the whitish throat and sides of neck. **Juvenile:** Similar to the female but have larger buffy patches on the forehead, and the breast and belly are tinged more deeply pale brown.
VOICE Calls include the *Xenopirostris* whistle, *tseeang* or *tseeeo*, a loud *whip* and quieter whistling or clucking alarm or contact calls.
HABITAT/BEHAVIOUR Found only in or immediately adjacent to primary western deciduous forest, where it preys on medium-sized and large invertebrates which are found by breaking off loose bark, opening dead branches, investigating dead leaf clumps and opening insect refuges. It often joins other vangas and insectivores in mixed-species flocks. The large cup-shaped nest is usually placed in the fork of a tree.
RANGE/STATUS Endemic to Madagascar. Globally Threatened and currently classified as **Vulnerable.** Monotypic. Apparently has a very patchy distribution. Found only at Ankarafantsika (Ampijoroa Forest Station is a part of this) and at Analamera, in the far north-west. There is much suitable forest between the two sites that has not yet been thoroughly investigated for birds, in particular the type locality for the species, near Ambaro Bay, on the mainland near Nosy Bé. Found from sea level to 150m.
WHERE TO SEE Only likely to be seen at Ampijoroa, where its loud calls make it fairly easy to find.
SIMILAR SPECIES A species that is easy to identify within its range, given the massive flattened bill and dark cap, but *Xenopirostris* vangas outside the known range should be described carefully. Pollen's Vanga has a dark chin and throat and a pale bill, while Lafresnaye's is more similar to Van Dam's but has a pale bill and is paler overall.

214 Sickle-billed Vanga *Falculea palliata*

DESCRIPTION Size: 32cm. The largest vanga. Sexes alike, plumage varies with age. **Adult:** Head, neck and underparts white. Upperparts glossy black with the exception of the rump which is white. Iris dark brown, bill pale bluish-white, paler at the tip, long, narrow and strongly decurved. Legs and feet strong and dark grey. **Juvenile:** Similar to the adult though the black back and wing feathers are tipped with buff.
VOICE Groups often call together. A range of loud chortling, crying and harsh screeching noises, delivered in chorus, particularly when the group is alarmed or going to roost. The most characteristic call is a loud *waaah* like a baby crying. When not calling, a feeding group may remain remarkably inconspicuous, startling the observer by flying up from a tree calling vigorously.
HABITAT/BEHAVIOUR Found in or near (though occasionally some way from) primary western deciduous or southern spiny subdesert, where Sickle-billed Vangas are often the most noisy and characterful members of the bird community. They often form groups of three to ten, sometimes up to forty, especially when roosting in the dry season. Feeding groups often mix with White-headed Vangas. 'Sicklebills' use their long bills to probe into holes and crevices in dead and live trees, lever off bark, and glean insects from surfaces. When flying between trees, their wide rounded wings and hoopoe-like flight are characteristic. The large cup-shaped nest is built high in the fork of a tree.
RANGE/STATUS Endemic to Madagascar. Not globally threatened. Monotypic. Common in and near western deciduous forests and spiny forests all over the west and south, and even occurs in scrubby forest adjacent to evergreen humid forest in the north-east. Found from sea level to 800m.
WHERE TO SEE Common at Ampijoroa, Kirindy, Ifaty and Berenty.
SIMILAR SPECIES The large size, unique bill shape, white head and black back render this species °unmistakable.

213. Van Dam's Vanga. 213a (left) adult male. 213b (right) adult male. 213c (inset) female on nest.

214a. Sickle-billed Vanga, adult.

214b. Sickle-billed Vanga, adult.

215 White-headed Vanga *Artamella viridis*

DESCRIPTION Size: 20cm. A medium-sized vanga. Plumage varies with sex and age. Two subspecies.
Adult male nominate: Plumage all white except for glossy black mantle, rump (except for a narrow white bar) and tail. Iris dark brown, bill solid and almost triangular, laterally compressed and bluish-white, paler at the tip. Legs and feet dark grey. **Adult female nominate:** Similar to the male except crown, nape, cheeks, and throat tinged greyish, usually paler on the throat. There is also often a black line through the eye.
Juvenile: Similar to adult male, with white head and breast, though shows a dark crown, and wide brown fringes to the back feathers. Older individuals differ from adult females only by having much browner upperparts lacking gloss. *A. v. annae*: Probably only distinguishable by having a marginally longer bill.
VOICE A variety of loud chucking and whistling calls, including a loud short monosyllabic *whert* and a repeated *weetee woo*.
HABITAT/BEHAVIOUR Found in all native forest types, sometimes including areas and wooded areas far from native forest. Social, often joining mixed-species flocks with other vangas. Feeds on insects, fruit and seeds and rarely small vertebrates such as chameleons. It obtains food by investigating insect refuges under bark and epiphytes, breaking open dead twigs and gleaning and sally-gleaning from leaves and branches. The cup-shaped nest is built high in the fork of a tree.
RANGE/STATUS Endemic to Madagascar. Not globally threatened. Widespread and common in all forest types.The nominate subspecies is found in evergreen humid forest in the east, subspecies *A. v. annae* is found all over the west and south from the Sambirano southward. Found from sea level to 1,500m.
WHERE TO SEE Common at most forest sites, including Perinet-Analamazaotra, Mantadia, Ranomafana, Masoala, Kirindy, Ifaty and Berenty.
SIMILAR SPECIES Only likely to be confused with Lafresnaye's Vanga, which however always has some blackish on the rear of the crown, and greyish rather than black upperparts.

216 Chabert's Vanga *Leptopterus chabert*

DESCRIPTION Size: 14cm. A small vanga. Sexes alike, plumage varies with age. Two subspecies. **Adult nominate:** Crown, cheeks, forehead, nape, and entire upperparts glossy blue-black. There is a variably wide, bright blue area of bare skin around the eye which is turquoise above the eye and ultramarine below. Underparts pure white. Iris dark red, bill pale blue, legs and feet blackish. **Juvenile:** Similar to adult though lacks the blue eye-ring, and has white shaft-streaks and tips to the black feathers on the head, making the head look pale, with just a dark line through the eye, and white fringes to back and wing feathers. These fringes are gradually lost, older juveniles just showing white edges to the wing-coverts. *L. c. schistocercus*: Differs from the nominate in having the outer tail-feathers white for two-thirds of their length.
VOICE The call, often given by several members of a group, is a highly characteristic mechanical, rhythmical, repeated note, 2-3 per second: *tch-tch-tch-tch*. This is often the first sign of a group flying overhead.
HABITAT/BEHAVIOUR Found in all native forest types, secondary regrowth, scrubby vegetation and plantations, sometimes long distances from native forest, although not found in Antananarivo. Feeds either as a sally-gleaning insectivore, with mixed-species flocks, or as an accomplished aerial sally-feeder, rather like a woodswallow (Artamidae). When feeding aerially, makes long elegant swoops in the air in pursuit of flying insects, often around flowering trees such as eucalyptus or acacias. Flies long distances between foraging sites in small groups, occasionally up to 30, with a characteristic bounding flight. The cup-shaped nest is placed on a branch high above the ground, often near the end of a horizontal branch.
RANGE/STATUS Endemic to Madagascar. Not globally threatened. The nominate subspecies is frequent in eastern evergreen humid forest and common in all other forest types. Probably most abundant on the edges of primary western forest. Subspecies *L. c. schistocercus* is restricted to the south. Commonest below 1,000m though may occasionally be found higher.
WHERE TO SEE Common at all regular forest sites, such as Perinet-Analamazaotra, Mantadia, Masoala, Ampijoroa, Kirindy, Ifaty and Berenty.
SIMILAR SPECIES A small and easily identified vanga, only likely to be mistaken for female Blue Vanga. However Blue Vanga lacks the bright blue eye-wattle of Chabert's Vanga and is always blue rather than black above. They also always have a brilliant blue or blackish rather than pale blue bill. Juvenile may be confused with young Blue Vanga but the latter species shows an orange tinge on the breast.

215a. White-headed Vanga, adult male.

215b. White-headed Vanga, adult female.

216a. Chabert's Vanga, adult.

216b. Chabert's Vanga, adult.

217 Blue Vanga *Cyanolanius madagascarinus*

DESCRIPTION Size: 16cm. A small vanga. Plumage varies with sex and age. **Adult male:** Crown, nape, ear-coverts, mantle, scapulars, wing-coverts, back, rump and base of tail brilliant pale blue. Flight feathers and tip of tail blackish. There is a black line through the eye, extending to the base of the bill and slightly over the forehead and under the chin. Underparts bright white. Iris bright blue, bill brilliant pale blue with a dark tip and cutting edge, legs and feet blackish. **Adult female:** Crown, nape, mantle, scapulars, back and rump dull mid-blue, with a slight brown tinge. Wing feathers and tail blackish brown. The blackish mask extends around the eyes to the base of the bill. The underparts are off-white, variably washed buffy or even pale orange on the breast. The female's bill is dark brown, and the iris brownish. **Juvenile:** Similar to the female though mottled brownish on the ear-coverts, crown and back, slightly darker on the wings, with pale fringes to the upperwing-coverts, and is tinged orange on the sides of the upper breast.
VOICE The only call made regularly by this species is a very characteristic angry and vowel-less rattle, *tccccccch*, often repeated two or three times in succession.
HABITAT/BEHAVIOUR Found in and adjacent to primary evergreen humid forest and western forest. It appears to be absent from the southern subdesert. Feeds in mixed-species flocks, by gleaning and sally-gleaning from leaves and branches, and most characteristically from the ends of thin branches, from which it hangs upside-down before dropping off backwards and executing a smart loop up to a new branch. The cup-shaped nest is placed on a branch high above the ground, often near to the end of a horizontal branch.
RANGE/STATUS Regional Endemic, occurring in Madagascar and the Comoros. The only vanga to occur outside Madagascar. Not globally threatened. Represented in Madagascar by the endemic nominate subspecies which is common in western deciduous forest and in eastern evergreen humid forest from sea level to about 1,200m, rarely (where there are big trees) to 1,600m.
WHERE TO SEE Common at Perinet-Analamazaotra, Mantadia, Ranomafana, Amber Mountain, Masoala, Ampijoroa, and Kirindy.
SIMILAR SPECIES Difficult to mistake for any other species, through a combination of the size and the blue upperparts. Could possibly be confused with Chabert's Vanga, which see for differences.

218 Bernier's Vanga *Oriolia bernieri*

DESCRIPTION Size: 23cm. A medium-sized vanga. Plumage varies with sex, juvenile plumage unknown. **Adult male:** Entire plumage iridescent blue-black. Iris whitish, bill pale blue, legs and feet pale grey. **Adult female:** Entire plumage bright rufescent brown, brighter rufous on the wings, with narrow black bands on all feathers, most conspicuous on the breast and upperparts. These plumages are known to refer to these sexes for most individuals. However some sexually mature males show barred brown plumage.
VOICE Poorly known. It includes a harsh series of chattering calls not unlike a White-headed Vanga and a repeated *chew*.
HABITAT/BEHAVIOUR Present only in lowland evergreen humid forest, usually in flocks with other vangas. Characteristic feeding method is reminiscent of a large nuthatch or woodpecker, stripping dead bark and moss from branches, investigating nooks and crannies for invertebrates, and tossing clumps of dead material from the base of palm and Pandanus leaves.
RANGE/STATUS Endemic to Madagascar. Globally Threatened and currently classified as **Vulnerable**. Monotypic. Known mostly from the northern half of the evergreen humid forest belt, from Marojejy to about Zahamena, but with an old record in Vondrozo (south-east of Ranomafana). It seems to occur only to about 1,000m, and even then it is rather scarce and patchy where it does occur.
WHERE TO SEE The most accessible site is Ambanizana on the Masoala Peninsula, but enterprising spirits prepared to explore would probably find it in mid-altitude or lowland forest anywhere from Brickaville north. It has not yet been recorded from Mantadia, where it may occur.
SIMILAR SPECIES Both sexes are extremely distinctive; males might conceivably be mistaken for Crested Drongo but they have a shorter square tail, white as opposed to red irides, lack the crest and have completely different behaviour.

7. Blue Vanga, adult male.

8a. Bernier's Vanga, adult female.

218b. Bernier's Vanga, adult male.

219 Helmet Vanga *Euryceros prevostii*

DESCRIPTION Size: 28-31cm. A large and extremely distinctive vanga. Plumage varies with age. **Adult:** Head, upperwing-coverts, flight feathers, rump, outer tail-feathers and underparts solid blue-black. On some individuals the black breast grades into a sooty grey belly. Mantle, scapulars and central tail feathers bright rufous. Iris pale yellow, bill bright pale blue with a blackish tip, massive, laterally flattened, with a large casque. Legs and feet black. **Juvenile:** Black areas on adult are pale buff in the juvenile, while the rufous areas are dark brown. Somewhat older birds have brown primary and secondary wing feathers and black body plumage. The bill is pale horn on young juveniles.

VOICE The most common call is a pleasant descending ripple, *pipipipewpewpew pew,* like that of the Rufous Vanga but not as long or well-phrased. Another frequent call is a pair of short rather off-key warbles, of about 2 seconds, the first in a different key to the second. Contact calls include a short whistled *phu,* a higher *tseeah,* like a high Hook-billed Vanga, and a Rufous Vanga-like *eesh,* possibly as an alarm.

HABITAT/BEHAVIOUR Found only in lowland and the lower reaches of mid-altitude evergreen humid forest. Feeds mostly by sally-gleaning large insects and invertebrates from leaves and branches, or by seizing prey from the ground. Usually perches between 3 and 10m from the ground, and often mixes with other large vanga species in flocks. Often perches motionless for long periods, when it is difficult to locate. The nest is usually built in the fork of a tree.

RANGE/STATUS Endemic to Madagascar. Globally Threatened and currently classified as **Vulnerable.** Monotypic. Fairly common in most lowland evergreen humid forest from at least Marojejy to Mantadia. Appears not to occur further south. Found from sea level to about 1,000m. Often difficult to find. Field studies indicate that this species may be most closely related to Rufous Vanga.

WHERE TO SEE Common and relatively easy to find in Masoala, very rare and much less frequently seen in Mantadia. Searches in lowland forest south of the Antananarivo-Toamasina road may yield the species. The quiet but far-carrying calls are a good way of finding this species.

SIMILAR SPECIES Completely unmistakable.

220 Nuthatch Vanga *Hypositta corallirostris*

DESCRIPTION Size: 13-14cm. A small, highly distinctive vanga. Plumage varies with age and sex. **Adult male:** Entire plumage mid-blue except for a black mark between the bill and eye and slightly over the forehead, and variable pale buff on the vent. Iris mid-brown, bill bright orange-red with a slightly darker tip to the culmen. Legs and feet dark grey. **Adult female:** Blue hind crown, mantle, scapulars, secondary wing-coverts and tail, buffy forecrown, chin, centre of breast, belly and rump, and lacking the clear black eyestripe. **Juvenile:** Similar to female, but young males show increasing amounts of blue on the sides of the breast and head with age.

VOICE A series of quiet hissing or squeaking notes including a *tsee see see* and a quiet rippling trill which increases in volume.

HABITAT/BEHAVIOUR Found only in lowland evergreen humid forest, where it is fairly common and seen regularly. Climbs medium and large tree-trunks like a nuthatch, searching for food on bark. Never faces head-down. Also occasionally forages along horizontal branches. May sometimes climb relatively narrow stems or even lianas. Almost always encountered in mixed-species flocks. Often aggressive to other members of the species, and chases are seen frequently. The nest is a cup attached to the main trunk of a tree.

RANGE/STATUS Endemic to Madagascar. Not globally threatened. Monotypic. It is present the length of the eastern evergreen humid forest belt but more common in the north than the far south. Found from sea level to about 1,000m and reportedly up to 1,800m.

WHERE TO SEE Common at Perinet-Analamazaotra, Mantadia, Masoala and elsewhere in lowland or mid-altitude evergreen humid forest.

SIMILAR SPECIES The behaviour, blue coloration and red bill of this species make it difficult to confuse with any other.

19a. Helmet Vanga, adult.

20a. Nuthatch Vanga, adult male.

219b. Helmet Vanga, adult.

220b. Nuthatch Vanga, adult female.

221 Tylas Vanga *Tylas eduardi*

DESCRIPTION Size: 21cm. Plumage varies with age, and possibly with sex in western race. Two subspecies. **Adult nominate:** Crown dark olive-grey, rest of head black, separated from the dark olive-grey upperparts by a narrow white collar. Wings and tail darker blackish brown. Chin, and throat blackish (or very rarely white), forming a black hood. Narrow white band on the upper breast, rest of the underparts vary from whitish to sandy orange. Iris typically dark brownish though occasionally pale, bill, feet and legs lead-grey to black. **Juvenile:** Similar to adult, though chin slightly paler, pale buffy fringes to wing feathers, yellow gape and pale orange bill base. Some young birds show some whitish on the forehead. *T. e. albigularis:* Similar to nominate, but almost always has just the cap dark, with the ear-coverts, cheeks, chin and throat whitish. The breast is typically pale pink-orange, though some are bright orange and some are almost white. These subspecies have been recognised on the basis that most birds in the areas concerned conform to these descriptions. However, there are records of white-throated birds from the east (usually with deep orange breasts), and at least one record of a black-throated bird from the west. In addition, in the highlands such as at Ambohitantely, there are both white- and black-throated birds.
VOICE A highly characteristic series of notes including at least one that is 'whiplashed': tu-too whirrit'. The contact call is a quiet *whit-whit-whit* or *quip-quip*.
HABITAT/BEHAVIOUR Found in eastern evergreen humid forest and deciduous forest in the west. A common bird in mixed-species flocks in evergreen humid forest. Feeds in the canopy and upper shrub layer, rather like a cuckoo-shrike, taking small and medium-sized invertebrates from leaves and small branches. The cup-shaped nest is usually built in the fork of a tree.
RANGE/STATUS Endemic to Madagascar. Not globally threatened. Eastern form found throughout. The western race is rare, one of the least frequently seen western forest birds, despite having a relatively wide distribution, from near the Mangoky to almost Mahajanga. Few breeding-season records from the west.
WHERE TO SEE The eastern form is common at most evergreen humid forest sites such as Perinet-Analamazaotra, Mantadia and Ranomafana. The western race is rare and unlikely to be found except possibly at Andranomena reserve just north of Morondava.
SIMILAR SPECIES Narrow black bill, olive upperparts, black hood and orange underparts make this species simple to identify. However, individuals with white underparts might be taken for Ashy Cuckoo-Shrikes, from which they differ in the olive back. Normally coloured adults are very similar to female Pollen's Vangas, with which they often associate. Pollen's Vanga differs by its large pale blue bill.

222 Littoral Rock Thrush *Monticola imerinus*

DESCRIPTION Size: 16cm. A small thrush. Plumage varies with sex and age. **Adult male:** Pale grey head, breast, mantle and lesser and median-coverts, grey-brown wings and dark brown tail. Inner webs of tail feathers dull orange. Underparts from lower breast dull orange. Iris dark brown, bill blackish, legs and feet blackish. **Adult female:** Dull grey-brown head and back, slightly darker on the wings. Underparts off-white with thin dark malar-stripes and lightly streaked darker on the mid-breast. The tail is mostly dark brown, with inconspicuous pale rufous inner webs to all except the central tail feathers are pale rufous. **Juvenile:** Similar to adult though the upperparts show narrow pale fringes, while the breast feathers are widely edged pale brown.
VOICE The typical song consists of various short scratchy phrases which are frequently repeated. These include a *cheearr tu-tu-tu* and longer phrases comprising of clear whistles mixed with scratchy notes. The calls include a quiet *kirr-tak-tak-tak* as an alarm.
HABITAT/BEHAVIOUR Found exclusively in coastal vegetation, usually in euphorbia bushes or low shrubs on sand or coral rag. Perches conspicuously, forages on the ground. Usually found singly or in pairs. Feeds on insects and berries. Builds a bowl-shaped nest from twigs.
RANGE/STATUS Endemic to Madagascar. Not globally threatened. Monotypic. Known from the Onilahy River south and west to Lake Anony, just to the west of Fort Dauphin, where it appears to be scarce. Restricted to coastal areas. Abundant in its rather limited range. Found from sea level to 200m.
WHERE TO SEE Abundant just around the hotel at Anakao, about 25km south of Toliara and just to the south of the Onilahy River. Also very common anywhere along the coast from Anakao to Cap Ste. Marie.
SIMILAR SPECIES Male very similar to male Forest and Benson's Rock Thrushes though there is no overlap in range. Can be distinguished by rather longer and stronger bill, paler grey head and breast and limited rufous coloration in tail. The song of the male is much more scratchy than the other three species.

221. *Tylas Vanga, adult.*

222. *Littoral Rock Thrush. 222a (left) adult male. 222b (right) adult female. 222c (inset) juvenile.*

223 Amber Mountain Rock Thrush *Monticola erythronotus*

DESCRIPTION Size: 16cm. A small forest thrush. Plumage varies with sex. **Adult male:** Blue-grey hood extending to lower chin, slightly paler supercilium. Dark maroon-chestnut on mantle and scapulars, rather browner on wing feathers, which have chestnut fringes. Rather long tail bright orange, with narrow dark brown streaks on the outer-tail feathers and dark brown central tail feathers with orange streaks in the webs. Underparts orange from the upper breast to the tail. Iris dark brown, bill blackish. Feet and legs pale brown. **Adult female:** Dull earth-brown head, mantle and scapulars, somewhat darker on wings, which are fringed chestnut. The tail feathers are mostly orange with narrow brown fringes to the outer feathers and darker central feathers. The underparts are washed orange on the breast, otherwise mottled brownish with whitish streaking on the lower throat. **Juvenile:** Unknown though likely to resemble juvenile Forest Rock Thrush.
VOICE Song is poorly known, but includes phrases similar to Forest Rock Thrush.
HABITAT/BEHAVIOUR Found in mid-altitude and montane evergreen humid forest. A rather quiet and shy bird foraging on the ground and in the understorey. Nest is in tree hollow or crevice under an overhang.
RANGE/STATUS Endemic to Madagascar. Conservation status not evaluated, as previously considered a subspecies of Forest Rock Thrush. Likely to be globally threatened due to the small known world range. Monotypic. Only found at Amber Mountain in the north of Madagascar, where it is fairly common. Found from about 800 to 1,300m.
WHERE TO SEE Fairly common around the forest station at Amber Mountain.
SIMILAR SPECIES Male easily separated from all other known Malagasy rock thrush species by the dark rufous back. In addition they are longer tailed than Forest Rock Thrush. Female differs in the brighter orange tail and from Forest Rock Thrush in lacking whitish streaking on the breast.

224 Forest Rock Thrush *Monticola sharpei*

DESCRIPTION Size: 16cm. A small forest thrush. Plumage varies with sex and age. One or two subspecies, the status of which are disputed. Nominate. **Adult male nominate:** Blue-grey head (slightly paler supercilium), mantle and upper breast, and variably on the lesser and median wing-coverts. Dark rufous-brown tinged grey on the primaries, secondaries, central tail feathers, and outer webs of the rest of the tail feathers. Orange uppertail-coverts and inner webs of the tail feathers and slightly brighter orange on the lower breast and belly. Iris dark reddish-brown, eye quite large. Bill blackish, sometimes with a pale orange base. Legs usually appear mid-brown, feet dark brown. **Adult female nominate:** Dark rufous-brown or earth-brown head, mantle, wings and central tail feathers. Variable but often conspicuous pale eye-ring. Pale brown breast and belly mottled and streaked darker, especially on the breast with whitish streaks on the throat and breast. Throat bordered by blackish malar-stripes. The inner webs of the outer tail-feathers are dark orange. **Immature:** Similar to the respective adults, but show pale fringes to all back, head and breast feathers, rather wider on the breast. **Juvenile:** Similar but have pale shaft-streaks to upper and underpart and wing feathers. *M. s. salomonseni*: Distinguishable only by size; other characters proposed for their separation do not appear to be consistent.
VOICE Song a wide variety of quiet thrush-like phrases, separated by gaps of several seconds. The phrases generally lack grating or scratching noises. The most common is a melancholy *teeooo teeooo teeooo*. The alarm call is a quiet *tseet-tak-tak* or *tak-tak-tak*. A common contact call is a high *hweet*, another a low *krrrrr*.
HABITAT/BEHAVIOUR Found in mid-altitude and montane evergreen humid forest. Feeds on the ground or by sally-gleaning from branches and leaves. Usually found in areas of larger trees, but also at forest edge and in open scrubby areas next to ericoid high-mountain forest. Rather quiet and discreet. Usually found singly or in pairs. Feeds on insects and berries. Builds a bowl shaped nest from twigs which is situated in a rock crevice or low in a bush.
RANGE/STATUS Endemic to Madagascar. Currently considered **Near Threatened** globally. Found in mid-altitude, montane and ericoid forest in the east, and in transitional forest on the high plateau. An as yet unidentified rock thrush at Bemaraha (western Madagascar) may be this species. Not rare, but patchyily distributed and elusive. Occurs from about 800m to 2,500m.
WHERE TO SEE Fairly common though elusive at Ranomafana, Mantadia and Maromizaha.
SIMILAR SPECIES For identification from Amber Mountain Rock Thrush, Common Stonechat and Madagascar Magpie-Robin, see those species. Male is rather difficult to separate from Benson's Rock Thrush though the head and breast are a duller grey in Benson's Rock Thrush, not blue. The belly is also a duller orange. Female Forest Rock Thrush is much warmer earth-brown than Benson's Rock Thrush. The ranges of these species are not known to overlap but further study may show that they do.

223a. Amber Mountain Rock Thrush, adult male.

223b. Amber Mountain Rock Thrush, adult male.

224a. Forest Rock Thrush, adult male.

224b. Forest Rock Thrush, juvenile.

225 Benson's Rock Thrush *Monticola bensoni*

DESCRIPTION Size: 16cm. Plumage varies with sex and age. **Adult male:** Head, mantle, throat, upper breast (to below the carpal joint of the wing), wing-coverts, tertial fringes, and flight feathers greyish-blue. The secondary fringes show as pale panel on closed wing. Throat slightly paler. Remainder of wings are dark brown. Uppertail-coverts, inner webs of tail feathers (except central ones), lower breast and belly dull orange. Central tail feathers and outer webs and tips to all others are dark brown. Iris dark brown, bill blackish. Legs and feet dark grey (though can appear paler). **Adult female:** Grey-brown head, mantle, wings and outer webs of tail feathers, dull off-white below with dark malar stripes and subtly scaled breast. More-or-less conspicuous pale eye-ring. **Immature:** As adult but with much paler fringing on head, mantle and belly. **Juvenile:** Shows pale centres to back and breast feathers. Young birds show pale at base of bill (pale pink in very young).
VOICE Song is a rather quiet rambling series of short whistled phrases, including odd chacks and scratchy strophes. Calls include a quiet *tak-tak-tak* apparently an alarm.
HABITAT/BEHAVIOUR Found in low scrubby vegetation near to rocks and cliffs. Occasional in denser vegetation, sometimes feeding in patches of high forest. Often sally-gleans from small shrubs or rocks, often flying long distances to capture insect prey. Males sing from conspicuous perch. Usually found singly or in pairs. Feeds on insects and occasionally fruit in winter. Builds a bowl shaped nest in a rock crevice.
RANGE/STATUS Endemic to Madagascar. Globally Threatened and currently classified as **Vulnerable**. Monotypic. Possibly occurs over a wider area than currently recognised, hence the necessity of field separation from Forest Rock Thrush. Found in the area between the Mangoky valley and Ihosy, with a population on the high mountain slopes of Andringitra possibly referable to this species. Most common in the southern part of the Isalo massif, around Ranohira. Found from 700m to 1,000m.
WHERE TO SEE Common on the path to the Piscine Naturel at Isalo, also in the grounds of the Relais de la Reine hotel, 15km west of Ranohira, and near the Oasis, between the two.
SIMILAR SPECIES For separation from Forest Rock Thrush, Littoral and Amber Mountain Rock Thrushes, Common Stonechat and Madagascar Magpie-Robin see respective species accounts.

226 Madagascar Magpie-Robin *Copsychus albospecularis*

DESCRIPTION Size: 18cm. Plumage varies with age and sex. **Adult male:** At least three plumage forms; all have black head, breast, mantle, wings and at least central tail feathers, and white lesser-coverts. The nominate form has a black belly, all-black tertials, median and greater coverts and a short all-black tail. *C. a. inexpectatus* has a whitish belly and under-tail-coverts, but is otherwise similar. *C. a. pica* is somewhat larger, with a white belly, greater coverts and outer fringes to tertials, and two white outer tail-feathers. The tail is also rather longer. In a putative fourth subspecies, *C. a. winterbottomi*, male looks like *C. a. pica* but has an entirely black tail. **Adult female:** Dark brown-grey crown, mantle, wings and tail, with white on the wings and tail following the male pattern, except in *C. a. winterbottomi* where female has white outer tail-feathers. Cheeks, throat, breast and belly are variably grey. **Juvenile:** As adult female, but more rufous, especially on wings and breast, with a pale orange gape-line. Juvenile male often shows dark on head and breast.
VOICE Male song is characteristic, a long sequence of pleasant high-pitched warbled and trilled thrush-like notes, often rather quiet and given in discrete, phrases separated by several seconds. Alarm call is a high, single off-key whistle, *tseeeeeeee*, which is quiet and difficult to locate but carries well in the forest.
HABITAT/BEHAVIOUR In forest or second-growth. The nominate subspecies occurs more in the forest interior, the other subspecies are common in areas of dense scrub in disturbed or secondary forest. Terrestrial, usually encountered in pairs. Feeds largely on insects and occasionally berries. Cup-shaped nest is built in a tree hole or other natural crevice.
RANGE/STATUS Endemic to Madagascar. Not globally threatened. Nominate form common around Bay of Antongil, and similar birds are found over much of the eastern evergreen humid forest. Intergrades with the next form occur widely within this area too. *C. a. inexpectata* occurs elsewhere in the eastern evergreen humid forest, and *C. a. pica* in the west, north, south and on the high plateau. *C. a. winterbottomi* is supposed to occur in the area around Ihosy, so might be expected in Isalo and Zombitse. Found from sea level to about 1,200m.
WHERE TO SEE Common at most forest sites.
SIMILAR SPECIES Generally unmistakable. Dark nominate female can look rather like female Forest Rock Thrush if whitish lesser coverts are not visible.

5. *Benson's Rock Thrush. 225a (left) male.   225b (inset) male.   225c (right) female.*

6. *Madagascar Magpie-Robin. 226a (left) adult male nominate. 226b (right) adult male C. a. pica. 226c (inset) adult female.*

227 Common Stonechat *Saxicola torquata*

DESCRIPTION Size: 14-15cm. A small open-country chat. Plumage varies with sex and age. Three endemic subspecies are currently recognised. **Adult male *S. t. sibilla*:** Brightly coloured and contrasted. Black hood (to upper breast), wings, tail, and mantle (edged with brown) contrast with white uppertail-coverts, patch on inner greater coverts, breast-side and neck-side, flanks and belly. Spot in centre of breast is bright dark chestnut. Iris dark brown, bill legs and feet blackish. **Adult male *S. t. ankaratrae*:** similar but larger. **Adult male *S. t. tsaratananae*:** Similar but differs in having lower breast blackish, with only tips of these feathers chestnut. **Adult female:** Similar in pattern to male, but the black is replaced by mid-brown streaked darker brown on hood, mantle, wings and tail. Breast, rump and belly are pale buffy-brown. **Juvenile:** Plumage very scaled when young. When older, similar to female but paler and more streaked, particularly on the head, mantle and breast.
VOICE Usual contact call is a series of harsh scratching notes, *tsak-tsak*. The male sings a 2 to 3-second phrase of scratchy notes from a conspicuous perch.
HABITAT/BEHAVIOUR Found in montane heathland and scrub, in open areas nearby, in eucalyptus scrub, degraded forest and second growth, and in high plateau towns. Common in reedbeds and marshes. Conspicuous, usually found in pairs or family parties. Perches conspicuously on the tops of small shrubs in open areas, often calling and tail-flicking. Feeds on insects. Nest is a bowl shaped structure which is situated in dense vegetation close to ground.
RANGE/STATUS Occurs in Europe, Asia, and Africa. Not globally threatened. Represented in Madagascar by three endemic subspecies: *S. t. sibilla* occurs from sea level to 2,500m and is common in the east and in high plateau towns but is scarce or absent in most of the west and south. *S. t. ankaratrae* is restricted to mountainous areas near Ankara and areas south and south-west of Antananarivo. *S. t. tsaratananae* is restricted to the Tsaratanana highlands.
WHERE TO SEE A few pairs occur in Antananarivo. Otherwise found at Perinet-Analamazaotra and Ranomafana, and particularly common in marshy areas near forest like Torotorofotsy and Vohiparara.
SIMILAR SPECIES Female and juvenile may be mistaken for female Forest Rock Thrush, which is larger, more even rufous-brown above, with blackish malar streaks, paler throat, mottled brown breast and lacks white patch on inner wing-coverts. In addition, Forest Rock Thrush is unlikely to be seen far from forest.

228 White-throated Oxylabes *Oxylabes madagascariensis*

DESCRIPTION Size: 17-18cm. A small understorey babbler. Plumage varies with age. **Adult:** Crown, cheeks and nape rufous-brown, contrasting with the dull dark brown back, wings and tail. Short white supercilium, mostly behind the eye which on males may be longer and more conspicuous. In front of eye there is just a small white spot. Throat white, breast and belly dull dark brown, warmer on the upper breast. Tail comparatively long, the wings short. Iris dark reddish-brown, bill fairly long and strong, dull dark grey. Long, strong legs and feet mid- or dark grey. **Juvenile:** Initially dark charcoal-grey head, rest of plumage dark olive-brown, with variable yellow spots on the side of the neck and green-yellow fringes to the wings, with a distinct yellow gape. Soon acquires pale buffy or buffy-yellow throat, variable in extent (sometimes extending to lower breast), and pale, dull rufous crown and nape, and loses green-yellow on wings.
VOICE Contact call is a characteristic, high-pitched sibilant trill, slightly descending *ssshhrewwww*. Adults have a duet song, one bird singing a short, loud whistled sequence, *whit-treet tirooet teeoo*, while the other comes in half-way through with a loud wooden rattled call. The two elements may also be heard separately.
HABITAT/BEHAVIOUR A characteristic, skulking and fairly shy species of understorey of evergreen humid forest. Moves in family groups or with Dark Newtonias, greenbuls and Madagascar Yellowbrows through dense ground vegetation. Often feeds on the ground or in dead leaf clumps up to about 5m from the ground. Feed on small or medium-sized invertebrates. The nest is a cup-shaped structure, usually 1-2m above the ground.
RANGE/STATUS Endemic to Madagascar. Not globally threatened. Monotypic. Common in eastern evergreen humid forest, over almost all the altitudinal gradient, from sea level to at least 2,000m, though most common between 800m and 1,600m.
WHERE TO SEE Easy to find at Perinet-Analamazaotra, Mantadia, Ranomafana and other similar sites.
SIMILAR SPECIES The adult is unmistakable. Juveniles, particularly those with pale throats, could be mistaken for Dusky Greenbul. They differ by lacking yellow eye-ring, their buffy rather than yellow throats, the rufous tinge to the head, longer tails and usually prominent pale gape.

227. Common Stonechat, adult male.

228a. White-throated Oxylabes, adult.

228b. White-throated Oxylabes, adult.

229 Madagascar Yellowbrow *Crossleyia xanthophrys*

DESCRIPTION Size: 15cm. A small terrestrial babbler. Sexes alike, plumage differs with age. **Adult:** Crown, nape, mantle and back dull dark olive-green, slightly blacker on the cheeks, which contrast vividly with a long, conspicuous, yellow supercilium which kinks up behind the eye. The wings and tail are slightly darker than the rest of the upperparts. Throat and upper breast yellow, tinged olive. The lower breast is darker yellow-olive, darkening on the belly and undertail-coverts. Iris dark brown, bill short, pale pink, long legs and feet strong, dull pink. **Juvenile:** Similar but rather duller, especially on the supercilium and breast, and the culmen and tip of the bill are dark brown.

VOICE Call is a characteristic, thin but very penetrating *tsip*, similar to the call of Forest Fody, though sharper and usually delivered from low down rather than from a bush or tree. The song is a peculiar series of very high-pitched whistled notes, *tsit tsit tseer tsee tsee tsit tit* and similar variations.

HABITAT/BEHAVIOUR A highly terrestrial babbler, often very difficult to see in the dense understorey of mid-and high-altitude forest, where it walks rapidly over the ground with a characteristic rolling gait. Often occurs in family groups with White-throated Oxylabes, Dark Newtonias, and greenbuls. Sometimes when mobbing an intruder or singing it will climb to 1 or 2 metres up a shrub. Feeds on insects. Nest is a cup-shaped structure, situated in leaf-litter or in dense liana tangles.

RANGE/STATUS Endemic to Madagascar. Globally Threatened and currently classified as **Vulnerable**. Monotypic. Generally rare; however, fairly common from about 800m to at least 2,000m in primary eastern evergreen humid forest and may have been overlooked due to its skulking nature.

WHERE TO SEE Fairly common in areas of dense understorey at Ranomafana, Maromizaha and Mantadia, though apparently absent from Perinet-Analamazaotra.

SIMILAR SPECIES A very characteristic species, unlikely to be mistaken for any other on account of its vivid yellow supercilium and ground-hugging habits.

230 Crossley's Babbler *Mystacornis crossleyi*

DESCRIPTION Size: 16cm. A small terrestrial babbler. Sexes differ and plumage varies with age. **Adult male:** Crown and nape mid-grey, contrasting with mid-brown back, wings and tail. A broad black line through the eye is punctuated with a small white spot over the eye. A broad white line runs from the base of the bill to the rear of the ear-coverts. Below this, the chin and throat are blackish, grading into grey on the belly and off-white on the lower belly and undertail-coverts. Iris dark brown, bill long, slim and slightly decurved at the tip, blackish with a dull grey cutting edge. Legs and feet long, strong and pinkish-grey. **Adult female:** Similar to the male, except that the crown is brownish, the band through the eye narrower and the chin and throat are off-white rather than black, though still contrast slightly with the white sub-moustachial stripe. This plumage may also be found in sexually mature males. **Juvenile:** Variable according to age. Very young birds are almost wholly chocolate-brown, somewhat paler below, though with age they soon develop adult characteristics.

VOICE The usual song is a loud, clear single-note whistle lasting about 2 seconds, very like that of Hook-billed Vanga but more modulated: *tsiiioeeeee*, dropping slightly then rising slightly. In addition gives a series of similar shorter single-note whistles, *tooee tooee tooee*, which are sometimes given in a rising series. Calls include a very high-pitched *peeeer*, and a loud chacking in alarm.

HABITAT/BEHAVIOUR Found in the understorey of primary evergreen humid forest, usually singly or in family groups, walking on the ground in rather open areas of understorey. Males are aggressive and can be attracted by a whistled imitation of the song. When not singing, may be discreet and difficult to see. Feeds on insects. The nest is built low down and is a rough cup-shaped structure built from twigs.

RANGE/STATUS Endemic to Madagascar. Not globally threatened. Monotypic. Fairly common but rather patchily distributed in all eastern evergreen humid forest blocks, from sea level to 1,500m.

WHERE TO SEE Fairly common at Perinet-Analamazaotra, Mantadia, Ranomafana and most mid-altitude evergreen humid forest sites.

SIMILAR SPECIES Adults are completely characteristic, with the combination of greyish crown, black line through the eye and white sub-moustachial stripe. Juveniles are less obvious, but when in uniform rufous plumage will almost always be accompanied by adults.

229a. Madagascar Yellowbrow, adult.

229b. Madagascar Yellowbrow, adult.

230a. Crossley's Babbler, adult male.

230b. Crossley's Babbler, adult female.

231 Brown Emutail *Dromaeocercus brunneus*

DESCRIPTION Size: 15cm. A tiny herb-layer warbler. Sexes alike, plumage varies with age. **Adult:** Rufous-brown crown, back and wings, grey ear-coverts (slightly paler supercilium in some individuals) and with a whitish chin and upper throat (sometimes to the upper breast), indistinctly streaked darker. Rest of the underparts orange-brown. Wings very short. Tail remarkable, long with very few lateral barbs, so that all that can usually be seen are the raches. Iris dark brown, bill blackish, legs and feet pinkish-brown. **Juvenile:** Entirely dark rufous-brown, with a conspicuous yellow gape, and fully-barbed tail.

VOICE The call is a 1 to 2-second rolling rattle, like Madagascar brush warbler but much less harsh, almost purring, and much higher. Song is extremely characteristic but rather variable; usually two or three short high initial *whit* or *wee* notes followed rapidly by a 1 to 2-second whirring *quirrrrrrrrrrr*, lower than the initial notes. This is actually a duet. Also a similar phrase - *whit wee wee chechechechechech*.

HABITAT/BEHAVIOUR Found in mid-altitude or montane eastern evergreen humid forest, in areas of dense damp herbaceous growth. Very skulking and difficult to see. Runs along the ground, when the resemblance to a mouse is extremely striking with the long barbless tail resembling that of a small rodent. Flies weakly, occasionally flying rapidly and low across paths and between clumps of vegetation. Feeds on small insects. The nest is built in dense vegetation close to the ground.

RANGE/STATUS Endemic to Madagascar. Currently considered **Near Threatened** on a global scale. Monotypic. Fairly common though elusive in eastern evergreen humid forests between 800 and 2,500m.

WHERE TO SEE Present on ridge-tops at Mantadia, Maromizaha and at Vohiparara in Ranomafana National Park.

SIMILAR SPECIES A small rufous warbler, easily distinguished from Dark Newtonia and Madagascar Brush Warbler by its voice, terrestrial habits, virtually unbarbed tail, rufous plumage and grey ear-coverts.

232 Grey Emutail *Amphilais seebohmi*

DESCRIPTION Size: 16-17cm. A small marshland warbler. No known plumage variation. Greyish-brown head and upperparts with more-or-less conspicuous blackish shaft-streaks. Poorly marked pale supercilium and darker eyestripe. Underparts pale buff, with a narrow but variable necklace of dark streaks on the breast. Undertail-coverts brownish. Tail almost lacking lateral barbs. Iris dark brown, bill greyish horn, legs pinkish.

VOICE The typical song is a duet, one bird giving a rattling *chuchuchuchuchuchuchu* call while the second bird gives a series of three to ten high-pitched and slightly descending notes - *treee-treee-treee*. Also a series of *cheep* notes which accelerate into the rattle described above given by a single bird.

HABITAT/BEHAVIOUR Found in mid- and high-altitude marshes, especially those with low dense rushes and herbs, though not in high papyrus or *Cyperus* sedge stands. Also in low montane ericoid forest at high altitudes, where it might overlap in habitat preference with Brown Emutail. A skulking species, usually seen singly. Feeds on small insects. The bowl-shaped nest is usually situated in a dense tuft of grass or sedge.

RANGE/STATUS Endemic to Madagascar. Not globally threatened. Monotypic. Found very patchily in marshes and high-altitude vegetation, above 700m all over the eastern evergreen humid forest block. Common where present, but probably not very abundant overall.

WHERE TO SEE Common at Vohiparara marsh at Ranomafana and Torotorofotsy marsh near Perinet-Analamazaotra.

SIMILAR SPECIES For identification from Madagascar Swamp Warbler and Madagascar Brush Warbler, see those species. From Brown Emutail by the greyer coloration and lack of contrasting grey ear-coverts. In addition, Brown lacks the dark shaft-streaks on the upperparts and the voice is also characteristic. However, note that the name Grey Emutail is somewhat misleading as the species shows essentially brownish upperparts.

231a. Brown Emutail, adult.

231b. Brown Emutail, adult.

232a. Grey Emutail.

232b. Grey Emutail.

233 Madagascar Brush Warbler *Nesillas typica*

DESCRIPTION Size: 17-18cm. A large understorey warbler. Sexes alike, plumage varies slightly with age. At least three subspecies, only two of which are distinguishable in the field. **Adult nominate:** Dull earth-brown (though variable) crown, cheeks, mantle, and back, slightly darker on wings and tail. Poorly marked dark eye-stripe and pale buffish supercilium to just behind the eye. Underparts off-white with a faint yellow-green tinge on breast, dull pale brown on belly, with indistinct streaking on upper breast. Wings rather short, tail loose and long. Iris mid-brown, greyer in juveniles. Bill dark brown on upper mandible, with paler cutting edge and pale horn base to lower mandible. Legs and feet mid-brown-grey or lead-grey. **Juvenile:** Even brown-grey all over, with yellow gape. *N. t. obscura:* Darker olive-green-brown, with little pale on throat and barely visible streaking; however some eastern birds approach this colour. Some western birds have yellow on supercilium. Isolated montane populations (such as at Ibity and Itremo) may be paler and greyer, and have been separated as *N. t. monticola.*
VOICE Loud rattling *trrrrrrrrrrrrk*, heard from September to January. Also a *trkatrk*, *trk* and variants.
HABITAT/BEHAVIOUR Found in dense primary and degraded forest, secondary growth, gardens and plantations. Rather secretive and difficult to find if not calling, but often tame and confiding. Flies between clumps of vegetation and across paths with heavy, rushed flight. Feeds low in dense understorey, gleaning small insects from clumps of leaves and sticks. Nest is built in dense vegetation close to ground.
RANGE/STATUS Regional Endemic, occurring in Madagascar and the Comoros. Not globally threat-ened. Nominate race is abundant in eastern evergreen humid forests, on high plateau and, outside forests, to sea level in east and north. Absent from lowland evergreen humid forest, most of the western forest except near Ampijoroa and the south. In calcareous western forests (Ankarana, Namoroka and Bemaraha), the western subspecies *N. t. obscura* is common. Found from sea level to 2,700m.
WHERE TO SEE Fairly common in Antananarivo, abundant at Perinet-Analamazaotra, Ranomafana, Mantadia, and other mid-altitude evergreen humid forests, Ampijoroa (only in degraded forest or scrub). The western form is most easily seen at Ankarana.
SIMILAR SPECIES For distinctions from Madagascar Swamp Warbler, see that species. From both emutails by larger size and fully feathered (although loose) tail. In addition, from Grey Emutail by lack of discrete streaking on the back and from Brown Emutail by the lack of rufous coloration on the underparts and lacking the contrasting grey ear-coverts. From Subdesert Brush Warbler by darker brown coloration, espe-cially the underparts, the less well-marked supercilium and much lower pitched voice.

234 Subdesert Brush Warbler *Nesillas lantzii*

DESCRIPTION Size: 17cm. A large understorey warbler. Sexes alike, plumage varies slightly with age. **Adult:** Crown, cheeks, mantle, wings and tail pale grey-brown, slightly darker on the flight feathers. Dull dark eyestripe and fairly clear pale supercilium to behind the eye. Underparts off-white with slight darker streaking on the upper breast. Iris mid-brown, bill dull mid-brown upper mandible, pale brown or dull pink lower mandible with a dark tip. Legs dull bluish-grey, feet slightly darker. **Juvenile:** Duller and more uniform grey-brown all over, with a conspicuous yellow gape.
VOICE Call similar in structure to Madagascar Brush Warbler but much higher pitched and thinner, almost whispering, lacking the rasping quality of the latter species.
HABITAT/BEHAVIOUR Similar to Madagascar Brush Warbler but only found in the arid habitats of the south. Typically in euphorbia forest, low coastal scrub, degraded forest and near Fort Dauphin in edges of lowland evergreen humid forest.
RANGE/STATUS Endemic to Madagascar. Not globally threatened. Monotypic. Common from the Mangoky river south to Cap Ste. Marie and from there east to Fort Dauphin, inland as far as the limit of southern subdesert forest. Found from sea level to 200m. Originally treated as a subspecies of Madagascar Brush Warbler, but differs in plumage and voice and occurs sympatrically with that species, for instance near Fort Dauphin and in Andohahela, and should thus be regarded as a good species.
WHERE TO SEE Very common in the degraded margins of *Didierea* forest at Ifaty, in euphorbia forest near St. Augustin and Anakao, and along the coastal strip from there to Fort Dauphin, where it is present in evergreen humid forest edges on Pic St. Louis.
SIMILAR SPECIES Very similar to but markedly paler than Madagascar Brush Warbler; call distinctive (see above). From Thamnornis Warbler by lack of pale green fringes to the wing and tail feathers, lack of pale tips to the outer tail feathers, less conspicuous pale supercilium, and less contrasted bill.

233. *Madagascar Brush Warbler, adult nominate.*

234a. *Subdesert Brush Warbler, adult.*

234b. *Subdesert Brush Warbler, adult.*

235 Madagascar Swamp Warbler *Acrocephalus newtoni*

DESCRIPTION Size: 18cm. A large, long-tailed reed warbler. Sexes alike, plumage varies slightly with age. **Adult:** Uniform mid-grey-brown on cap, cheeks, nape, mantle, back, and tail, slightly darker on the wings. Head with a rather diffuse dark eyestripe and pale supercilium. Underparts off-white tinged buffy especially on the flanks and belly, with a variable but usually neat gorget of streaks across the upper breast. Iris reddish-brown, fairly strong and long bill dark grey on the upper mandible, paler, pinkish on the base of the lower mandible. Legs dark grey, feet dull horn. **Juvenile:** Similar to the adult, though the iris is darker and may appear more uniform, lacking the breast streaking.
VOICE Song a loud short series of notes, the first high, followed by a series of short, ringing, mellow whistles *teeeee-tew-tew-tew-tew* repeated irregularly. These are often interspersed with low, throaty and chacking notes. Calls short and chacking, sometimes repeated in a series.
HABITAT/BEHAVIOUR A slightly aberrant, long-tailed *Acrocephalus* reed-warbler. Often found climbing around in stands of *Cyperus* sedge or *Phragmites*, singing from reed-tops and flying between clumps with low laboured flight. Also found in trees, dense vegetation near marshes and on the edges of mangroves, coastal scrub and very locally in low ericoid forest on mountain-tops. Feeds on insects. The nest is usually situated in dense vegetation, low over water.
RANGE/STATUS Endemic to Madagascar. Not globally threatened. Monotypic. Common in all shrubby riverside, reedbed and marsh habitats in the east and west, less common in the south. Rarely on the tops of high mountains in ericaceous habitat. Found from sea level to at least 2,000m.
WHERE TO SEE Common in small marshes and old rice-paddies at Perinet-Analamazaotra, Ranomafana, Ampijoroa, Mantadia, and on the coast near Toliara.
SIMILAR SPECIES Distinguished from Madagascar Brush Warbler and Grey Emutail, both of which may be common in marshy habitats, by a combination of the long, fully-feathered tail and discrete streaks on the breast (though these are variable), orange-red eye and thicker, more solid bill. The mellow song is a further distinction from Madagascar Brush Warbler.

236 Thamnornis Warbler *Thamnornis chloropetoides*

DESCRIPTION Size: 15cm. A large understorey warbler. Plumage variation unknown. **Adult:** Head greyish, with a distinct paler supercilium and darker eyestripe. Mantle, wings and tail slightly darker, with very characteristic green-yellow fringes to all wing and tail feathers. Tail quite long. Outer tail-feathers tipped white. Underparts whitish, slight and indistinct streaks on the throat. Iris brown, bill quite long, strong and pointed, slightly decurved, dark horn on the upper mandible and pale orange on the lower. Legs strong, pale horn, feet slightly darker.
VOICE Call a rattling trill rather like Madagascar Brush Warbler (i.e. lower and more rattling than Sub-desert Brush Warbler), but quieter. Song, often given from the top of a *Didierea* stem, is a long rattle (like the call) followed by a rapid *tewtewtewteetewteetewtewteeteetew...*, lasting for 10 to 30 seconds, running slightly up and down the scale.
HABITAT/BEHAVIOUR Found in spiny subdesert and, in the north of its range, the scrubby edges of western deciduous forest. Often scarcer in low coastal euphorbia scrub, where Subdesert Brush Warbler is often abundant. Behaviour is similar to Subdesert Brush Warbler, feeding low in dense vegetation and even on the ground, but singing from a high perch is characteristic. Feeds on insects. The nest is built in dense shrubbery close to the ground.
RANGE/STATUS Endemic to Madagascar. Not globally threatened. Monotypic. Common in spiny subdesert and margins of western deciduous forest from just south of Morondava to just west of Fort Dauphin, inland to Vohibasia and Parcel 2 of Andohahela. Found from sea level to 800m.
WHERE TO SEE Common at Ifaty, north of Toliara, in spiny subdesert.
SIMILAR SPECIES Similar to Subdesert Brush Warbler, but head is larger and tail proportionately slightly shorter. The grey head and supercilium are conspicuous, as are the diagnostic green-yellow edges to the wing and tail feathers and the white tips to the outer tail-feathers. In addition, may be separated by the pale orange lower mandible on the strong and decurved bill, and the loud, extremely characteristic song.

35. Madagascar Swamp Warbler. 235a (inset) adult. 235b (left) adult. 235c (right) juvenile.

36. Thamnornis Warbler, adult.

237 Rand's Warbler *Randia pseudozosterops*

DESCRIPTION Size: 12cm. A small, arboreal, forest warbler. Plumage variation poorly understood but minor. **Adult:** Crown, nape, mantle, and tail cold mid-grey-brown, slightly darker on the wings, with darker centres to the coverts and tertials, the latter with obvious pale fringes. Noticeable dark eyestripe and a short, wide whitish supercilium. Underparts even off-white, slightly buffer on the breast. Iris dark brown, bill fairly strong for a small warbler, gives the impression of being slightly decurved. Upper mandible dark horn, lower variable bright pale horn. Legs and feet greyish-brown. **Juvenile:** Similar to adult but bill darker.
VOICE Calls include a sequence of strange high-pitched twittering notes, possibly a food-begging call. When foraging, though occasionally gives a loud *chick* which is similar to Cryptic Warbler. Song is characteristic, but easily confused with Stripe-throated Jery. It consists of a regular, slightly descending series of four to eight notes, *tew-tew-tew-tew-te*, typically given from the top of a riverside tree. Stripe-throated Jery's song is longer and more varied, (although may be abbreviated), the notes are less well separated (better modulated), and the song usually goes up in pitch. In addition there are often two song phrases, the first ascending and the second descending. Both species sing for several hours at a stretch, often from adjacent, or even the same trees, often moving together when changing song post.
HABITAT/BEHAVIOUR Occurs in lowland and mid-altitude eastern rain-forest, in areas of large trees. Usually in the canopy, rarely lower than 5m above the ground. Rand's Warbler has a habit of searching for invertebrates along horizontal branches by looking over alternate sides of the branch at the underside. This behaviour is very mechanical and rapid, and extremely characteristic. Also gleans insects from small stems and leaves in the canopy. A characteristic member of canopy mixed-species flocks. No data available on nesting behaviour.
RANGE/STATUS Endemic to Madagascar. Currently considered **Near Threatened** globally. Monotypic. Common in lowland and mid-altitude forest from sea level to about 1,200m (rarely to 1,500m), along the length of the eastern evergreen humid forest.
WHERE TO SEE Common at Perinet-Analamazaotra, Mantadia and Ranomafana, and may be found at all lowland or mid-altitude sites with large trees. May be overlooked if the song is not known.
SIMILAR SPECIES Similar to Cryptic Warbler and the jeries, especially Green. Distinguished from them all by lack of green or yellow in the plumage, fairly conspicuous whitish supercilium, rather thick, slightly decurved bill, and unique feeding behaviour.

238 Common Newtonia *Newtonia brunneicauda*

DESCRIPTION Size: 12cm. A small shrub and canopy-layer insectivore. Sexes alike, plumage varies slightly with age. Two subspecies but these are not distinguishable in the field. **Adult:** Crown, ear-coverts, mantle, wings and tail cold grey-brown. Head and wings appear uniform (except slightly darker primaries). Outer tail-feathers slightly paler. Underparts mostly pale buff, warmer on the centre of the breast and on the flanks. Iris conspicuously pale, whitish-yellow. Bill blackish, legs and feet grey. **Juvenile:** Upperparts browner, with variable rufous-brown tips to the greater coverts and slight ginger tips to the tertials. May also show a pale rufous panel in the secondaries. Underparts browner, with a strong but variable rufous tinge to the breast. Iris duller, brown-grey
VOICE The song is a 2 to 3-second rattling, *kitrikitrikitrikitrik*, given while the bird is feeding or from the top of a shrub or tree. Calls include an irritated *bzz bzz bzz bzz bzz* as an alarm.
HABITAT/BEHAVIOUR Feeds on small arboreal insects gleaned from leaves and small branches in the shrub-layer, lower canopy and canopy of all native forest types. A characteristic member of mixed-species flocks. The nest is a deep cup hidden in shrub-layer vegetation.
RANGE/STATUS Endemic to Madagascar. Not globally threatened. Very common in eastern evergreen humid forests, western deciduous forest and southern subdesert. One of the commonest forest birds, but scarce or absent outside native forest. Nominate subspecies occurs throughout most of range, replaced by *N. b. monticola* in the highland forests of the Ankaratra range. Found from sea level to 2,300m.
WHERE TO SEE Common at all regular forest sites
SIMILAR SPECIES Adults could be mistaken for Dark, Archbold's and Red-tailed Newtonias, but are characterised by the combination of wholly dark bill and (usually) legs, a complete lack of rufous coloration in the upperparts and a conspicuously pale iris. Juveniles may present more problems, but the only noticeable rufous coloration on the upperparts of most is a greater-covert wingbar. Never shows red in the tail or brown around the eye. The song is very distinctive.

237. Rand's Warbler, adult.

238a. Common Newtonia, adult.

238b. Common Newtonia, adult.

239 Dark Newtonia *Newtonia amphichroa*

DESCRIPTION Size: 12cm. A small warbler-like understorey species. Sexes alike, plumage varies slightly with age. **Adult:** Crown, ear-coverts, nape, mantle, back, wings and tail dark brown-grey, wings with paler, warmer brown-olive fringes to the flight feathers. Underparts paler brown, but this may be difficult to see in the dark understorey when the bird may appear completely dark. Iris mid-yellow-orange, actually quite pale but again this is difficult to see in the field when the eye often appears dark. Bill blackish, legs and feet dark grey. **Juvenile:** For a short period after fledging, are much more rufous than adults, especially on the rump and underparts, with paler shaft-streaks on the crown and mantle and often showing a paler wing-bar.

VOICE The characteristic contact or alarm call is a penetrating *schreep*, given in a series, often in tandem with a quiet repeated *pit*. Song is a loud rolling warble, *weetaweetawetachui-wit chui-wit cheweechewee* and similar variations. Each phrase typically lasts for 3 to 5 seconds. Less rattling and more varied and warbling than Common Newtonia and more like Red-tailed, but distinguished from the latter by being more varied.

HABITAT/BEHAVIOUR Almost always seen in areas of dense understorey, in primary or dense secondary, mid-altitude or montane evergreen humid forest. Occurs in family groups with other understorey birds, particularly White-throated Oxylabes and Spectacled Greenbul. Feeds on small insects. The nest is a deep cup hidden in low vegetation.

RANGE/STATUS Endemic to Madagascar. Not globally threatened. Monotypic. Common in eastern evergreen humid forest from 600m or 800m to 2,300m. Scarce in real lowland forest where the understorey is less dense.

WHERE TO SEE Common at Ranomafana, Perinet-Analamazaotra, Mantadia, and Amber Mountain, though difficult to locate except by voice.

SIMILAR SPECIES Usually appears as a small uniformly dark brown bird moving through the low understorey. When feeding higher could be confused with Common Newtonia, but is always browner, especially on the upperparts, and the eye usually appears darker, orange rather than whitish. The calls and song are immediately characteristic.

240 Archbold's Newtonia *Newtonia archboldi*

DESCRIPTION Size: 12cm. A small, grey-brown warbler-like bird. Sexes alike, plumage varies with age. **Adult:** Crown, ear-coverts, mantle, back, tail and wings mid-grey-brown. A prominent eye-ring and variable narrow band on the forehead is darker rufous-brown. The crown may also be somewhat warmer brown than the mantle. Underparts buffy, with a variable pinkish tinge on the breast and flanks, slightly darker than on Common Newtonia. Iris pale whitish-yellow, bill blackish, legs pale or mid-grey. **Juvenile:** Similar to adult but with a strong, dark rufous greater-covert wingbar and conspicuous pale rufous edges to the secondaries. In addition the breast may be brighter pink.

VOICE Calls include a harsh scolding rather like a Souimanga Sunbird. The song is a very distinctive, variable four- or five-syllable warble, *tee-too tehew* or *chichichich wit-tee tew*.

HABITAT/BEHAVIOUR Found in southern *Didierea* forests, and adjacent scrubby vegetation, and in the northern part of its range, in the degraded fringes of western deciduous forest. Scarce or absent in coastal euphorbia forest. Feeds by gleaning insects from the leaves of shrubs and low trees, like Common Newtonia. The nest is a deep cup hidden in low dense shrubbery.

RANGE/STATUS Endemic to Madagascar. Not globally threatened. Monotypic. Found within about 100km of the coast from just south of Morondava to just west of Fort Dauphin. Found from sea level to 100m.

WHERE TO SEE Fairly common in suitable spiny forest habitat at Ifaty and also present around Berenty.

SIMILAR SPECIES Can be difficult to distinguish from the completely sympatric Common Newtonia, but the latter species lacks the conspicuous rufous feathering around the eye found in Archbold's Newtonia. This often appears as a dark eye-ring. Otherwise, Archbold's Newtonia is warmer coloured and has a slightly longer and stronger bill and a longer tail, giving a longer silhouette. The songs and calls of the two species are completely characteristic.

239. Dark Newtonia, adult.

240a. Archbold's Newtonia, adult.

240b. Archbold's Newtonia, adult.

241 Red-tailed Newtonia *Newtonia fanovanae*

DESCRIPTION Size: 12cm. A small warbler-like canopy species. Plumage presumably varies with age but juvenile plumage unknown. **Adult:** Crown, cheeks and nape grey-blue, contrasting with the greyish-brown mantle, scapulars and rump. No strong face markings. Wings slightly darker on the primaries, and the edges to the secondaries are conspicuously buff or orangish, showing as a conspicuous pale panel on the closed wing. Tail and uppertail-coverts mostly reddish, with duller outer fringes to the inner webs and tips of most feathers. Underparts whitish, with a variable bronze wash on the sides of the breast. Iris dark brown, bill dark horn on the upper mandible, paler grey on the lower. Legs and feet dark horn.

VOICE Song a rather clear and far-carrying series of descending notes, of two kinds; either *sweep-sweep-sweep-sweep-sweep-sweep-sweep-sweep-sweep*, with between five and fifteen notes, or *pitchi-pitchi-pitchi-pitchi-pitchi-pitchi*, also between five and fifteen notes. Often the two phrases are alternated by the same bird. Calls poorly known but include an irritated buzzing like Common Newtonia.

HABITAT/BEHAVIOUR Similar to Common Newtonia, but more likely to be seen higher in the canopy, and more acrobatic, often sally-gleaning or hovering off the ends of branches, almost always in the company of other species such as jeries, newtonias and small vangas. Only seen in lowland evergreen humid forest, in areas of high trees. Feeds on insects. No data available on nesting behaviour.

RANGE/STATUS Endemic to Madagascar. Globally Threatened and currently classified as **Vulnerable.** Monotypic. Until 1989, known only from a single specimen from near Moramanga. Rediscovered in lowland evergreen humid forest at two sites, near Andohahela and north-west of Tamatave, at almost the same time, and now known from the far north (Anjanaharibe-sud) to the far south. However, it seems to be rare or absent above 800m, and in several sites it appears not to be present above 500m. If this altitude preference holds up over all of its range, it is the only species restricted to true lowland forest. However, its distribution is probably patchy.

WHERE TO SEE Probably present in low densities in mid-altitude forest (700-800m) in the area around Perinet-Analamazaotra and Andosibe an'ala, and has been recorded at the Masoala Peninsula. Present in addition near Andohahela, and could be looked for at any evergreen humid forest site below about 800m.

SIMILAR SPECIES A rather clean and smart newtonia, easily distinguished from the other species by the grey head contrasting with the browner mantle, the red tail, the dark eyes and the pale lower mandible. Very similar in coloration to the female Red-tailed Vanga, and at a distance (for instance in a mixed-species flock), could easily be mistaken. However, female Red-tailed Vanga can be distinguished by the larger, more thickset body, slower gleaning behaviour, thick black bill, the pale eye-ring, lack of a pale panel in the wing, and calls and song.

242 Madagascar Cisticola *Cisticola cherina*

DESCRIPTION Size: 12cm. A small grassland warbler. Plumage varies slightly with age, males average slightly larger than females. **Adult:** Upperparts mid-grey brown, slightly buffy, with conspicuous darker feather-centres on the crown, mantle, rump, uppertail-coverts and greater, median and lesser wing-coverts. The cap and wings are slightly darker, the tail grey-brown with black subterminal marks and conspicuous white tips. Cheeks and underparts are whitish, with fine narrow streaking on the sides of the breast. Some birds show buff on the underparts, particularly on the undertail-coverts. Iris mid-brown, bill dark brown on the upper mandible with greyer cutting edges and a greyer lower mandible. Legs pinkish and conspicuous. **Juvenile:** Similar to the adult, though typically more boldly streaked on the upperparts and buffer on the underparts.

VOICE The call is a high off-key *tsit, tit*, or sometimes a hoarser *cheep*, elongated into a display-flight over grass or reeds, where the birds call *tsit....tsit....tsit....tsit....* Also wingsnaps, using the wing feathers to produce a sharp buzzing sound.

HABITAT/BEHAVIOUR Found in all kinds of grassland, marshes, swampy areas and savanna. Often perches high on a dead stalk, but feeds low down. Display flight up to 30m into the air. Feeds on small insects. The pyramidal shaped nest is built low down in dense grass or similar dense vegetation.

RANGE/STATUS Regional Endemic occurring in Madagascar, the Comoros and Aldabra. Monotypic. Not globally threatened. Abundant throughout in areas of open grassland and swamp. Not found in primary forest except sporadically in degraded spiny bush. Found from sea level to 2,000m.

WHERE TO SEE Common in all suitable open habitats, at all likely birding sites.

SIMILAR SPECIES A small grassland warbler with a short tail, often conspicuously displayed to show off the white and black margins beneath. Much smaller than Grey Emutail, with a short, fully feathered tail.

241. Red-tailed Newtonia, adult.

242a. Madagascar Cisticola, adult.

242b. Madagascar Cisticola, adult.

243 Common Jery *Neomixis tenella*

DESCRIPTION Size: 10cm. A small warbler-like bird. Sexes alike, plumage varies with age. Four subspecies. **Adult nominate:** Crown bright pale greenish, cheeks paler, with a slight dark line through the eye and a pale yellowish supercilium to just behind the eye. Rear ear-coverts, nape and sides of neck clear pale grey, contrasting with the bright pale green lower mantle, scapulars and rump. Wing feathers and tail slightly darker, with narrow, paler yellowish fringes. Underparts mostly whitish, with a yellowish throat and a variable but often brilliant pale yellow wash over the upper breast, and usually some narrow olive streaking in the centre of the breast. Iris pale brown or orange. Bill quite strong for a small insectivore, slightly decurved. Upper mandible dark horn, and lower variable pale orange, almost to the tip. Legs pale or mid-pink or orange. *N. t. orientalis:* Darker than the nominate, slightly duller green above and with rather less vivid yellow on the breast. *N. t. decaryi:* Duller olive-green again, and is washed olive-green on the flanks, has less yellow on the throat and more streaking, mostly on the centre of the breast, over a dull olive-yellow wash. *N. t. debilis:* The dullest race, with clearly olive flanks and quite strong streaking over the dull yellow breast. **Juvenile:** All races resemble the adult nominate, with fairly bright green upperparts, a limited amount of fairly bright yellow on the breast, usually no streaking on the breast but show a darker iris.

VOICE A very high-pitched descending series of 'seeping' notes followed by a single lower note, *tseee-tseee-tseee-tseee-tseee tsirrup*, often mixed with a lower sunbird-like *dzheee*, possibly an alarm. Song, heard mostly in the early morning and delivered from the top of a high tree or shrub, is a compounded series of the 'seeping' notes, starting with a slightly lower note and fading away at the end.

HABITAT/BEHAVIOUR A small insectivore, characteristic of the canopy or upper shrub layer in most forests. Also ventures out into degraded and secondary areas well away from primary forest. It often occurs in small family groups with other jeries, white-eyes, and newtonias. It is one of the few endemic species to occur all over the high plateau, being reasonably common in Antananarivo.

RANGE/STATUS Endemic to Madagascar. Not globally threatened. One of the commonest forest birds in Madagascar. Common in the east, west and south; in the east evergreen humid forest from sea level to about 1,300m in degraded and secondary areas somewhat higher.

WHERE TO SEE Common at all low- and mid-altitude forest sites.

SIMILAR SPECIES This species is most likely to be confused with Green and Stripe-throated Jeries, and Cryptic Warbler. It is unique in having a conspicuously contrasted grey nape and upper mantle and, in addition, can be distinguished from Green Jery in having a strong yellow tinge to the throat, from Stripe-throated Jery by the pale lower mandible, and from Cryptic Warbler by its pale legs and shorter tail.

244 Green Jery *Neomixis viridis*

DESCRIPTION Size: 10-11cm. A small insectivorous warbler-like bird. Sexes alike, plumage varies slightly with age. Two subspecies. **Adult nominate:** Bright dark green crown, nape, and upperparts, with a slight pale supercilium and a slight dark line through the eye. The wings and tail are slightly darker green. The underparts are whitish on the throat and upper breast, with inconspicuous dull olive-yellow streaks on the lower breast and belly, merging to olive-grey on the flanks. Iris orange. The bill is rather long and thin, dark horn on the upper mandible and pale on the lower, almost to the tip. The legs and feet are bright pale orange, sometimes appearing very bright if the sun is shining through them. *N. v. delacouri:* Slightly darker on the back. **Juvenile:** Similar to adult, though bill paler and iris darker.

VOICE Call is a surprisingly loud irregular *tick...tick...tickit*, a very hard clean note. Song is highly characteristic, a short rising series of high-pitched 'seeping' notes that ends sharply in lower clicking notes; *tsee- tsee-tsee-tsit-tsitick*. Song is similar to Cryptic Warbler, though the latter is louder and more strident.

HABITAT/BEHAVIOUR A canopy or sub-canopy species, only found in primary forest or adjacent secondary growth. Often feeds high up and not often seen lower down. Feeds by gleaning and sally-gleaning, with the occasional hover-glean. Very active and difficult to follow. Frequently in mixed-species flocks.

RANGE/STATUS Endemic to Madagascar. Not globally threatened. Common in eastern evergreen humid forest from sea level to about 1,400m, somewhat less common at higher altitudes.

WHERE TO SEE Common at Perinet-Analamazaotra, Ranomafana, Mantadia, Masoala, and at most other lowland or mid-altitude forest sites. Also present at Ambohitantely, on the western edge of the high plateau.

SIMILAR SPECIES Rather shorter tailed than Common and Stripe-throated Jeries and Cryptic Warbler with a more rotund shape. In addition the tail often appears notched. The bill appears somewhat finer than Common Jery. The song and call are characteristic.

243a. *Common Jery, adult nominate.*

243b. *Common Jery, adult nominate.*

244. *Green Jery, adult nominate.*

245 Stripe-throated Jery *Neomixis striatigula*

DESCRIPTION Size: 12cm. A small canopy insectivore. Sexes alike, plumage variation with age poorly known. At least two subspecies recognised. **Adult nominate:** Dull mid-green cap, mantle and upperparts. Strong blackish line through the eye and a short, conspicuous yellowish-white supercilium. Ear-coverts pale whitish-grey. Wings and tail rather darker green-brown. Underparts pale whitish-grey, suffused with yellow, on the throat and upper breast, and with variable olive streaking on the breast and throat. Iris mid-brown. Bill quite strong and slightly decurved, dark greyish-horn on both upper and lower mandibles, although may have a small pale area at the base of the lower mandible, and appears dark and heavy. Legs and feet mid-brown. *N. s. pallidior:* Similar to the nominate subspecies, though paler dull green above, and paler, more yellow below, especially on the throat.

VOICE The song is characteristic and only likely to be mistaken for Rand's Warbler. It is a long continuous series of blended, trilled buzzy notes that rise and then descend a scale. Often a second song-phrase linked to the first climbs back up the scale.

HABITAT/BEHAVIOUR Occurs in evergreen humid forest, coastal euphorbia scrub, and *Didierea* thickets, and secondary western forest. Does not occur in primary western deciduous forest, only at the limits and in secondary areas adjacent. In the east, rarely seen except when singing from the top of a high tree. Otherwise occurs in canopy mixed-species flocks, rarely descending below sub-canopy level. Feeds on insects which are gleaned actively from leaves and twigs.

RANGE/STATUS Endemic to Madagascar. Not globally threatened. Occurs the length of the eastern evergreen humid forest from Antalaha to Fort Dauphin (nominate race), between sea level and about 1,200m, occasionally higher. *N. s. pallidior* occurs in the south from just west of Fort Dauphin to about the Tsiribihina river, 100km north of Morondava from sea level to 800m.

WHERE TO SEE The eastern race is common at Perinet-Analamazaotra, Mantadia, Ranomafana and other low- and mid-altitude forest sites. The southern race is abundant near Ifaty, north to Morondava.

SIMILAR SPECIES A large, stocky jery, most easily distinguished by the dark eyestripe, strong supercilium and heavy blackish bill, and darker iris than Common Jery. The song is extremely characteristic.

246 Cryptic Warbler *Cryptosylvicola randrianasoloi*

DESCRIPTION Size: 12cm. A small, long-tailed canopy warbler. Sexes alike, plumage varies with age. **Adult:** Dull dark green on the crown, nape, mantle and upperparts. A slight pale supercilium contrasts with a poorly-marked dark eyestripe. The wings and tail are slightly darker brown-green, the flight feathers with narrow pale fringes. The underparts are mostly whitish, with a variable yellow wash over the throat and upper breast, indistinct streaking on the upper breast and throat and a dull olive wash over the lower breast and flanks. Iris brown, bill dark horn on the upper mandible, pale pink on the basal half of the lower. Legs and feet are dark pinkish-brown. **Juvenile:** Very young birds are dark dull green-grey on the back and head, slightly greener on the mantle and browner on the wings. Lacks the supercilium and eyestripe of the adult. The underparts are dull pale grey and slightly mottled on the breast, but without any trace of yellow. The bill is all-dark, with a pale orange gape, and the feet and legs dark horn.

VOICE The song is a loud, far-carrying, rasping *chick tss-tss-tss-tss-tss-tss-tss*, slightly fading away, with rather the rhythm of a car turning over prior to starting. The call is an equally distinctive *tsick* or *chick* or *chick-ess*.

HABITAT/BEHAVIOUR A species of the mid-altitude and montane evergreen humid forests, often occurring along steep ridges or in areas of bamboo. Often joins mixed-species flocks with jeries, newtonias, Rand's Warbler and small vangas, sally-gleaning from leaves and twigs, often flicking its wings while foraging. Singing birds often move and forage, along a ridge, where they may spend a few minutes at one perch before moving on. Often sings in a peculiar posture with the bill pointing diagonally downwards and the tail pointing upwards. The nest is a globular structure situated in the understorey.

RANGE/STATUS Endemic to Madagascar. Not globally threatened. Monotypic. Only described in 1996, but appears to be widely distributed from near Andapa in the north to Andohahela near the southern tip of the eastern evergreen humid forest belt. Fairly common from about 1,000m to the limit of forest at around 2,000m, though may be seen slightly lower than this, for example at Ranomafana.

WHERE TO SEE Common at Mantadia (on ridge-tops) and at Vohiparara and present near the main camp at Ranomafana. Appears not to occur on the high plateau.

SIMILAR SPECIES This species is similar to Common, Green and Stripe-throated Jeries, but differs from them all in its darker legs and feet, rather long and loose, slightly graduated tail and characteristic song.

5a. *Stripe-throated Jery, adult nominate.*

245b. *Stripe-throated Jery, adult nominate.*

6a. *Cryptic Warbler, adult.*

247 Wedge-tailed Jery *Hartertula flavoviridis*

DESCRIPTION Size: 12cm. A small, understorey warbler-like species. Sexes alike, plumage varies slightly with age. **Adult:** Crown olive green, contrasting with mid-grey ear-coverts and a pale greyish supercilium. Nape, mantle, scapulars, wings and tail mid-olive green. Underparts yellow, brightest on the throat, off-white on the belly and undertail-coverts. Tail rather long and loose, slightly wedge-shaped, often with the outer tail-feathers held splayed. Iris dark brown, bill conical, pale greyish-blue, legs and feet flesh-grey. **Juvenile:** Similar to adult, but greyish cheeks indistinct or lacking, and back slightly brighter green.

VOICE Song a loud, rapid and rather random series of trills and squeaks, unlike any other Malagasy bird, but not heard very often. Call similar to Spectacled Greenbul, a rather thin descending spluttering trill and also a soft, liquid *pwit.*

HABITAT/BEHAVIOUR Occurs in the understorey of eastern evergreen humid forest. A frequent member of understorey mixed-species flocks, feeds in tit-like fashion and is the only species that habitually feeds by hanging upside-down from dead-leaf clumps. Feeds on insects which are gleaned from leaves. Nest is a suspended globular structure usually 1-2m above the ground.

RANGE/STATUS Endemic to Madagascar. Currently considered **Near Threatened** on a global scale. Monotypic. Fairly common in most mid-altitude eastern evergreen humid forest (except probably the Sambirano). Most common between about 600 and 1,400m. Distinctly scarce or absent in most lowland forest, and seems to be absent from mossy forest at high altitude.

WHERE TO SEE Fairly common at Perinet-Analamazaotra, Mantadia, and Ranomafana.

SIMILAR SPECIES Similar to other jeries, but conspicuously larger; no other jery habitually forages in understorey shrubs or has grey ear-coverts. Resembles a small greenbul in behaviour, though differs in grey ear-coverts, small size, conical pale grey bill, habit of hanging upside-side from dead-leaf clumps and loose, slightly graduated tail.

248 Ward's Flycatcher *Pseudobias wardi*

DESCRIPTION Size: 15cm. A very characteristic monarch flycatcher. Sexes alike, plumage varies slightly with age. **Adult:** Glossy black crown, cheeks, nape, mantle, scapulars, and tail. Wings with broad white fringes to the greater coverts and tertials, forming a long white stripe on the closed wing. The underparts are white, but for a wide black breast-band. Iris dark brown surrounded by a broad fleshy bright blue eye-ring. Bill pale blue-grey, legs and feet blackish. **Juvenile:** Very similar to the adult, except that the eye-ring is narrower and duller (and may even be difficult to see), and the breast-band may be more diffuse.

VOICE An extremely characteristic flat, dry, metallic trill, *ttttttttttttttt,* slightly descending.

HABITAT/BEHAVIOUR Occurs in primary and adjacent secondary, eastern evergreen humid forest. Fly-catches for its insect prey from canopy perches or tree-fall gaps. Usually seen singly or in small groups. Rarely seen lower than the sub-canopy, but easy to see as it often chooses conspicuous perches. Often joins mixed-species flocks.

RANGE/STATUS Endemic to Madagascar. Currently considered **Near Threatened.** Monotypic. Common in evergreen humid forest between sea level and 1-500m (although scarcer below 600m), from Andohahela to the northern limit of the evergreen humid forest.

WHERE TO SEE Common at Perinet-Analamazaotra, Ranomafana, Masoala, and most mid-altitude sites.

SIMILAR SPECIES Could only be confused with the white-phase Madagascar Paradise Flycatcher, from which Ward's Flycatcher differs by its white throat, black breast-band, and lack of long central tail feathers, and Chabert's Vanga, from which it differs by its black breast-band, white in the wing and flycatcher habits. The call is particularly distinctive.

47. *Wedge-tailed Jery, adult.*

48. *Ward's Flycatcher, adult.*

249 Madagascar Paradise Flycatcher *Terpsiphone mutata*

DESCRIPTION Size: 18cm (with up to 12cm elongated central tail-streamers) A medium-sized monarch flycatcher. Plumage differs with age and season. **Adult male:** Occurs in approximately equal numbers in two plumage phases. 'White phase' black on the crown, (with a variable amount of bluish iridescence) nape, chin, and cheeks; the mantle is usually white in western birds and black in eastern birds, but variation occurs. Wings black with broad white fringes to the wing-coverts, tertials and (more narrowly) primaries. Rump and uppertail-coverts white, as are the elongated central tail feathers and the rest of the underparts. The other tail feathers are black, edged whitish on the inner margins. Iris dark brown with a brilliant blue eye-ring. Bill blue with a black tip, legs and feet blackish. 'Red-phase' males are rufous with an iridescent bluish-black crown and cheeks, darker brown wings with wide white fringes to the outer greater coverts, and long, white, central tail feathers. Bare parts as white male. **Adult female:** Mostly rufous, slightly darker on the wings, with a blackish iridescent cap and a narrow bluish eye-ring. **Juvenile:** Similar to female. Young males may have a small amount of white in the wing.
VOICE Call is a characteristic *retret retret retretret*, frequently repeated. Song is a loud, characteristic scolding series of whistled notes which are given in a descending series.
HABITAT/BEHAVIOUR Found in all native forest types except montane forest and more rarely in other wooded habitats such as plantations. Usually observed sallying for small insects. Often joins mixed species flocks. Both sexes make typical monarch-flycatcher tail-fanning and wing-spreading manoeuvres. Feeds on a variety of insects. Nest is deep bowl-shaped structure bound to narrow branches, 1-5m above the ground.
RANGE/STATUS Regional Endemic, occurring in Madagascar and the Comoros. Not globally threatened. Represented in Madagascar by endemic nominate subspecies found in native forest, from sea level to 1,600m.
WHERE TO SEE Common at all forest sites.
SIMILAR SPECIES Difficult to confuse with any other species.

250 Souimanga Sunbird *Nectarinia souimanga*

DESCRIPTION Size: 10-11cm. A small sunbird. Plumage varies with age, sex and season. Two subspecies. **Adult male nominate breeding:** Head, upper breast, mantle, upper scapulars and lesser coverts iridescent blue-green. Rest of wings and tail dull brown. Lower breast-band reddish, with narrow blackish band below. Rest of the underparts dull yellowish. Iris dark brown, bill, legs and feet dark grey or black. From January to July, male may show an eclipse plumage which resembles female except with traces of iridescent or dark feathers on the breast. **Adult female:** Dull olive-green crown, nape, mantle and wings, with a slight paler supercilium. Flight feathers and tail slightly darker. Underparts dull pale yellow or whitish, slightly streaked dark brown. **Juvenile:** Resembles the female but has a slightly shorter, pale-based bill and slight pale fringes on the wing feathers. **N. s. apolis:** Slightly paler, particularly on underparts which may be whitish.
VOICE The song is a short, loud explosive warbled phrase and is commonly heard. Also gives typical sunbird chirping and scolding notes. The single-note call is usually a loud *chiup*, but sometimes this species may give a more off-key hoarse *tchiew* which sounds similar to the call of Long-billed Green Sunbird.
HABITAT/BEHAVIOUR Found in all types of wooded vegetation, including secondary forest and plantations in east, west and south. Fairly common in Antananarivo. Feeds on nectar, especially baobabs, eucalyptus, and species of Leguminosae and *Bakerella* in evergreen humid forest. Also eats small insects gleaned from leaves and spiders webs. Found in mixed-species flocks in forest. Small oval-shaped nest situated 1-5m above the ground.
RANGE/STATUS Regional Endemic, occurring in Madagascar, the Comoros and in the Seychelles. Not globally threatened. Abundant everywhere except in open savanna areas and parts of the south. The nominate subspecies occurs throughout, except in the south, and also on the Comoros. The endemic subspecies *N. s. apolis* is restricted to the south. Found from sea level to 2,300m.
WHERE TO SEE Easily observed at all forest sites and in Antananarivo.
SIMILAR SPECIES Likely to be mistaken only for Long-billed Green Sunbird, and the sunbird-asities. Males yellow underparts and reddish breast-band are distinctive. The female differs from female Long-billed Green Sunbird in that the latter has longer, stouter bill, is larger overall and shows much more streaking on the underparts and usually paler supercilium. Long melodious call of Souimanga Sunbird is characteristic. Souimanga Sunbird is easily distinguished from the sunbird-asities by a combination of the longer tail, larger size, longer, and thicker bill, and characteristic calls. Male Souimanga differs additionally in the colourful breast-band and lack of eye-wattles.

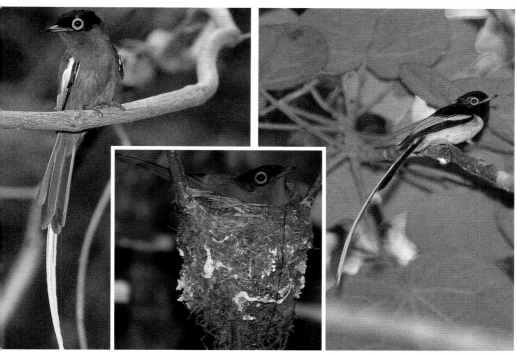

249. *Madagascar Paradise Flycatcher.* 249a (left) adult male red phase. 249b (right) adult male white phase. 249c (inset) female on nest.

250. *Souimanga Sunbird.* 250a (inset) adult male. 250b (left) adult male. 250c (right) adult female.

251 Long-billed Green Sunbird *Nectarinia notata*

DESCRIPTION Size: 14cm. A large, long-billed sunbird. Plumage varies with age, sex and season. **Adult male:** Head, chin, throat, upper breast, nape and mantle brilliant iridescent green, the wing-coverts more bluish. Rest of plumage blackish. Eclipse males are mostly olive-brown with scattered iridescent feathers on the breast and back. Iris dark red-brown, bill, legs and feet dark brown. **Adult female:** Dull olive-brown crown and upperparts, darker on the wings and tail, with a fairly well-marked pale supercilium and a dark line through the eye. The underparts are whitish, fairly heavily streaked with dark brown on the breast. **Juvenile:** Similar to the female though less well marked, more olive and with a shorter, pale-based bill.
VOICE Only one call seems to be used at all frequently, a loud, penetrating, peevish *tchew* or variants such as *tchiup*, usually given singly at 2 or 3-second intervals, sometimes in a long agitated sequence.
HABITAT/BEHAVIOUR Like Souimanga Sunbirds, active and conspicuous when feeding on flowers. Found in all types of native vegetation except high mountains but mostly less common than Souimanga Sunbird. Often males call loudly from the tops of isolated trees. The oval-shaped nest is situated 2-10m above the ground.
RANGE/STATUS Regional Endemic, occurring in Madagascar and the Comoros. Not globally threatened. Represented in Madagascar by the endemic nominate subspecies which is fairly common in eastern evergreen humid forest from sea level up to about 1,500m, patchy but sometimes abundant in western and the northern part of the southern forests. Scarce in the south. More common in Antananarivo than Souimanga Sunbird.
WHERE TO SEE Fairly common and easy to see at Perinet-Analamazaotra, Ranomafana, Mantadia, Ampijoroa, Kirindy and near Ifaty.
SIMILAR SPECIES Adult males and females are fairly easy to separate from Souimanga Sunbird (see that species). During moult into and out of the eclipse plumage, males may resemble Souimanga Sunbirds in having the lower breast and belly paler, off-white, with an iridescent breast. However they differ in lacking the reddish breast-band, and are larger with stouter, longer bills and a different voice.

252 Madagascar White-eye *Zosterops maderaspatana*

DESCRIPTION Size: 11-12cm. A small warbler-like bird. Plumage varies slightly with age. **Adult:** Face, crown, nape, mantle and back bright olive-green, slightly yellower on the rump and darker on the wings and tail. The eye is surrounded by a wide, bright white eye-ring, broken by a slight black line that runs through the eye. The chin and throat are bright yellow, as are the undertail-coverts, the rest of the underparts are bright white. Iris mid-brown, the rather stout bill is dark blackish-brown, legs and feet mid-grey. **Juvenile:** Slightly brighter green above, and when very young shows a pale orange gape.
VOICE The call is a characteristic series of slightly peevish low *sweet* notes, often given in a chorus by a group of birds. The song is very different, a pleasant wandering warble, lasting about 10 seconds, without much tonal variety.
HABITAT/BEHAVIOUR Found in all native forest formations, including evergreen humid forest, western dry forest, southern subdesert, plantations, secondary forest and scrub. Often in large groups, particularly on the edge of primary forest, where bands of up to fifty may be seen in mixed-species groups. Forages for insects, nectar, and small fruits in the canopy and understorey, and may congregate at fruiting trees, for instance at Traveller's Palm, where it eats (with difficulty) the bright blue fruits. The nest is a deep bowl-shaped structure situated 3-25m above the ground in the fork of a tree.
RANGE/STATUS Regional Endemic, occurring in Madagascar, the Comoros, the Iles Glorieuses and the Seychelles. Not globally threatened. Represented in Madagascar by the nominate subspecies which is common to the Iles Glorieuses. Abundant all over the eastern evergreen humid forest and in native vegetation and plantations on the high plateau, including in Antananarivo. Much more localised and scarce in the west and south, being commonest in gallery forest and plantations, where there are fruiting and flowering trees. Found from sea level to at least 2,200m.
WHERE TO SEE Common at most forest sites.
SIMILAR SPECIES Only likely to be confused with jeries or Cryptic Warbler, but instantly identifiable by the combination of bright white eye-ring and yellow throat and undertail-coverts.

251a. *Long-billed Green Sunbird, adult male.*

251b. *Long-billed Green Sunbird, adult female.*

251c. *Long-billed Green Sunbird, juvenile.*

252. *Madagascar White-eye, adult.*

253 Common Waxbill *Estrilda astrild*

DESCRIPTION Size: 11-13cm. A small estrildid finch. Sexes similar, plumage varies slightly with age. **Adult:** Grey crown separated from the pale grey cheeks by a conspicuous red eye-stripe. Entire upperparts, including wings and longish tail, brown with close, fine, blackish bars. Throat off-white, rest of underparts buff tinged pink with a reddish patch in the centre of the belly, browner flanks with fine dark barring and blackish undertail-coverts. Iris reddish-brown, bill bright waxy-red, legs and feet blackish. **Immature:** Similar to adult, though tends to be paler with less distinct barring, lacks red on the belly and has a black bill which turns red after a few months.
VOICE Typical calls include a sharp *pit* and a nasal *cher-cher-cher.*
HABITAT/BEHAVIOUR Inhabits open areas including grassland, marsh edges and crops. Gregarious, usually seen in small groups. Feeds on seeds. No proof of nesting in Madagascar.
RANGE/STATUS Occurs widely in sub-Saharan Africa and has been introduced widely including southern Europe, Brazil, the Caribbean and various Pacific and Indian Ocean Islands. Not globally threatened. In Madagascar the subspecies present is probably the nominate subspecies. Recently sighted (in 1983 and 1989) on Nosy Be, these sightings presumably relate to introduced individuals and it is not known whether or not a population has/will become established. Observed at and around sea level.
WHERE TO SEE Only known from Nosy Bé where a small population may still exist.
SIMILAR SPECIES A small, long-tailed, seed-eating passerine which is easily recognised by its closely barred brown plumage, red eye-stripe and in all but juveniles, the bright red bill.

254 Madagascar Mannikin *Lonchura nana*

DESCRIPTION Size: 10cm. A tiny estrildid finch. Sexes similar, plumage varies with age. **Adult:** Black lores contrast with the rest of the head which is grey with some faint blackish mottling on the crown. Upperparts brown with blackish flight feathers and tail and a yellowish rump which appears dull yellow due to the visible blackish bases to the feathers. Black chin and upper throat forms a neat black bib. Rest of the underparts pinkish-buff with indistinct darker mottling on the breast and undertail-coverts. Iris dark-brown, bill shows a blackish upper mandible and a pale horn lower mandible. Legs and feet pink. **Immature:** Plainer and more uniform than the adult, lacking the dark lores and bib and grey head and showing an all-black bill.
VOICE Calls include a soft *tsit* and a thin *tsip-tsirip* in flight. The song is a short rattling burst of notes which is often repeated.
HABITAT/BEHAVIOUR Occurs in a variety of open areas including grassland, forest edge, open woodland, marsh edges and crops and sometimes around villages. Gregarious, usually seen in small groups, sometimes mixed with other seedeaters such as Madagascar Red Fody. A ground feeder, diet consists chiefly of grass seeds. The nest is constructed from grass and usually situated in a tree or shrub.
RANGE/STATUS Endemic to Madagascar. Not globally threatened. Monotypic. Occurs commonly in suitable habitat throughout the island, though is more common in the north. Found from sea level to 2,000m.
WHERE TO SEE Widespread and easily seen at a number of sites. Regularly encountered at sites such as Perinet-Analamazaotra, Ranomafana and Ampijoroa.
SIMILAR SPECIES A tiny, brown seed-eating passerine. The adults are easily recognised by the distinctive black lores and bib. Immature best identified by tiny size, uniform brown plumage and stubby black bill. Unlikely to be confused with any other species.

53. *Common Waxbill, adult.*

54. *Madagascar Mannikin, adult.*

255 Nelicourvi Weaver *Ploceus nelicourvi*

DESCRIPTION Size: 14-15cm. A stocky forest weaver. Sexes differ and plumage varies with season and age. **Adult male breeding:** Black crown and ear-coverts are surrounded by bright golden-yellow which extends from the chin to the throat and round the ear-coverts forming a complete collar across the nape. Upperparts olive, slightly darker on the flight feathers. The olive of the upperparts extends across the upper breast forming an olive breast-band under the yellow throat. Rest of the underparts smoky grey with deep rufous undertail-coverts. Iris dark brown, bill stout, black, legs and feet dark grey. **Adult male non-breeding:** Similar to breeding male, though duller and with a less well-marked head pattern, lacking the black hood. Forehead yellow grading into the olive crown. Yellow supercilium and ear-coverts are separated by an olive eye-stripe and there is an olive patch at the rear of the ear-coverts. **Adult female:** Similar to non-breeding male. **Immature:** Similar to adult female, though duller with much of the yellow around the head sullied with olive and the bill paler, yellowish.

VOICE Has a characteristic weaver *swizzling* call.

HABITAT/BEHAVIOUR Inhabits both primary evergreen humid forest and adjacent areas of second growth. Usually seen singly or in pairs, sometimes with mixed-species flocks. Feeds largely on insects which are gleaned from trees. The nest is typical for a weaver being a bulky grass structure with an entrance tunnel which is suspended over an open area such as a trail or river.

RANGE/STATUS Endemic to Madagascar. Not globally threatened. Monotypic. Fairly common in evergreen humid forest in the north-west, north and east. Found from sea level to 2,000m.

WHERE TO SEE Frequently encountered at all suitable sites such as Perinet-Analamazaotra and Ranomafana with the nests being frequently visible over trails.

SIMILAR SPECIES The distinctive plumage renders the species unmistakable.

256 Sakalava Weaver *Ploceus sakalava*

DESCRIPTION Size: 13-15cm. A typical weaver. Sexes differ and plumage varies with season and age. Two subspecies, nominate and *P. s. minor* which differ only in the smaller size and slightly smaller bill of the latter. **Adult male breeding:** Vivid yellow head with bright, pinkish-red bare skin around the eye. Upperparts grey-brown with darker feather centres with indistinct pale buff median- and greater-covert wing-bars. Chin to the upper breast bright yellow, concolorous with the head. Rest of the underparts greyish. Iris brown, bill stout, bluish-grey, legs and feet pink. **Adult male non-breeding:** Rufous-brown crown, eye-stripe and moustachial stripe with duller pink skin around the eye. Supercilium, rest of face, chin, throat and breast greyish-buff. Rest of plumage as in male breeding. **Adult female** and **immature:** Similar to non-breeding male, though less prominent bare skin around the eye.

VOICE Vocal, especially around colonies, when males wing-quiver while calling. The call/song is a rather monotonous, sparrow-like, *chi-chi-chi-chi*. Also gives a short, emphatic *tswieck* in flight.

HABITAT/BEHAVIOUR Open habitats including savanna, crops, thorn scrub, lightly wooded areas and village surrounds. Gregarious, often seen in moderate or even large flocks. Adaptable and able to exist near humans, often feeding in rice paddies. Feeds largely on seeds though will also take insects. Nests colonially, in a tree or stand of trees, with many, loosely constructed, spherical grass nests, each with an entrance tunnel, situated in close proximity to one another.

RANGE/STATUS Endemic to Madagascar. Not globally threatened. Two subspecies are recognised, the nominate which is common in the north and west and *P. s. minor* which is common in subarid areas in the south-west and south. Found from sea level to 1,000m.

WHERE TO SEE Common and easy to see at most sites in the west such as around Toliara and at Ampijoroa.

SIMILAR SPECIES The bright yellow head of the male in breeding plumage renders it unmistakable. In other plumages, may be confused with female/non-breeding male Madagascar Red Fody but is relatively easily identified by its larger size, large grey-blue bill, rufous-brown tones to the head and pinkish bare skin around the eye, though the latter is not always conspicuous.

255. *Nelicourvi Weaver, adult male breeding.*

256a. *Sakalava Weaver, adult male breeding.*

256b. *Sakalava Weaver, adult female.*

257 Madagascar Red Fody *Foudia madagascariensis*

DESCRIPTION Size: 13-14cm. Sexes differ and plumage varies with season and age. **Adult male breeding:** Vermilion-red head; black patch around the eye. Mantle and scapulars red with black feather centres. Rump and uppertail-coverts red. Wings and tail blackish with narrow, pale buff fringes. Underparts red, often paler on belly. Red areas occasionally replaced by orange or yellow. Iris brown, bill stout and black, legs and feet pinkish. **Adult male non-breeding:** Olive-brown crown, eye-stripe, moustachial-stripe and indistinct dark malar-stripe contrast with prominent yellowish-buff supercilium and yellowish-washed ear-coverts and throat. Mantle and scapulars grey-brown to olive-brown with blackish feather centres. Rump and uppertail-coverts uniform olive-brown. Wings and tail blackish with broad pale creamy-buff fringes to each feather, particularly on wing-coverts where two wing-bars are usually apparent. Underparts pale greyish-olive washed with yellow, particularly on undertail-coverts. Bill horn coloured. In transitional plumage, males show patchy red. **Adult female** and **immature:** Similar to non-breeding male except bill pale horn. **VOICE** Short, high-pitched *chit chit chit* notes which vary slightly in pitch and may accelerate into rapid trill. Flight call a penetrating *tsit*. **HABITAT/BEHAVIOUR** Open habitats including savanna, scrub, lightly wooded areas, forest edge and towns. Gregarious, often seen in flocks particularly when roosting. Adaptable and able to exist near humans, often feeding in rice paddies. Feeds largely on seeds, though will also take insects and nectar of flowering trees. Constructs loose, spherical grass nest in tree or shrub. **RANGE/STATUS Endemic to Madagascar.** Introduced to other islands including the Seychelles. Not globally threatened. Monotypic. Very common. From sea level to 2,300m. **WHERE TO SEE** Common, widespread and easy to see, even in the capital, Antananarivo. **SIMILAR SPECIES** Breeding male unmistakable; otherwise difficult to separate from Forest Fody, though the former shows a smaller bill, tends to be paler, particularly around the face and underparts, and is less green than Forest Fody which typically shows brighter olive upperparts. Also shows paler, creamy-buff as opposed to olive fringes to the wing-coverts and tertials and thus typically shows clearer wing-bars. Forest fragmentation has allowed the two species to meet in unnaturally high numbers leading to widespread hybridisation. Some birds resembling Forest Fody may show red on mantle or undertail-coverts, suggesting a hybrid origin. The voices of two species are subtly different. Non-breeding birds may be confused with female House Sparrow and non-breeding Sakalava Weaver, which see for differences.

258 Forest Fody *Foudia omissa*

DESCRIPTION Size: 14-15cm. Sexes differ and plumage varies with season and age. **Adult male breeding:** Vermilion-red head, chin, throat and upper breast forms a red hood broken only by black patch around eye. Mantle and scapulars olive with black feather centres contrasting with pale orange-red rump and uppertail-coverts. Wings and tail blackish with narrow olive fringes feather and pale olive tips to coverts forming wing-bars. Greyish lower breast and belly demarcated from red upper breast. Undertail-coverts washed with yellow. Iris brown, bill massive, blackish, legs and feet pinkish. **Adult male non-breeding:** Olive-brown crown, eye-stripe and moustachial-stripe, with slightly paler olive-yellow supercilium and olive-grey ear-coverts. Upperparts similar to breeding male, though rump and uppertail-coverts are olive. Underparts greyish-olive washed with yellow, particularly on undertail-coverts. Bill horn coloured. **Adult female** and **immature:** Similar to non-breeding male except bill pale horn. **VOICE** Calls are similar to Madagascar Red Fody, though are higher-pitched and faster. **HABITAT/BEHAVIOUR** Restricted to evergreen humid forest. Usually seen alone, or in small flocks, sometimes joining mixed-species flocks. Spends much of the time in the middle and upper canopy, though also feeds low down. Feeds on insects and seeds, also nectar of flowering trees. **RANGE/STATUS Endemic to Madagascar.** Not globally threatened. Monotypic. Fairly common. Found from sea level to 2,000m, though more common at higher altitudes. It is likely that Forest Fody is disappearing through hybridisation with the adaptable Madagascar Red Fody and its continued existence may depend upon protection of large tracts of undisturbed evergreen humid forest. Some consider Forest Fody to be conspecific with Red-headed Fody *F. eminentissima* of Aldabra and the Comoros. **WHERE TO SEE** A scarce and declining species. Most likely to be found in the forest interior at Perinet-Analamazaotra, Ranomafana or Mantadia, though apparent hybrids occur at these sites. **SIMILAR SPECIES** Breeding males are distinctive but care must be taken to eliminate hybrids or transitional Madagascar Red Fody (which see for differences).

257a. Madagascar Red Fody, adult male breeding.

257b. Madagascar Red Fody, adult male transitional plumage.

257c. Madagascar Red Fody, adult female/immature.

258. Forest Fody, adult male breeding.

259 House Sparrow *Passer domesticus*

DESCRIPTION Size: 14-15cm. A typical sparrow. Sexes differ and plumage varies slightly with season and age. **Adult male breeding:** Grey crown bordered by a broad chestnut band which extends from behind the eye to the nape. Lores, chin and throat black, highlighting the whitish cheek. Upperparts mostly chestnut with black feather centres, though the rump and uppertail-coverts are grey and there is a prominent whitish median covert wing-bar. Underparts greyish with dark chevron markings on the undertail-coverts. Iris dark brown, bill blackish, basally pinkish, legs and feet pinkish-brown. **Adult male non-breeding:** Similar to breeding male, though pale fringes to the fresh plumage obscures the black throat and gives the bird an overall paler and duller appearance. Bill generally paler. **Adult female:** Crown and nape greyish-brown, rest of face pale greyish-buff with a prominent buff supercilium. Rest of plumage similar to male non-breeding, though bill tends to be pinkish. **Immature:** Similar to adult female, though tends to be paler and shows a prominent yellowish gape.
VOICE Call and song is a monotonous *cheep, chirp* or *chiseep*. Also gives a scolding *cher-r-r-r-r* in alarm.
HABITAT/BEHAVIOUR Restricted to urban environments and their surrounds in Madagascar. Gregarious, usually seen in small groups. Adaptable and able to coexist with humans. Feeds largely on seeds, though will take advantage of other available food. The nest is constructed from grass and is typically situated in a roof cavity or similar location.
RANGE/STATUS Occurs across Europe and western Asia, though has been introduced widely including the Americas, Australia and parts of Africa. Not globally threatened. In Madagascar the subspecies present is uncertain but likely to originate from either the nominate form or *P. d. indicus*. Recently introduced with the first sighting coming in 1985, it is currently restricted to the area within 50km of Toamasina. Found at and around sea level.
WHERE TO SEE Only known from the Toamasina area on the east coast.
SIMILAR SPECIES The distinctive head pattern and chestnut plumage of the male render it unmistakable. The female could be confused with female/non-breeding male Madagascar Red Fody but is relatively easily identified by its larger size, proportionately smaller bill and buff hue to the upperparts.

260 Wattled Starling *Creatophora cinerea*

DESCRIPTION Size: 21cm. A medium-sized starling. Sexes differ and plumage varies with season and age. **Adult male breeding:** Head bald and black with a large black wattle on the throat and a large patch of bright yellow skin on the hind crown. Upperparts greyish-buff with a conspicuously paler, off-white rump. Wings and tail black, the former showing a white patch at the base of the primaries. Underparts greyish-buff, slightly paler than the upperparts and becoming whitish on the undertail-coverts. Iris dark brown, bill pinkish-grey, legs and feet pinkish-brown. **Adult male non-breeding:** Similar to the female, though may show remnants of the breeding head adornments and black lores. **Adult female:** Similar to male, though lacks the head adornments, having a grey-buff head with a yellow eye-ring and a small patch of bare yellow skin behind the eye. **Immature:** Similar to the female, though drabber and browner.
VOICE Unlikely to be heard in Madagascar, though flocks give various hisses and thin squeaky warbles.
HABITAT/BEHAVIOUR Prefers open grassland and sparsely wooded areas. Highly gregarious and likely to appear in flocks despite its vagrant status. Feeds on a variety of invertebrates, flowers and small fruits. Only recorded near to sea level.
RANGE/STATUS Occurs in eastern, central and southern Africa and is highly nomadic throughout its range. Not globally threatened. Monotypic. In Madagascar it is a rare vagrant with just one record of a flock of eight to ten north of Toliara.
WHERE TO SEE A rare vagrant and hence no regular sites.
SIMILAR SPECIES Readily identified from the two other species of starling occurring on Madagascar by the pale grey-buff body plumage and contrastingly pale rump.

259a. House Sparrow, adult male.

259b. House Sparrow, adult female.

260. Wattled Starling, adult male breeding.

261 Common Myna *Acridotheres tristis*

DESCRIPTION Size: 25cm. A large starling. Sexes alike, plumage varies slightly with age. **Adult:** Black head, chin, throat, nape and hindneck with a conspicuous patch of bare yellow skin around and behind the eye. Rest of plumage dark brown but for black flight feathers and tail and white undertail-coverts, patch at the base of the primaries and tail-tip (except for the central tail feathers). Iris yellowish, bill, legs and feet yellow. **Immature:** Similar to the adult though duller, lacking the black hood and showing reduced bare yellow skin around the eye.
VOICE Vocal, giving a variety of loud calls including various hisses and piercing harsh calls as well as a frequently repeated *keewoo keewoo keewoo*. Also a good mimic of species such as Lesser Vasa Parrot.
HABITAT/BEHAVIOUR Prefers open habitats, sparsely wooded areas, paddies and village surrounds. Gregarious, usually seen in small groups, though forms large communal roosts. An opportunistic feeder, frequently seen with livestock. Feeds on a variety of invertebrates, small vertebrates, fruits and seeds. Nests in a tree cavity.
RANGE/STATUS Occurs in southern Asia though has been introduced widely into other areas including parts of Africa, New Zealand and the Seychelles. Not globally threatened. Represented in Madagascar by the nominate subspecies which is native to India and south-eastern Asia and is common in the north-west, north, east and south and is gradually spreading. Found from sea level to 1,600m.
WHERE TO SEE Common and widespread in its spreading range, even now present in the capital Antananarivo.
SIMILAR SPECIES A large, stocky dark starling which is easily distinguished from Madagascar Starling by its larger size, yellow bare parts and extensive white wing-patches and white tail-tip.

262 Madagascar Starling *Hartlaubius auratus*

DESCRIPTION Size: 21cm. A small slender starling. Sexes differ and plumage varies slightly with age. **Adult male:** Uniform chocolate-brown head. Upperparts brown, slightly paler than the head. Wings dark brown with a slight green gloss. The primaries are blue with white outer webs though this is often concealed when perched. Long slightly notched tail, brown with a blue gloss and white outer tail-feathers. Underparts brown, grading into the white belly and undertail-coverts. Iris dark brown, bill slender and black, legs and feet black. **Adult female:** Similar to the male though drabber and less well marked, the head being concolorous with the rest of the upperparts. **Immature:** Similar to the adult female.
VOICE Only heard infrequently. The calls include a repeated, high-pitched, trisyllabic whistle *tee tree-tee* and a loud metallic *plick* which is often repeated. A quiet warbling song is sometimes given at roosts.
HABITAT/BEHAVIOUR Inhabits natural forest types including undisturbed and degraded areas and even sparse woodland around villages. Gregarious, usually seen in small groups and sometimes joins mixed-species flocks. Generally found in tree tops and forest edge, often perching on prominent branches. Feeds predominantly on small fruits and occasionally invertebrates. Nest is situated in a tree hollow.
RANGE/STATUS **Endemic to Madagascar**. Not globally threatened. Monotypic. Distributed in suitable habitat throughout and is fairly common in the north-west, north and east, and rather scarce elsewhere, particularly in the south and on the high plateau. Found from sea level to 1,200m, rare at higher altitudes.
WHERE TO SEE Usually relatively easy to find in forested sites of the east such as Perinet-Analamazaotra, Ranomafana and the Masoala Peninsula. It is also seen frequently at Zombitse Forest.
SIMILAR SPECIES Unlikely to be confused with the two other species of starling on Madagascar, which see for differences. Madagascar Bulbul is superficially similar though shows uniform dark grey plumage with a red bill and lacks white in the wings and tail.

261. Common Myna, adult.

262a. Madagascar Starling, adult male.

262b. Madagascar Starling, adult female.

263 Eurasian Golden Oriole *Oriolus oriolus*

DESCRIPTION Size: 24cm. A brightly coloured oriole. Sexes differ and plumage varies with age. **Adult male:** Entire bird golden-yellow but for black lores, wings and tail. There is a yellow patch on the primary-coverts and all but the central tail feathers show yellow tips. Iris reddish, bill pinkish-red, legs and feet grey. **Adult female:** Similar to the male though drabber. The head and upperparts are olive-yellow, brightest on the rump, the wings and tail show a similar pattern to the male though the black is replaced by dark olive. Underparts whitish, streaked lightly with olive and suffused with yellow which is brightest on the belly and undertail-coverts. Bare parts as male. **Immature:** Similar to the female though drabber, less yellow and with duller, brownish bill and iris.
VOICE The song, which is unlikely to be heard on Madagascar is a fluty, melodic yodelling *tuu-klee-chooee*. The alarm call is a harsh mewing *kla-eik*.
HABITAT/BEHAVIOUR Most likely to be seen in Madagascar in coastal trees where the species favours dense canopy. Feeds on a variety of invertebrates.
RANGE/STATUS Breeds across Europe, northern Africa and Asia, wintering in sub-Saharan Africa and southern Asia. Not globally threatened. Presumably represented in Madagascar by the nominate subspecies which is found in the western part of its range. It is a rare visitor to Madagascar with a few scattered records mainly from the west coast during the austral summer. Most records come from near to sea level.
WHERE TO SEE A rare vagrant with few records and no regular sites though perhaps most likely to be seen on the west coast.
SIMILAR SPECIES The distinctive black or olive and yellow plumage renders this thrush-sized species unmistakable.

264 Crested Drongo *Dicrurus forficatus*

DESCRIPTION Size: 26cm. A typical drongo. Sexes alike, plumage varies slightly with age. **Adult:** Entire plumage blackish. The flight feathers are tinged brown and the rest of the plumage shows a blue sheen. There is a conspicuous tuft of feathers above the bill forming a crest and the long tail is deeply forked. Iris red, bill, legs and feet blackish. **Immature:** Similar to the adult though differs in the shorter and less prominent crest, shorter tail and the crown, wing-coverts and underparts show variable whitish fringes.
VOICE A highly vocal species with a very varied repertoire. Typical phrases include a jumbled, rapid group of shrill nasal notes and various whistled phrases interspersed with nasal notes. Sometimes mimics other species.
HABITAT/BEHAVIOUR Occurs in a variety of habitats with trees from forest to sparsely wooded terrain and plantations. Usually seen singly or in pairs and frequently accompanies mixed-species flocks. Hunts from an exposed perch, usually in the mid-canopy and will undertake fly-catching sallies. Feeds on a variety of invertebrates. The small bowl-shaped nest is usually constructed high in a tree.
RANGE/STATUS Regional Endemic, occurring in Madagascar and Anjouan in the Comoros. Not globally threatened. Represented in Madagascar by the nominate subspecies which is endemic. Common in suitable habitat throughout, though rare on the treeless parts of the high plateau. Found from sea level to 1,600m.
WHERE TO SEE Common and widespread, easily seen at most sites.
SIMILAR SPECIES The only drongo in Madagascar, easily recognised by its all-blackish plumage, slender silhouette, prominent crest and deeply forked tail.

63. Eurasian Golden Oriole, adult male.

64. Crested Drongo, adult.

265 Pied Crow *Corvus albus*

DESCRIPTION Size: 50cm. A large, black and white crow. Sexes alike, plumage varies slightly with age. **Adult:** Entire plumage glossy black except for a white hind collar which joins the white lower breast and upper belly. Iris dark brown, bill, legs and feet black. **Immature:** Similar to the adult though differs in overall drabber plumage which is less contrasting.

VOICE Gives loud cawing calls *kwaaarr* or *kwoork*, typical of the genus.

HABITAT/BEHAVIOUR Occurs in a variety of open habitats such as sparsely wooded terrain, open savanna and village surrounds. Gregarious, especially outside the breeding season when usually seen in small, loose groups. Feeds mainly on the ground though is an agile and powerful flyer and frequently soars. An omnivorous and opportunistic feeder, the diet consisting of carrion, invertebrates, small vertebrates, seeds and fruit. The large stick nest is usually situated high in an isolated tree.

RANGE/STATUS Occurs in sub-Saharan Africa, Madagascar and some adjacent islands. Not globally threatened. Monotypic. In Madagascar it is common in suitable habitat throughout, though less common on the high plateau. Found from sea level to 2,000m.

WHERE TO SEE Common and widespread in open habitats.

SIMILAR SPECIES The only crow in Madagascar and unlikely to be confused with any other species. In flight, may appear superficially similar to a raptor at a distance though on closer inspection the black and white plumage and stout black bill are unmistakable.

65a. Pied Crow, adult. 265b (inset) Pied Crow, adult.

APPENDIX A
SPECIES RARELY RECORDED IN MALAGASY WATERS

Cape Petrel *Daption capense*

DESCRIPTION Size: 38-40cm. Wingspan: 81-91cm. A medium-sized stocky petrel which is unlikely to be confused with any other species. Head sooty black, black mantle merges into the white back, rump and tail base, all of which are mottled with black chevrons. Underparts white. Upperwings black with white patches on the secondary-coverts and at the base of the inner primaries, giving the upperparts a distinctive piebald appearance. Underwings mostly white with a narrow dark border.
RANGE/STATUS Circumpolar in the southern oceans where it is abundant and widespread from the pack ice to the Tropic of Capricorn. Not globally threatened. Occasional migrant in Malagasy waters.

Barau's Petrel *Pterodroma baraui*

DESCRIPTION Size: 38cm. A medium-sized stocky petrel with a strong wheeling flight. White forehead contrasts with the dark cap. Upperparts grey with a distinct blackish 'M' marking on the upperwing and a dark rump. Underparts and underwings white with dark tips to the primaries and a narrow, diagonal dark bar across the-coverts. Similar to Soft-plumaged Petrel though easily separated by the predominantly white as opposed to dark underwings. Easily separated from prions by the larger size and stronger, wheeling flight.
RANGE/STATUS Indian Ocean, though exact pelagic distribution unknown. Globally Threatened and currently classified as Critically Endangered. One record from a boat north-east of Fort Dauphin in December 1991.

Soft-plumaged Petrel *Pterodroma mollis*

DESCRIPTION Size: 34cm. Wingspan: 89cm. A medium-sized stocky petrel with a strong wheeling flight. White forehead, rest of upperparts dark grey with an indistinct distinct blackish 'M' marking on the upperwing. Underparts white with a noticeable grey breast-band and dark underwings which at close range show a pale flash across the base of the primaries and secondary-coverts. May be confused with Barau's Petrel, which see for differences.
RANGE/STATUS South Atlantic and Indian Oceans. Not globally threatened. One record of four individuals seen from a boat south of Madagascar in July 1991, and one old specimen record.

Antarctic Prion *Pachyptila desolata*

DESCRIPTION Size: 25-27cm. Wingspan: 58-66cm. A small weak petrel with an erratic weaving flight low over the waves. Head dark blue-grey with a short, white supercilium and a thick, dark, blackish eye-stripe. Chin, throat and the rest of the ear-coverts white. Upperparts including upperwing blue-grey with a narrow blackish 'M' marking on the upperwing and a black terminal band on the tail. Dark blue-grey wash on the hindneck extends to the sides of the breast forming a distinct half-collar. Underparts white. Bill large and blue. The six species of prions are notoriously difficult to identify at sea. The two species to have been identified from Madagascar, this and Slender-billed Prion are almost impossible to separate at sea, though Slender-billed shows less grey on the sides of the breast, a paler grey head with a less well-marked eye-stripe and has a thinner bill. Soft-plumaged and Barau's Petrels are superficially similar, though differ in their plumage and stronger, more wheeling flight.
RANGE/STATUS Circumpolar in southern oceans, occurring north to the Tropic of Capricorn. Not globally threatened. Probably an occasional migrant to Malagasy waters, where it has been reportedly captured along the coasts.

Slender-billed Prion *Pachyptila belcheri*

DESCRIPTION Size: 26cm. Wingspan: 56cm. Almost identical to Antarctic Prion though tends to show less grey on the sides of the breast thus forming less of a collar and the bill is much slimmer. See comments under identification for Antarctic Prion.

RANGE/STATUS Occurs in southern oceans though the exact distribution is unclear. Not globally threatened. Probably a rare migrant to Malagasy waters. Recorded from carcasses found on Nosy Satrana in 1985 which were initially identified as Salvin's Prion (*P. salvini*).

Jouanin's Petrel *Bulweria fallax*

DESCRIPTION Size: 31cm. Wingspan: 79cm. A medium-sized, long-winged and long-tailed petrel. Flight is strong and swift moving over the ocean in broad arcs. Plumage wholly blackish-brown though at close range a paler diagonal covert bar may be visible on the upperwing. Separated from Great-winged Petrel by the more slender, long-winged and long-tailed shape. Separated from Wedge-tailed Shearwater by the smaller size and faster, more direct flight.

RANGE/STATUS Occurs in the Arabian Sea and north-west Indian Ocean. Not globally threatened. Two records from boats north-east of Fort Dauphin in December 1991 and January 1992.

Cory's Shearwater *Calonectris diomedea*

DESCRIPTION Size: 46cm. Wingspan: 113cm. A large heavy shearwater with a slow lazy flight. Grey head merges into white underparts. Upperparts greyish brown with paler fringes to the upperwing-coverts, a variable white band on the uppertail-coverts and darker tail and flight feathers. Underparts white with a dark greyish border to the underwings. Bill large and yellow. The only large shearwater with white underwings occurring in Malagasay waters.

RANGE/STATUS Breeds in the north Atlantic and disperses to the south Atlantic and south-west Indian Oceans. Not globally threatened. One record of ten birds seen from a boat south-west of Cap Ste. Marie in December 1991.

Flesh-footed Shearwater *Puffinus carneipes*

DESCRIPTION Size: 43cm. Wingspan: 103cm. A large heavy shearwater with a slow effortless flight. Plumage wholly blackish-brown. Bill and legs yellowish flesh. Very similar to Wedge-tailed Shearwater, which see for differences.

RANGE/STATUS Breeds in the south Pacific and Indian Oceans dispersing north in the non-breeding season. Not globally threatened. One record of two birds seen from a boat south-west of Cap Ste. Marie in December 1991.

White-faced Storm-petrel *Pelagodroma marina*

DESCRIPTION Size: 20cm. Wingspan: 42cm. A medium-sized storm-petrel. Dark crown and eye-stripe contrast with a prominent white supercilium. Upperparts grey-brown with a paler grey covert bar and pale grey rump which contrast with the blackish flight feathers and tail. Underparts and underwings white but for blackish underside to the flight feathers and tail. Easily separated from all other storm-petrels occurring in Malagasy waters by the grey-brown upperparts and patterned, whitish face.

RANGE/STATUS Widespread in all three oceans. Not globally threatened. Two records of three birds from a boat close to Nosy Bé in May 1991.

Black-bellied Storm-petrel *Fregetta tropica*

DESCRIPTION Size: 20cm. Wingspan: 46cm. A large storm-petrel. Dark, blackish upperparts except for a conspicuous greyish bar across the secondary greater coverts and a conspicuous white rump band. Underparts and underwing blackish except for the belly, flanks and underwing-coverts which are white with a black line running down the centre of the breast and belly which joins the blackish undertail-coverts. Flight direct and low, often with legs dangling and body swaying from side to side. The feet project beyond the tail in flight. Slightly larger than Wilson's Storm-petrel from which it differs by the extensive white on the underparts. Similar to White-bellied Storm-petrel which differs in having paler upperparts and an unmarked white belly which lacks the central black stripe.
RANGE/STATUS Widespread in southern oceans and recorded regularly as far north as the equator. Not globally threatened. Regularly recorded near to the Madagascar coasts, records probably referable to *F. t. melanogaster*.

White-bellied Storm-petrel *Fregetta grallaria*

DESCRIPTION Size: 20cm. Wingspan: 46cm. A large storm-petrel, similar in flight and jizz to the previous species. Dark, brown upperparts except for an inconspicuous greyish bar across the secondary greater coverts and a conspicuous white rump band. Underparts and underwing blackish except for the belly, flanks and underwing-coverts which are white. See Black-bellied Storm-petrel for identification discussion.
RANGE/STATUS Widespread in southern oceans and recorded regularly as far north as the equator. Not globally threatened. One record of five birds from a boat 40km off Nosy Bé in May 1991.

Red-billed Tropicbird *Phaethon aethereus*

DESCRIPTION Size: 45-50cm. (+ 46-56cm tail-streamers). Wingspan: 99-106cm. Very similar in size and shape to the two regularly occurring tropicbirds. Head white with a conspicuous black mask. Rest of the upperparts white with narrow blackish vermiculations and bars. Tail white, upperwing white with a black wedge formed by the outer four primaries and their coverts and some black barring on the inner secondary-coverts and secondaries. Underparts white with some greyish barring on the flanks. Bill red. Juvenile differs from adult in having a yellowish, black-tipped bill, more extensive black masks which join across the nape, broader and coarser barring on the upperparts and a black-tipped tail which lacks streamers. Adult easily separated from the two other tropicbirds by a combination of the red bill, barred upperparts and long white tail-streamers. Juvenile separated from juvenile White-tailed by its larger size, black nape and coarsely barred upperparts. Juvenile Red-tailed Tropicbird lacks the black nape and shows very restricted black in the primaries.
RANGE/STATUS Found in tropical and subtropical zones of the north-west Indian, east Pacific and Atlantic Oceans. Not globally threatened, though the least numerous of the tropicbirds. The only records in Madagascar are a doubtful record from near Antsirabe and at least one nineteenth-century specimen record.

Masked Booby *Sula dactylatra*

DESCRIPTION Size: 86cm. Wingspan: 152cm. A large seabird, similar in flight and jizz to the two other booby species occurring in Malagasy waters. **Adult:** Plumage all-white but for black primaries, secondaries and tail and a conspicuous black mask. Bill large and pale. **Juvenile:** Similar to juvenile Brown Booby, which see for differences. May only be confused with the two other species of booby occurring in Malagasay waters, which see for identification discussions.
RANGE/STATUS A widespread, pantropical species. Not globally threatened. A rare visitor to Malagasay waters with just one record of a single bird seen from a boat east of Sambava in January 1994.

APPENDIX B

SPECIES NOT RECORDED WITHIN THE LAST 50 YEARS

Long-crested Eagle *Lophaetus occipitalis*

DESCRIPTION Size: 52-58 cm. This medium to large raptor is highly distinctive. When perched it appears sooty-brown with white undertail-coverts and a long and distinctive crest which is usually held vertically. In flight, its dark plumage with white barring in the tail, and broad, rounded wings with prominent white 'bulls-eyes' in the primaries are unmistakable.

RANGE/STATUS This species is known from one sight record near Anjimanoro in 1868. Long-crested Eagle occurs in Africa south of the Sahara and is largely sedentary, although to some extent nomadic in the non-breeding season. Although an unlikely candidate for vagrancy, the record is considered to be reliable.

Snail-eating Coua *Coua delalandei*

DESCRIPTION Size: about 65 cm. Slightly larger than the Giant Coua which, in the east, has not been recorded further north than Mandena, just to the north of Fort Dauphin. Differs from the Giant Coua in having distinctly blue upperparts and a paler, whitish coloration on the upper breast. There may also have been differences in the colour of the bare parts but of course these are not well preserved in museum specimens.

RANGE/STATUS The Snail-eating Coua was last reported in 1834 and has never been reliably recorded away from Ile Sainte-Marie off the east coast of Madagascar, where it is certainly extinct. However, it is just possible that it occurred on the mainland. If so, then it might still be found in the lowland forest around the Bay of Antongil.

Lesser Striped Swallow *Hirundo abyssinica*

DESCRIPTION Size: 16 cm. A highly distinctive, long-tailed swallow which is easily recognised by its blue upperparts, orange-rufous head and rump, and off-white underparts boldly streaked with black.

RANGE/STATUS This species is known from one specimen record (pre-1925) and one sight record in 1947. This species occurs in Africa south of the Sahara where it is largely sedentary, although it is a breeding visitor to the northern and southern parts of its breeding range and its movements are poorly understood.

GLOSSARY

aerial: in the air

allopatric: relating to two or more usually closely related species whose ranges do not overlap

allospecies: a group of two or more closely related species with non-overlapping ranges

aquatic: water-living

arboreal: tree-living

axillaries: the feathers at the base of the undersides of the wing (the 'armpit')

bar: a narrow line

bare parts: the parts of a bird with no feathers, including the bill, legs, feet, iris and any naked parts of the head

cap: a distinct patch of colour covering all or part of the top of the head, usually a larger area than the crown

carpal bar: a contrasting line extending from the carpal joint across the secondary wing-coverts to the body

carpal (joint): the bend on the leading edge of the open wing

casque: an enlargement of the upper part of the bill or on top of the head

cere: a bare wax-like or fleshy patch of skin at the base of the upper mandible into which the nostrils open; only present on some birds such as raptors and pigeons and often brightly coloured

circumpolar: all the way round one of the earth's poles

cline: a geographical gradient between individuals of a species in a feature such as size or colour

collar: a band of dark or light contrasting colour around the front or back of the neck

crepuscular: active around dawn and dusk

crest: a tuft of feathers on the top of the head which, in some species, may be raised or lowered

crown-stripe: a distinct line from the forehead along the centre of the crown

cryptic: having colouring or patterning which provides camouflage

culmen: the ridge or upper part of the upper mandible on a bird's bill

cutting-edge: the area where the upper and lower mandibles of the bill meet

deciduous: of a tree or plant that sheds its leaves annually

decurved: curved downwards

dimorphic: having two distinct plumage forms, usually colour related, as in light and dark morphs

diurnal: active during daylight hours

emergent vegetation: plants which grow in water but extend out above the water's surface

endemic: restricted to a particular area

eye-ring: a contrasting ring around the eye

face: the sides of the head including the lores, orbital area, ear-coverts and malar area

feral: a formerly domesticated species or population now living wild

fledging: the point at which a young bird leaves the nest or has attained its first full set of feathers

flight feathers: the primary and secondary wing feathers

foliage: leafy vegetation

foreneck: the front side of the neck

frontal shield: a plate of often raised and often contrastingly coloured bare skin on the forehead - found in species such as coots

frugivore: fruit eater

gape: the fleshy interior of the bill

gonys: the prominent ridge towards the tip of the lower mandible formed by the fusion of the two halves of the lower mandible; particularly prominent in species such as gulls

gorget: a distinctively coloured patch on the throat or upper breast

gregarious: sociable, lives in groups

guttural: from the throat

hindneck: the upper or rear side of the neck

hood: a dark-coloured head and (usually) throat

insectivore: insect eater

jizz: a combination of characters which give the bird a distinct appearance in the field

leading edge: the forward edge of the open wing

lore: the area between the base of the upper mandible and the eye

mandible: either the upper or lower part of the bill

marine: of the sea

mask: a dark patch on the side of the head, usually including the ear-coverts

mesial: pertaining to the middle and usually used when referring to throat markings. A mesial throat stripe is a stripe along the centre of the throat

migrant: a species which undertakes a movement between its breeding and non-breeding areas

monotypic: of one form, not having subspecies

montane: of the mountains

morph: a distinct, genetically determined plumage form or type

nail: the hardened tip of the upper mandible, usually referred to on ducks

nocturnal: active during the night

notches: used as a descriptive term for feather markings - usually pale markings on a dark background along the edge of a feather giving a 'notched' effect

occipital crest: a crest on the hindcrown and/or nape

omnivore: an eater of food from plant and animal origin

orbital ring: a ring of bare skin around the eye

pantropical: distributed around the world's tropics

passerine: a bird belonging to the Order Passeriformes, usually referred to as 'perching birds' which are recognised by the structure of the foot with three toes facing forward and one toe facing back

pelagic: of the open ocean

plume: an elongated feather, usually used in display

polymorphic: having more than one distinct plumage morph

race: a colloquial term for subspecies

rachis: the central 'shaft' of a feather (plural raches)

raptor: a bird of prey

rictal bristles: stiff, bristle-like feathers which surround the gape of certain species such as nightjars

sally-gleaning: a short flight culminating in the capture of prey from the foliage

scalloped: with crescent-shaped plumage markings

sole: the underside of the foot

speculum: a contrasting, often iridescent, patch on the inner secondaries of a (duck's) wing

streamers: greatly elongated tail feathers or tail feather projections

subantarctic: region adjacent to and north of the Antarctic

submontane: lower elevations and foothills of mountains

subsong: a subdued version of the normal territorial song

subterminal: the area just before the tip

terrestrial: ground-living

territory: the area a bird establishes for itself and defends from others

trailing edge: the hind edge of the wing

underparts: the under-surface of the body including the throat, breast, belly, flanks and undertail-coverts

understorey: the lower level of a forest, i.e. the undergrowth

underwing: the underside of the wing including the coverts and flight feathers

upperparts: the upper surface of the body including the mantle, wings, back and rump

upperstorey: the higher level of a forest, i.e. the canopy

upperwing: the upperside of the wing including the coverts and flight feathers

vagrant: accidental to the region

vent: the area including the undertail-coverts and the lower belly and rear flanks

vermiculations: fine, wavy plumage markings

washed: suffused with a particular colour

wattle: a fleshy lobe of skin, often brightly coloured, around the face or base of the bill or neck

web: the broad surface of a feather, the inner web being on the inner side of the shaft and the outer web on the external side of the feather shaft; also, the fold of skin stretched between the toes of some aquatic birds

wing-bar: a narrow line across a wing, often formed by paler tips to the secondary-coverts

wing patch: a coloured area on a bird's wing

Selected Bibliography

The following is a list of references which contain useful information about the birds of Madagascar. It is not exhaustive but contains all the main sources of reference which were consulted during the preparation of this book. A much more complete bibliography can be found in Putnam (1997, see below) and this is obtainable from the World Wide Fund for Nature in Antananarivo (see Useful Addresses).

Attenborough, D. (1961) *Zoo Quest to Madagascar.* Lutterworth Press, London.

Benson, C. W., Colebrook-Robjent, J. F. R., & Williams, A. (1976-77) Contribution à l'ornithologie de Madagascar. *Oiseaux et R.F.O.* 46: 103-134; 47: 41-61, 167-191.

Bradt, H., Schuurman, D. and Garbutt, N. (1996). *Madagascar Wildlife: A Visitor's Guide.* Bradt Publications, Buckinghamshire.

Brown, L. H., Urban, E. K. and Newman, K. (1982) *The Birds of Africa.* Vol. 1. Academic Press, London.

Chantler, P. and Driessens, G. (1995) *Swifts: A Guide to the Swifts and Treeswifts of the World.* Pica Press, Sussex.

Clement, P., Harris, A. and Davis, J. (1993) *Finches and Sparrows: An Identification Guide.* Christopher Helm, London.

Collar, N. J., Crosby, M. J. and Stattersfield, A. J. (1994) *Birds to Watch 2: The World List of Threatened Birds.* BirdLife International, Cambridge.

Dee, T. J. (1986) *The Endemic Birds of Madagascar.* International Council for Bird Preservation, Cambridge.

del Hoyo, J., Elliott, A. and Sargatal, J. (eds.) (1992) *Handbook of the Birds of the World.* Vol. 1. Ostrich to Ducks. Lynx Edicions, Barcelona.

del Hoyo, J., Elliott, A. and Sargatal, J. (eds.) (1994) *Handbook of the Birds of the World.* Vol. 2. New World Vultures to Guineafowl. Lynx Edicions, Barcelona.

del Hoyo, J., Elliott, A. and Sargatal, J. (eds.) (1996) *Handbook of the Birds of the World.* Vol. 3. Hoatzin to Auks. Lynx Edicions, Barcelona.

Dowsett, R. J. and Dowsett-Lemaire, F. (1993) *A Contribution to the Distribution and Taxonomy of Afrotropical and Malagasy Birds.* Tauraco Press, Liège, Belgium.

Dowsett, R. J. and Forbes-Watson, A. D. (1993) *Checklist of Birds of the Afrotropical and Malagasy Regions.* Vol. 1. Species Limits and Distribution. Tauraco Press, Liège, Belgium.

Eguchi, K., Yamagishi, S. and Randrianasolo, V. (1993) The composition and foraging behaviour of mixed species flocks of forest-living birds in Madagascar. *Ibis* 134: 91-96.

Enticott, J. and Tipling, D. (1997) *Photographic Handbook of the Seabirds of the World.* New Holland, London.

Evans, M. I., Duckworth, J. W., Hawkins, A. F. A., Safford, R. J. Sheldon, B. C. and Wilkinson, R. J. (1992) Key bird species of Marojejy Strict Nature Reserve, Madagascar. *Bird Conservation International* 2: 201-220.

Fry, C. H., Fry, K. and Harris, A. (1992) *Kingfishers, Bee-eaters and Rollers.* Christopher Helm, London.

Fry, C. H., Keith, S. and Urban, E. K. (eds.) (1988) *The Birds of Africa.* Vol. 3. Academic Press, London.

Goodman, S. M. (ed.) (1997) A floral and faunal inventory of the eastern slopes of the Réserve Naturelle Intégrale d'Andringitra, Madagascar; with reference to elevational variation. *Fieldiana: Zoology,* new series. Number 85.

Goodman, S. M. and Langrand, O. (eds.) (1994) *Inventaire biologique; Forêt de Zombitse.* Recherches Pour le Développement, Série Sciences biologiques, No. Spécial. (Centre d'Information et de Documentation Scientifique et Technique, Antananarivo, Madagascar).

Goodman, S. M., Pidgeon, M., Hawkins, A. F. A. and Schulenberg, T. S. (1997) The birds of south-eastern Madagascar. *Fieldiana: Zoology,* 87: 1-132.

Goodman, S. M. and Patterson, B. D. (eds.) (1997) *Natural Change and Human Impact in Madagascar.* The Smithsonian Institution, Washington.

Hancock, J. and Kushlan, J. (1984) *The Herons Handbook.* Croom Helm, London.

Harrison, P. (1983) *Seabirds: An Identification Guide.* Christopher Helm, Kent.

Harrison, P. (1987) *Seabirds of the World: A Photographic Guide.* Christopher Helm, Kent.

Hawkins, A. F. A. in press. Altitudinal and latitudinal distribution of east Malagasy forest bird communities. *Journal of Biogeography.*

Hawkins, A. F. A., Chapman, P., Ganzhorn, J. U., Bloxam, Q., Tonge, S. and Barlow, S. (1990). Vertebrate conservation in Ankarana Special Reserve, Northern Madagascar. *Biological Conservation* 54 (2): 83-110.

Hayman, P., Marchant, J. and Prater, T. (1986) *Shorebirds: An Identification Guide to the Waders of the World.* Croom Helm, Kent.

Howard, R. and Moore, A. (1991) *A Complete Checklist of the Birds of the World.* 2nd edition. Academic Press, London.

ICBP (1992) *Putting Biodiversity on the Map: Priority Areas for Global Conservation.* International Council for Bird Preservation, Cambridge.

Jenkins, M. D., (ed.) (1987) *Madagascar - an environmental profile.* International Union for the Conservation of Nature, Cambridge, UK and Gland, Switzerland.

Jolly, A. (1980) *A World Like Our Own; Man and Nature in Madagascar.* Yale University Press, New Haven.

Jolly, A., Oberlé P., and Albignac R. (eds.) 1984 *Madagascar.* IUCN Key Environments Series. Pergamon Press, Oxford.

Jonsson, L. (1992) *Birds of Europe with North Africa and the Middle East.* Christopher Helm, London.

Keith, S., Urban, E. K. and Fry, C. H. (eds.) (1992) *The Birds of Africa.* Vol. 4. Academic Press, London.

Lambert, F. and Woodcock, M. (1996) *Pittas, Broadbills and Asities.* Pica Press, Sussex.

Langrand, O. (1990) *Guide to the Birds of Madagascar.* Yale University Press, New Haven and London.

Langrand, O. and Sinclair, J. C. (1994) Additions and supplements to the Madagascar avifauna. *Ostrich* 65: 302-310.

Lanting, F. (1991) *Madagascar - a world out of time.* Robert Hale, London.

Lekagul, B. and Round, P. D. (1991) *A Guide to the Birds of Thailand.* Saha Karn Bhaet Co., Bangkok.

Madge, S. and Burn, H. (1988) *Wildfowl: An Identification Guide to the Ducks, Geese and Swans of the World.* Christopher Helm, Kent.

Madge, S. and Burn, H. (1993) *Crows and Jays: A Guide to the Crows, Jays and Magpies of the World.* Christopher Helm, London.

Milon, P., Petter, J.-J., and Randrianasolo, G. (1973) *Faune de Madagascar 35: Oiseaux.* ORSTOM and CNRS, Tananarive and Paris.

Mittermeier, R. A., Tattersall, I., Konstant, W. R., Meyers, D. M. and Mast, R. B. (1994) *Lemurs of Madagascar.* Conservation International, Washington, D.C.

Morony, J. J., Bock, W. J. and Farrand, J. (1975) *Reference List of the Birds of the World.* American Museum of Natural History, New York.

Nicoll, M. and Langrand, O. (1989) *Madagascar: Revue de la Conservation et des Aires Protégées.* WWF International, Gland, Switzerland.

Oberlé, P. (ed.) (1981) *Madagascar: Un Sanctuaire de la Nature.* Librarie de Madagascar, Antananarivo, Madagascar.

Olsen, K. M. and Larsson, H. (1997) *Skuas and Jaegers: A Guide to the Skuas and Jaegers of the World.* Pica Press, Sussex.

Preston-Mafham, K. (1991) *Madagascar - A Natural History.* Facts on File, Oxford.

Putnam, M. S. (1997). *Une bibliographie ornithologique de Madagascar.* Recherches pour le Développement, Series Sciences Biologiques, no. 11. World Wide Fund For Nature - Centre d'Information et de Documentation Scientifique et Technique, Antananarivo.

Rand, A. L. (1936) The distribution and habits of Madagascar birds. *Bull. Amer. Mus. Nat. Hist.* 72:143-499.

Safford, R. J. and Duckworth, J. W. (eds.) (1990) *A Wildlife Survey of Marojejy Reserve, Madagascar.* ICBP Study Report No. 40. International Council for Bird Preservation, Cambridge.

Schulenberg, T. S., Goodman, S. M. and Razafimahaimodison, J.-C. (1993) Genetic variation in two subspecies of *Nesillas typica* (Sylviidae) in south-east Madagascar. *Proceedings VIII Pan-African Ornithological Congress:* 173-177.

Sinclair, I. and Davidson, I. (1995) *Southern African Birds: A Photographic Guide.* Struik Publishers, Cape Town.

Turner, D. A. and Dowsett, R. J. (1988) Additions and Corrections to Afrotropical and Malagasy Avifaunas 1. Western Indian Ocean Islands. *Tauraco* 1 (1): 130-138.

Urban, E. K., Fry, C. H. and Keith, S. (eds.) (1986) *The Birds of Africa.* Vol. 2. Academic Press, London.

Urban, E. K., Fry, C. H. and Keith, S. (eds.) (1997) *The Birds of Africa.* Vol. 5. Academic Press, London.

Useful Addresses

The BirdLife ZICOMA project
(Zones d'Importance pour la Conservation des Oiseaux à Madagascar)
BP 1074, Antananarivo 101, Madagascar.

ASITY
La Ligue Malagache pour la protection des Oiseaux de Madagascar, Section Oiseaux,
Parc Botanique et Zoologique de Tsimbazaza, BP 4096, Antananarivo 101, Madagascar.

Jersey Wildlife Preservation Trust
BP 8511 Antananarivo 101, Madagascar.
JWPT have an active conservation programme working extensively in wetlands and the forests of the central west, with programmes based around the captive and in-situ conservation of threatened species, including the Madagascar Teal.

World Wide Fund for Nature Madagascar
BP 738, Antananarivo 101, Madagascar.
WWF has many important site-based conservation projects, and has highly effective conservation education and training programmes. The WWF office is the base of the Working Group on Birds in the Madagascar Region, which publishes a biannual newsletter.

Conservation International
BP 5178, Antananarivo 101, Madagascar.
CI concentrate their activities on two major site-based projects, Ankarafantsika, home to the Van Dam's Vanga, and Zahamena, in the eastern rainforest.

The Peregrine Fund
BP 4113, Antananarivo 101, Madagascar.
The Peregrine Fund works in two major areas, the Masoala peninsula and the lakes around Antsalova, on the conservation of the habitats of the two most threatened raptors of Madagascar, the Madagascar Serpent Eagle and the Madagascar Fish Eagle, using a community-based approach.

The Working Group on Birds in the Madagascar Region
This group produces a newsletter twice-yearly. Contact:
Steve Goodman, WWF Madagascar, BP 738, Antananarivo 101, Madagascar,
or Field Museum of Natural History, Roosevelt Road at Lakeshore Drive, Chicago, IL 60605, USA.

INDEX

Figures in bold refer to the main species accounts.